DEVOTIONS

Devotions

PATRICIA BARRIE

Halts by me that footfall:
Is my gloom, after all,
Shade of His hand, outstretched
    caressingly?
Francis Thompson, 'The Hound of Heaven'

Chatto & Windus

LONDON

Published in 1986 by
Chatto & Windus Ltd
40 William IV Street
London WC2N 4DF

British Library Cataloguing in Publication Data

Barrie, Patricia
Devotions.
Rn: Wendy Barber   I. Title
823'.914[F]   PR6052.A72/

ISBN 0-7011-3029-6

Typeset at The Spartan Press Ltd
Lymington, Hants
Printed in Great Britain by Redwood Burn Ltd
Trowbridge, Wiltshire

For my husband

Chapter One

Last night I danced with a beautiful woman. Last night? Blue night. Bright, dark, velvy, veldt, velvet blue night. In my arms. In my arms. Dance, dancing. Last night.

Last night I danced with a beautiful woman. Was it real or a dream, a blue nightmare turning dread, red and shallow? Hello.

'Bu!'

'All right, Mr Knighton? All right, love? Your daughter'll be here soon.'

'Bu-bu-bu.'

'That's right, that's right.'

Right? It can't be right. It can't be real. But she looks real enough, that smiling woman, that nurse purse person. And she sounds real enough, though coarse, and too loud. My daughter will be here soon, she said, and that seems good, except that I have no daughter, only my wife, my wife. Her name is Emma and I call her Emily, which she hates, and blushes when I say it – which is why I say it. She blushes easily for me. She is like a lute in my hands. Touch her, and she sings the tune, hating my power, loving it too, for she knows her power is the greater. She can live without singing. I cannot live without the music she makes for me.

Emma, Emily. She is here. My vision is a little blurred and I cannot see clearly, but I recognise her shape, small and compact, the way she holds her head; her voice, 'Good afternoon,' clear and precise. She is a powerful woman. When she speaks she has more courtesy than princes and commands respect with a single word. It is real! It is not a dream, for in dreams so much joy is not possible. Emma!

'Bu-bu-bu!'

I cannot speak! And it is not a dream, for she is close to me now and I see her black hair, her brown eyes, her sweet little mouth and her smile. Emily? No, not Emily . . . My daughter.

There are tears on my face. My throat is twisted in knots and I am weeping. So is she, but she smiles too, and holds me in her arms as though I were a child.

'There, Daddy. It's all right.'

All right? All right? All bright and beautiful, and her face glowing blood-red explodes, darkens and comes together piece by piece. Peace.

My daughter, my child. I am floating on a warm, salt sea, loving and loved; but fear takes my heart and grief downweighs me. The sea is cold, cold, and has no end.

'We won't be beaten, Daddy, will we?'

Won't we? I think perhaps you are wrong, little girl; for if this is real, we are beaten now and there is no hope for us. Is it real? Tell me.

She holds my hand and says nothing. Her smile tells all, as sad as death, pitying me, loving me more than Emma ever did before she died, long ago. How and why does this child love me? Does she not realise that my love for her is counterfeit, given not for her soul but for her hair, her eyes, her voice? She is a carbon of Emma, of her mother, a perfect ghost of my beloved dead. Don't you know, little girl, how much I have hated you? You have kept me in agony all your life, every word, every gesture of yours a knife in my heart, a goad to my dying manhood. I have wounded you, rejected you, hurt and punished you for your innocent likeness to the woman I loved, and you have forgiven me everything – thank God, for I think I need you now.

She is shy, and very courteous to me, trying to anticipate the things I would ask if I could speak. She tells me the name of the hospital, the names of the nurses. She tells me that I have had a stroke, that I cannot speak, cannot walk, cannot move my right arm.

'But it will all come back,' she says, as if she were talking of the spring. 'It will take a little while, but it will all come back.'

Does she believe it? Oh God, does she believe it?

I am drowning.

'Bu! Bu!' I am angry, little girl, and would send you cowering if the sound of my voice did not disgust me, if my senseless burbling did not terrify me so. I would send you cowering if I did not need to feel your hand in mine.

Poor child, she sees my frown and thinks I am anxious for her. She has never learned that in my world there is room for only one, and that it is me.

'I'm all right,' she says brightly. 'Mrs Lear has been helping me, and I've taken some money from your wardrobe.'

She blushes, but she knows I am helpless, and how could she live without taking my money?

I am cursed. All my life I have been the victim of a curse, but never the victim of persons. Now I am . . . just a victim. And this child is my master. What kind of master will she be? I have not been kind to her.

8

Who knows how sincerely she has bestowed her forgiveness? Who knows how deep are the wounds I have inflicted on her mind? Will she take her revenge on me? How am I to suffer now?

Relief! Here is a man I know. His name is Bob Hurley, and although his mind is as narrow as a clothes line, he is clever too. We are friends for his cleverness. No, we are friends because I am half in love with his poor, cowed wife, who reminds me sometimes – when she laughs – of Emily. I do not like Bob Hurley, but we are friends because I love his wife.

Ah, I can smile, and must say hello, and shake his hand.

'Bu-bu-bu.'

My hand, of course, does not move.

Bob looks at me from the corner of his eye and pulls up a chair. He speaks to the child, not to me.

'How is he, Ann?'

Her name is Anna, but he never says it. Sometimes I think he calls her Ann out of spite. He does not like her. He thinks she is spoiled, a snob. I have told him she is shy, but he does not believe me, and perhaps, in a way, he is right. For although she is not spoiled, she is powerful. She has Emily's power: a directness of eye, a clarity of voice, an indefinable grace of which she is wholly ignorant. Now she is master she will learn her power and use it.

Against me?

'How is he, Ann?' (Bob is afraid of powerful women.)

Anna smiles. 'He is much better,' she says softly. 'But why don't you ask him? He can nod and shake his head, and soon he will learn to speak again, if we help him.'

Bob frowns. 'Don't be silly,' he says sternly. 'Face the facts, Ann. He isn't going to get better. He won't last the week, and you know it.'

My bowels have dissolved.

Anna's face burns. 'Hush!' she whispers. 'He isn't deaf! He can hear you! You can hear, Daddy, can't you?'

I do not want to die! Even if what he says is true, I do not want to die! I am afraid! I am too afraid to move; and she is wrong, for I cannot nod, cannot shake my head!

'You're fooling yourself, Ann.' Bob smiles a sneer of pity for her unworldliness. 'Don't you know what a stroke is? It's brain damage. *Brain* damage! He has no more understanding than a vegetable!'

Ah! Ah, I cannot bear this! If this is what living will mean to me, I think I prefer death – and hell. Hell must be better than this.

9

Anna is standing now. Her lips are trembling, and she has taken my hand. Her hands are very small and I do not know whether she holds my hand to give strength or to take it. I know only that I am glad she is holding me, because that hand is the one I can move, and if she did not hold it I would smash it into Bob Hurley's face. What will Anna do? Will she weep and beg his help, his comfort, the strength of his manly arms to support her in her grief? I am terrified, for in turning to him she must turn from me, and she is all I have.

She is all I have!

'You callous, ignorant, stupid man,' Anna says in Emily's perfect voice, which comes like a hymn to my ears. 'How *dare* you?' She is shaking with rage.

Rage! It is one thing she did not inherit cleanly from her mother. Emily had a great rage when she was moved. So have I. Anna has inherited them both, and has her own personal baby rage too. Bob is getting only three of their nine lashes because we are in a public place and Anna knows discretion. But her discretion has limits, and Bob knows it. He is twisting with fear and resentment. He would kill her if he could.

'Get out of here,' Anna says now, very quietly; 'and please don't ever come back. My father does not need such friends as you.'

How did she say that? How did she do it? She is blazing like a saint at a stake. I am saved by a five-foot-two giant!

'If he lives,' Bob hisses through his teeth, 'you'll need all the friends you can get, madam! And when that time comes, I'll remember this!'

He pushes his chair backwards, leaning toward her, wagging his finger an inch from her face. How can he treat her so? She is seventeen, just a little girl. And she loves me. How can he speak to her, of me, like this?

Perhaps he knows that I am half in love with his wife. Perhaps this is his revenge – for she is more than half in love with me. I will never see her again and do not want to. I am a courtier; a gallant, devilish fellow with sparkling eyes and a lopsided smile. I am a dandy. Tall and elegant with never a hair out of place. I am a rake, a seducer. Women are clay in my hands.

How can I live without that?

How can I see Bob Hurley's wife again, like this, weeping?

Anna takes my weeping face in her small hands and kisses my eyes. She cradles my head against her small breast and rocks me, rocks me, even though she is weeping too, and I can't tell which tears are whose.

Then she is mopping us up, smiling, her lips drawn stiffly back from her teeth. Oh, God, which of us is suffering most?

'Damn him!' she says encouragingly. 'If you're a vegetable, I'm a . . . a . . .' (she has always been a trifle inarticulate; no confidence; my fault) '. . . a haddock!' she declares at last. 'And no one's going to make fish and chips out of us!'

Chapter Two

When I was thirteen, fourteen, fifteen and longing to be grown up, my father told me I would be grown up when I was sixteen, and not a minute before. When I was sixteen, he told me that growing up was not the work of a moment. The law said (he said) that I would not be grown up until I was twenty-one; but seeing the outrage on my face, he agreed that I might *begin* at sixteen.

'How?' I asked, daring a hint of sarcasm.

He smiled and traced his finger teasingly from my ear to the point of my chin. 'You can wait up for me when I go out.'

I loved him too much to be ungrateful.

He was never very late. Eleven o'clock, perhaps. Sometimes he would be gloomy and send me to bed. Sometimes he would be cheerfully aggressive – which meant that he was very unhappy – and he would talk to me: occasionally about politics; more often about God, whom he didn't believe in; and sometimes – though very rarely – about me. He usually began with flattery. He would say I was pretty, or clever, or good, and as I basked in his praise (for I never learned) he would slowly take my virtues apart, holding them up to the light which was my mother and finding the flaws in them, one by one.

I told my friend Jenny about this one Sunday when we took her dog for a walk on the beach. I was still aching from having my virtues dissected the night before, and wanted some sympathy.

'That's terrible!' she said. 'Don't you hate him for doing that to you?'

No, it had never occurred to me to hate him for it. My father was the sun, my mother a ghostly, perfect moon, and it was my duty to aspire to her perfection. It was my purpose, the challenge upon which the whole of my life had been founded – for unless I became the moon, how else could I absorb my father's light and reflect it for his pleasure?

I did not say all this to Jenny. My ideas are sharp enough, but I am frequently tongue-tied when asked to express them. 'No,' I said, a little surprised; and she said I was crazy. This was true, so I didn't argue the point. I knew I was crazy, because although he had taken my virtues apart, I was glad simply that he had talked to me.

Our day-to-day lives did not include conversation. My curiosity about him was rarely satisfied. Once, having heard Jenny's mother say it to Jenny's father, I asked as we sat down to dinner, 'Did you have a good day, Daddy?'

He raised his eyebrows, and a slow smile tipped his mouth to one side. He was apt to smile a very similar smile when I asked impossible favours. It called me a presumptuous little madam.

'Yes, thank you,' he said.

He always tried to be courteous, even when he was flaying the soul from my body.

So these nights when I waited up for him were like meat to the starving. I lived in dread that he would come home gloomy and silent, and when he spoke, no matter what he said, I ate his words and was grateful. Whilst he talked, I waited for a word that he loved me, trusted me, approved of me. I waited to hear his secrets. He told me only three; but I discovered afterwards that they were not secrets at all: everyone knew that he was a political conservative, a religious rebel, a man who had loved his wife. At sixteen and seventeen, half fledged to woman-hood, I, his daughter, knew scarcely more about him than the man who served behind the bar at the Watersmeet Hotel.

When I knew he could no longer speak, my most poignant grief was that he would never, now, tell me his secrets, never allow me to enter the hallowed places of his soul. And I admit now, with even greater sadness, that had he lived to be ninety, with the power of speech intact, he would never have said more.

The early years of my adolescence were agonising, and my father did nothing to make them easier. It was the first time in my life I wished my mother were alive, and it was the first time I knew I was glad she was dead. She died when I was four. I remember her.

I slept in a cot beside her bed and sometimes, when I cried, my father would lift me up and carry me to sleep with him, pushing me into the curve of his hips. I imagine he did it to quieten me so that my mother need not waken. But one night she woke first. I suppose I could speak; I suppose I must have made it plain that I wanted to sleep in my father's arms. 'No,' she said. I do not remember anything else, only the sense of being cheated and betrayed. I was jealous of her, and only later, under my father's priest-like tutelage, did I learn to worship her memory.

If I had had an ounce of sense I might have realised that my mother, had she lived, would in all probability have been very like Jenny's mother: warm and busy, giggling at our silly, schoolgirl jokes, occasionally carping about our faults. Instead, whenever I thought of her, she was characterised by the cold, rather severe smile and the immaculately tailored suit which she wore in one of her pre-marriage photographs; and the only word she ever said was *no*.

I was glad she was dead. Life was complicated enough without her. I did want a mother though. A mother like Jenny's, who could sweep up adolescent problems like crumbs from the tablecloth and blow them away with a laugh or a word of comfort. But the cosy and intimate instruction Jenny received on the subject of puberty was delivered to my unworldly ears without the benefit of motherly tact. Omitting as 'rather tedious' the careful groundwork of her mother's revelations, Jenny cheerfully informed me that when my time came I would bleed for a week, every month, until I was fifty. I felt as though my whole life had been shovelled up and hurled into a sewer.

At first I did not believe her. Wouldn't one die if one bled for a week?

'Oh, it's not much!' Jenny assured me. 'Just a little drop. But every day. For a week.'

'Oh.'

I didn't like the sound of it at all, and Jenny's throw-away phrase – 'It's just one of the crosses we women must bear!' – made it seem even worse. I was already weighed down with crosses. This one would almost certainly break my back. Perhaps Nature would forget me, and leave me out if I prayed hard enough? I prayed very, very hard, and full of faith in God, I forgot all about it.

My father was at his most efficient in the mornings, I at my loathsome worst, and in order to combat my sleepy bumblings, he had devised a routine to ensure that we both arrived in our appointed places at nine o'clock, properly clothed, fed and organised. Having established quite early in my life that it was counter-productive to stand at the foot of the stairs shouting 'Anna!' until he was blue in the face, he now simply marched into my room, threw the window wide open and tore the covers off me – which could be quite embarrassing at times.

'Get up!'

If my nightie had reached its favourite resting place – somewhere in the region of my armpits – I needed no further encouragement to get

13

up, and my father would leave without giving any. But one morning, when I was thirteen, he halted half-way to the door, whirling around with a look of horror on his face. I followed his gaze and my heart did a swallow-dive into a pool – a pool! – of blood and cold terror.

'All right,' my father said quietly. 'Stay there. Don't panic.'

He went out and returned a few moments later carrying a box and a closely printed leaflet. 'Do you know what these are?'

I hadn't a clue. Jenny had neglected to tell me about sanitary towels.

'Do you know why you're bleeding?'

I nodded, keeping perfect time with the chattering of my teeth. I wondered, vaguely, why my father did not look worried, why he hadn't asked what was wrong with me, why he wasn't rushing to call the doctor. I assumed he was being brave, merely waiting for me to explain how I had cut myself so badly before taking action. *Action?* I almost fainted. Somehow I had to tell him what was happening, before he volunteered to administer first aid!

'It's an egg!' I wailed, and was convinced of my father's complete ignorance on the subject when his jaw dropped with astonishment. 'And it has to come out so I don't have a baby before I'm grown up!'

My father said, 'Yes. I see,' without moving his lips, and turned away abruptly to drum his fingers on the dressing table. 'Well, in that case, there's no need for you to cry, Anna. Have a bath, read these, er, instructions, and do precisely what they tell you to do.'

When I arrived at school, still trembling with shock and convinced that the minuscule pad between my legs was not enough to stem the flood, Miss Hamshire, the headmistress, was waiting for me in the junior cloakroom.

'Your father telephoned,' she informed me kindly. 'Shall we have a little chat before prayers?'

Our little chat ironed out most of my misconceptions, but the damage was done. It was months before I came to terms with my condition, and every time it happened, I felt my stomach turn with revulsion.

I became depressed and felt very bitter towards God, who had given Nature its foul way with me in spite of my prayers. If He had not been able to prevent my periods, I reasoned, then He was not as powerful as the Sunday-school teachers claimed. Some things were apparently beyond His skill, and if that were so, what was He for? What use were prayers if He couldn't answer them?

I asked my father this while he was mowing the lawn – not a wise move, because gardening was one of his least favourite pursuits and he was invariably in a foul mood whilst he was doing it.

He snapped, 'I send you to church, Anna, precisely so that you need not ask me such questions. Ask the rector. That's what he's for. And stop scuffing your shoes!'

'I thought he might call me a heretic.'

My father glanced towards heaven. 'Give me strength!' he prayed nastily, and gave the lawn mower a vicious shove, taking a swathe of flowers clean off the border of candytuft which had seeded itself from last year.

I knew my father did not believe in God, but he frequently prayed for strength and patience when things became too much for him. Was that the answer? Perhaps one should not ask God to interfere with Nature, but only for the means of dealing with it.

'What I mean is,' I ventured, 'if I asked God to, er, turn the grass, say, pink – well, He couldn't. Could He?'

'No, Anna,' my father said through his teeth, irritated, I knew, less by the question than by my clumsiness in asking it.

'So He isn't completely om-omni-, er, powerful, is He?'

'Omnipotent! You should know *that* by now – it's in all the hymns, Anna!'

'Omnipotent,' I whispered, wishing I had never started. 'I do know it. I just wasn't . . . sure.'

'If you don't take risks with words, you'll never learn which are the right ones, will you?'

I bit my lip on a violent retort and managed to look humble. I knew the word 'justice' had no place in my father's vocabulary, because he had scorched my ears off only the day before for risking 'eligible' when I meant 'illegible'.

'God?' I prompted gently, hoping to steer the conversation from my shortcomings to those of my Maker. My father glared at me.

'I can't think why you consider me such an expert,' he said bitterly. 'But, if you insist, I suppose God has too much common sense to turn the grass pink for a whim of yours. If He kept the blasted stuff from growing it would be of more use.' He gave the lawn a venomous look, as if hoping, by sheer malice, to stunt its growth for the remainder of the summer.

'Besides,' he went on in a milder tone, 'if you asked me to give you a box of chocolates, my refusal wouldn't mean that I was powerless to grant your request. It would simply mean that I judged it bad for your teeth, for your digestion – and for my plan of things. If you believe in God, you have to give Him the right to reject as well as to grant your prayers. Some things aren't good for you, and some things have nasty repercussions elsewhere. For instance, if the grass suddenly turned pink the cows wouldn't eat it and we'd have no milk.'

'I think cows are colour-blind, Daddy.'

'Thank you, madam professor! Now, if you don't mind!' He gave the lawn mower another shove and then stopped, his eyes narrowed suspiciously. 'Why?' he demanded sharply. 'What have you been praying for?'

'Nothing. I just . . . wondered.'

I trailed away to the bottom of the garden, still wondering, though in fact my father had answered everything very neatly. God – like my father – was not in the business of answering prayers. He had a plan, as incomprehensible to me as my father's was, and He would let nothing change it; He *could* not, because of 'nasty repercussions'. Perhaps some poor, prehistoric slave, praying for his load to be lightened, had invented the wheel just because God had not answered his prayer, thus literally setting the wheels of progress in motion. My father's reason for sending me to church was that civilisation had been founded on religion, was inextricably tied up with it. I had thought he meant that God's power had created civilisation, but perhaps he had meant God's *lack* of power.

I sat in the long grass under the apple trees, clenching and unclenching my fists as the ideas came, popping in my mind like fireworks in a dark sky. Yes. Yes! I leapt up, smiling. God had made us in His image, and after that we were on our own. God's power was *in* us, because He had made us like Himself! And He *had* answered the slave's prayer, by turning it inwards, making the slave find his *own* strength to invent the wheel! That was the plan! Having made it, God could do nothing to change it, and the only thing we could ask of Him was strength enough to exist within it!

I ran back up the garden path, waving my arms and all but crying 'Eureka!'

'Daddy! I've worked it out! You know what you said about your plan of things? Well, I suppose you meant that God has a plan too, and I think I know what it is!'

At this point, my father was supposed to sit back on his heels and say, 'Gosh! Really! Tell me more!' But the lawn mower had seized up and he was crouching over it with a screwdriver, in a worse mood than ever, although for a moment he hid it rather well. He tilted his head, looking at me quite sweetly.

'Do you know what my plan is, Anna?'

'No . . .' I held my breath. Was all my enlightenment to come in a single day?

'I'll tell you,' he said grimly. 'My plan is to slap you and send you to bed if you bother me again. Can't you see I'm busy? Read a book; go for a walk; write to your cousins; be quiet.'

'Yes, but it won't take long, and I want –'

'Go to bed.' He hated the lawn mower, but he bestowed upon it an affectionate smile, as if suddenly appreciating that, for all its faults, at least it did not talk. 'I'll slap you later, when my hands are clean.'

I did not want to believe him and tried not to, although I knew from experience that his threats were never idle. There was no point in praying that he did not mean it; but judging that this might be a good time to begin my new relationship with God, I looked heavenward and said fervently, 'Give me strength!'

A split second later my father was depositing large, oily handshapes all over the seat of my dress, and ten minutes after that I was in bed, staring hopelessly at the ceiling and trying to summon strength enough not to cry.

I suppose this would have been an appropriate time to wash my hands of God completely, but I did not. For one thing, I was too proud of my recent theosophising to abandon it at the first hurdle, and for another, the conclusions I had reached were comforting and good. God was no longer remote and frightening, but close and intimate, loving me because He was a part of me. He understood me, and since I could now understand Him, we were friends. My father, on the other hand . . . His power was infinite; I worshipped and feared him; he was beyond my reach and beyond my understanding.

Looking back, I'm not surprised I was confused, but that I survived to be a reasonably sane adult amazes me. Sometimes I felt that I was existing in a different world than that of the rest of my generation. I scrabbled fiercely to gain a toe-hold on that other world, and although my father inevitably dragged me back, my success was that I at least saw what was going on and knew what I was aiming for. I had also some power – I still do not know what it was – of attraction; so that although I was shy and could never make the first move away from myself, people moved toward me, and, in spite of my shortcomings,

17

they usually stayed. I always had a 'best friend' and a small circle of second-bests, and I learned through them, at envious second-hand, the normality of life where mothers, fathers, brothers and sisters existed in a melting-pot of laughter, bickering and rough justice.

Without realising it until I was much older, I learned something else, which my friends seemed quite unaware of. I learned that in normal life women were the dominant sex. This – I cannot call it an idea, because I never consciously thought of it – this feeling was probably underlined by my father's oft-repeated litany to my mother's virtues, and by my awareness that he was incomplete without her. My friends were continually saying, 'My mother . . .', virtually ignoring the existence of their fathers, except as other dependants within the family circle. As a general rule it seemed that fathers were the servants of their wives and children, criticised, ridiculed and scolded. I often heard them praised, but it was usually the praise of patronage, not respect. I once tried to imagine my mother telling my father to wipe his feet, cut his toe-nails and hang up his clothes, with the result that I became, more than ever, glad she was dead. A woman who could say such things to my father and get away with it, was too terrifying to contemplate.

It also helped to realise that my friends were not significantly happier than I was, even though their sufferings took place on a completely different level. They fought their parents for extra pocket money, new clothes, ear rings and ice skates, and to the best of my knowledge never lost much sleep over the mysteries of God and Nature. I do not claim to have been innocent of material lusts, but wanting a pair of ear rings (which I did) came into the same category as wanting a sports car (which I did also). They were dreams, unattainable until I was grown up – which would happen on my sixteenth birthday, and not a minute before.

'Oh, they all say that,' Jenny informed me breezily when we discussed it at school. 'But they give in eventually, if you nag hard enough.'

'Nag?' I affected an hysterical laugh to indicate that nagging my father was like yelling obscenities at a police inspector.

'Tell him you'll run away.'

'He'd help me pack.'

'Tell him he doesn't love you. That usually works. They hate being told they don't love you.'

'If I told him he didn't love me, he'd say, "How right you are, Anna," and slap me for being cheeky enough to mention it. That's the difference between you and me. You know they love you, and I know he doesn't.'

That was the difference. My friends were assured of their parents' love and could risk losing some of it over quite trivial matters, like ear rings and ice skates. I knew that I was accepted on sufferance alone, and that if I went too far I would risk losing everything.

What was everything? My father was everything. Freedom was everything. I wanted him to love me and I wanted to take an equal part in the life of my own generation. These two desires were in total opposition, and if I worked towards either one of them, I put myself in grave danger of losing the other. I dangled helplessly in the middle, while on one side my father, and on the other freedom, passed me by.

When I was small, my symbol of freedom was the view from my bedroom window. Our house overlooked a tumbled landscape of trees and fields and hills which continually tempted me to lose myself in it and be free. When I saw people far off, ploughing or haymaking, walking their dogs, they seemed tiny and remote; but when I was walking in the landscape I felt much bigger, more obvious, infinitely more vulnerable – and very lonely. I always came home again to my father. Freedom was empty without him.

Later, when I was growing up, the countryside lost its attraction, and the symbol of freedom became my sixteenth birthday. My mother had been sixteen when my father fell in love with her. It seemed logical to hope, therefore, that when I was sixteen I could have my cake and eat it as well: win my father's love and my freedom too. Sixteen was the eve of the holiday, when all the rules would be erased from the book and the pages be strung up like bunting. Sixteen would loosen my tongue, liberate my ideas and make me tall and stately with a big bust. My father would call me darling with every breath, take me dancing at the Watersmeet Hotel – and I would live in a rainbow land, full of boyfriends, sports cars and high-heeled shoes.

But it was foggy that day, and no rainbow appeared. 'Growing up is not the work of a moment,' my father said. And he allowed me to wait up for him, like the moon, his wife. Sometimes he was gloomy, sometimes aggressive and sometimes – though I could not remember such explosive moods from my childhood – he was angry. The heightened colour and blazing eyes of these quick, ungovernable tantrums saddened me as nothing else had ever done. It was as if he had given up all hope of happiness, all hope of me, and was now raging helplessly against despair as some men rage helplessly against death.

But one night, when I was almost eighteen, he came in laughing and took me in his arms.

'Da, da, de-da,' he sang, and waltzed me around the room. He smelled of whisky and cigars and his ice-white collar cut into the darkly flushed skin of his neck. 'Da, da, de-da. I've danced all night, Anna! I've danced all night!'

He went on dancing, and I, who had never waltzed in my life, moved like a feather across the floor, guided by him in the dance as implacably as I had been guided by him through my days. It was the most extraordinary feeling. There was no question of being pushed and pulled, no fear of tripping, or of stepping on his feet. I was weightless, powerless, and as exhilarated as if, from the pinnacle of a tower, I had fallen and found myself effortlessly flying.

I suppose we danced for rather less than a minute, but it is a minute which still exists for me with all its joy intact. It was a minute of revelation, in which I saw him not as a father, but as a man; a man of endless strength, endless love, who could melt women's hearts with his eyes or crush their bones with the tips of his fingers. It was my first moment of desire, my first experience of forces within me beyond my control; but I did not recognise anything except that it was the happiest minute of my life.

My father lifted me up, crossing his arms tightly around my waist. He kissed my chin, my mouth, the tip of my nose and my eyes; each kiss a blessing, a gift and a release.

'Anna, Anna,' he said huskily, 'oh Anna; I thought I would never be happy again!'

He put me down and gathered me under his arm, leading me to the stairs. I did not know what had made him so happy and I did not care, for he was sharing it with me, who had never before shared anything.

'You must go to bed,' he said. And then, with another laugh, 'And I am going out to supper. Sleep well, my darling.'

My joy was uncontainable, and when he had gone out again I sang the tune of our waltz, and hugged myself, nestling into the world of my own arms to feel again the world of his.

Chapter Three

It would appear that my life has been saved, and now they are trying to save my dignity. I try to encourage them, and am encouraged. Almost I begin to believe that it can be saved, and that hell might at last be turned from its purpose. Like the spring, as my daughter promised, certain things have come back. I can walk. My leg dragged at first, but Anna – how like her mother – said, 'Nonsense,' very coolly, when I wept for my dragging leg. 'You're not trying, Daddy.'

The nerve!

My temper, like my tears, is beyond my control and I pushed her away, not caring for the whiteness of her face and the pain in her eyes. She stumbled; then she pressed her trembling lips together and came back to me, smiling.

'Shall we try it again?' she asked sweetly.

Damn her. She makes me laugh, and how can I laugh with hell at my door?

The leg no longer drags, and I can move my shoulder, grip a sponge feebly with my hand. I cannot speak. I cannot read or write. It amazes me. It is terrifying. The smallest of my needs can no longer be met without another person's kind anticipation. I am hungry, thirsty, I need the lavatory, a shave. I have a headache, double vision, diarrhoea; and I am frightened, frightened. For I cannot say a word.

'Bu-bu? Bu-bu-bu?'

I am asking, child, what are you doing for money? Is there any left in the wardrobe? Has anyone contacted you from the company? Am I being given sick pay, a pension? Do you know anything? Are you quietly starving out there all alone? Have you paid the electricity bill? How? With what?

'Bu? Bu-bu-bu?'

'Do you want a cup of tea, Daddy?'

'Bu! Bu!'

No, damn and blast you! Tell me about the money!

Ah, mime it! Mime? I can't.

Oh! The hospital ward falls, is falling, splitting into kaleidoscopic, tropic fragments, pieces of glass. Anna is far away, luminous and blazing, seen through a sheet of orange glass. Anna is blazing. Emily is blazing, blazing and naked as the day. Breasts sweet peach halves and a triangle of dark fire coaxing my lust through the glass. Glass? Or flames? Games. He's playing games! Oh, games? Where am I? Where has the world gone? Where was I?

Thinking, thinking, setting things to rights, nights in the glass . . . Park, dark . . . Ask!

Money! Mime it! How the hell do you mime with only one hand? How do you mime 'pension'? Anna is afraid of me. I can't blame her. There is nothing more frightening than a man afraid. Nothing more

21

fertile than two fears twining, breeding, conjuring up new fears like maggots to eat, grow, twine and breed and fill the world with madness. One of us – but I can't. One of us – must!

I grab her hand, paying out imaginary notes into her palm like a crazed bookie on odds of one hundred to one.

Anna frowns, her big eyes pleading with God – that devil – to send her inspiration. 'Wash?' she offers tremulously. 'Do you want to wash your hands?'

You stupid *bitch*! 'Bu!' No! No! I am asking –

I am not an idiot. Why then does it take half an hour to think of reaching for my wallet? My heart is racing like a sweat-shop sewing machine. I am going to have another stroke! I reach for my wallet and throw it at my child, cursing, 'Bu! *Bu!*'

And she smiles, the little girl, and says, 'Oh! Money! Do you want me to buy something for you?'

Jesus!

I turn away from her, curling my raw bones into a shield against her stupidity, her callous power. I don't deserve this! You foul, tainted bastard, God! I don't deserve this! What did I *do*?

'Daddy?'

Go to hell!

Yes, yes, I know what I did. But I did it because . . .

Oh, why did you take Emma, my Emily? She was my soul, and what man is any good without his soul? What did I do to deserve that?

I know, I know, there were dozens of women, and there have been dozens since, but I loved only one, only *one*!

'Daddy? Please . . .'

All right, two; but Anna doesn't count for Emily. Anna is *this* hell. *This* hell! Oh, and it is hell. I would rather be dead and in hell. At least then I should know where I was.

'Daddy, is it a big worry or a small one? The wallet, I mean.'

Tenacious little brat. She always was stubborn. Look at her, Max. Her face, pinched with fright, and her eyes, glowing with the old, determined flame which I never managed to beat quite out. She has always terrified me.

'You have to help me, Daddy. You have to help me to understand. If it's a big worry, open your hand. If it's a small one, clench your fist.'

Clever girl. Brave girl. What did she say? Big worry, open my hand. It must be an hour since I asked the question, and at last she is answering. The company directors have been to see her. Their wives ask her to Sunday lunch. My salary is still being paid. The bills are paid. She is eating properly. What more can I ask? I clench my fist and Anna weeps. So do I.

The speech therapist is a vision, doing more to retrieve my dignity than all the rest of the staff put together. She is tall and blonde, very cool, very warm. I am at least half in love with her, for she is my life, my life-line, and she loves me. They all do. Did. I am in the past tense. I must try to remember it. I must forget it or go mad.

'My name is Myra.'

I know. You've told me three times.

'You say it. *My-ra*.'

'Bu-bu.'

'No. My-ra. Mmmm-'

'Bu. Ooooo.' Damn. 'Mmmmm-' Hey!

'Mmmmy-ra. Mmmy-ra. Myra.'

'Mmmmy-ah!'

'Whoopee!'

I laugh. I weep. She takes no notice and begins to explain the mechanics of speech loss, the problems of retrieving it from the battered mess of my bloody brain cells. *B*, *p* and *m* are the easiest sounds to retrieve and we will begin with those. I am going to learn a word, a big word, two syllables, and say it to Anna when she visits again. Myra says the word and laughs.

Hell's teeth! I blush like a baby.

'Go on,' she grins. 'Say it.'

To Anna? Are you crazy? She'll creep away on her hands and knees and never come near me again!

'Go on.'

'Bu-bu-bu!'

'Good! Good! You nearly did it! Try again!'

I did not nearly do it, Myra, you delicious witch. I was telling you that I have never sworn at my child, never will swear at her. She is an innocent, a protected little *bud* of a girl. Good Lord, woman, isn't it bad enough that she . . . But she doesn't know that, and I don't admit it.

'Mr Knighton,' Myra says drily, 'say it. It is the one word you can say and, damn it all, you haven't so much choice that you can afford to be precious about it. What's more,' she narrows her eyes, 'you are not quite the gentleman you pretend to be, so you needn't try pulling any wool over my eyes.'

Vicious! Quite right, too. But you are a woman of the world, Myra. What will become of us when Anna discovers that I am not quite the gentleman I pretend to be? Eh?

'Right!' She picks up her briefcase. 'I wash my hands of you.'

She's a wonderful actress. Central School of Speech and Drama. Why on earth did she concentrate on Speech? With that hair, that face, that figure, she could be in films, making her fortune.

'Well?' she demands.

If I had the use of both arms and could be certain what my mouth was doing, I'd snatch her to my heart and kiss her. Then we'd see who was boss. But if I had the use of my arms, my voice, there'd be no snatching and grabbing. I play a subtler game. *Played.* Oh yes, Myra. *My* game, *my* game! And I am – was – a better actor than you will ever be.

'I'm going!'

She is, too, the devil! I smile. I frown. She's got me.

'Oh, *bugger!*'

It explodes out of me, and we laugh until I cry.

Chapter Four

I awoke to pitch darkness, my heart pounding with terror. The banging noise which had woken me was repeated, and I sat up, staring into the darkness. Where was my father? Had he come back from supper? If he had, why hadn't he switched on the lights? And what was that awful noise?

'Daddy?' It was a whisper, terrifyingly loud in the darkness.

Another series of disjointed knocking sounds convinced me that we had burglars, and that my father (who slept like a guard dog, and could wake at the fall of a pin) could not yet have come home.

'Daddy?'

No reply. Was I alone in the house with the burglars?

I crept out of bed, my body jerking to the pounding of my heart. My room was the smallest in the house. It was ten feet long and I walked only eight of them to reach the door. It seemed to take an hour. The landing window presented an arch of smoky orange light, reflected from the main road.

Knock, knock.

It was coming from my father's room.

I leaned against the wall, holding my breath, feeling sweat running down my back like melting ice. I began a prayer, 'Oh God,' but could get no further with it. My mind had seized upon terror and nothing else could move in there. Snaking my arm across the door pillar I turned the knob and pushed, then, doubled up with the pain of my fear, I waited. Nothing happened. No axe-wielding burglar rushed out to murder me.

'Daddy?' There was no reply.

I crept inside. It was not dark here. The window was large and allowed a dim suffusion of orange light to penetrate from the sky. My father lay in a sprawled heap beside the bed, his arm stretched out to the wardrobe, knocking it feebly. I switched on the light. He was grey, wet, his face resting helplessly in a pool of vomit.

I stooped, lifted his head. He was insensible, but his hand jerked convulsively against the wardrobe door, tapping out, as if prompted by instinct, the call for help. I was very calm. My body was shaking itself into fragments, but my mind was cool and calm. I dragged my father sideways to pull him clear of the vomit. He was six feet two, slim, but too heavy for me. It was difficult to turn him on his side, to arrange his arms and legs for balance. His pyjamas were gaping and soaked with urine. I pretended not to see. I was too shocked to confess I had seen. I pulled the thick eiderdown from the bed and covered him snugly. It was August, warm and humid. I was freezing.

The doctor came. He wore pyjamas, a raincoat, leather mules on his naked, blue-veined feet; but he had been formed in my father's mould, and even in disarray seemed distinguished. He knelt on the floor, lifted my father's eyelids, sniffed his breath.

'How much has he had to drink?' he muttered.

No one replied. Mrs Lear stood with her back to the wall, clutching her throat. Tears stood in her eyes, but they did not fall. Mr Lear and the doctor lifted my father to the bed. He had had a fit, the doctor said, or perhaps a stroke. We must wait until morning, and then we would know. A spark of instinct formed words in my mind: take him to hospital; play safe; be sure. But I said nothing, and the doctor patted my shoulder and went home to bed.

Mrs Lear, who lived next door, swallowed her tears and buttoned her dressing gown to the throat. She was suddenly very capable and stern. She said I did not need to be comforted, and I knew she was right because nothing could comfort me until my father sat up and said

25

'Anna? What the devil's going on?' Which, as yet, he showed little sign of doing.

Mrs Lear said I did not need to be comforted. I needed to do something. She made me help strip my father, wash him, change the sodden sheets. Mutely I obeyed her, but I could scarcely believe what I was doing. I blushed and shook. The novelty of having my father naked and helpless under my hands was too much for me.

Mrs Lear said she did not wish to be cruel, but I was a grown woman now and, if the the worst came to the worst, I might thank her for this. My father had spoiled me, she said. I stared at her as at an intruder. She chuckled. 'Oh, don't get on your high horse, miss. I know he's been strict with you. Too strict. But he's protected you too much, Anna. Clever you might be, I don't deny it; but you have no more idea of life than a babe in arms.'

She spoke as if it were entirely my fault. I wished my father would wake up and tell Mrs Lear it wasn't my fault, but he hadn't moved for three hours and his breathing was strange and harsh.

Mrs Lear bowed her head. 'He was so happy,' she whispered.

'Why was he happy?' To the best of my recollection, these were the only words I spoke all night. Mrs Lear gave no answer.

'Look at him,' she said gently. 'If he's had a fit, I'm a Dutchman. You're going to have to grow up fast, Anna. You are not a little girl, Daddy's little girl, any more.'

I grew up, as I had done most of the things I was bidden to do, blindly, seeing the details, not the whole. My father died for three days and I accepted his death passively, praying only that God would allow him to go to heaven to see my mother again. I knew, if only vaguely, that my father was not a particularly good man, that his beauty and strength were based on vices rather than virtues; but I do not know why I knew this. Perhaps his worship of my mother's virtues had prevented him boasting of his own. Perhaps he had never told me about his own goodness. I knew he drank and that he played cards for money; but these things were peripheral. I did not see them as essential traits of his nature. He was my father; that was his role, his essence. The drinking and the gambling were little hobbies which did not detract from his dignity, his heroism. If I had grown up less blindly I might have seen that they were his life's blood. But he was at the centre of my world. Perhaps I could be excused for forgetting that I was at the very edge of his.

He was an engineer, a very skilful, clever man; but I realised now that I knew nothing about his work or whom I should inform of his illness and impending death. I telephoned. I stammered my name, his name, the news; and then someone at the other end took over. A Mr Grant came to see me. He sat down and talked to me gently until he had established that I was not a half-wit, and then he gave me a crash course in domestic economy which ended with a visit to my father's bank. I was seventeen, almost eighteen, and I had never possessed more than five pounds in my life. Now I was to draw cheques against my father's salary and with a panicky surge of freedom, I realised that there was nothing – nothing at all – to prevent my buying a fur coat. I'm not certain what stopped me. Perhaps only the awareness that my father was not yet dead and might still rise up to catch me.

Being alone in the house was very strange. I wasn't frightened, but I was alert, sensitive, aware of an unnatural silence which even the radio could not kill. The silence was a garment I wore next to my skin. It was knitted from wire wool and it was three sizes too small. I walked from room to room, trying to shake it off, to escape it; but it was everywhere, and in my father's room the coils tightened to choke me. I reasoned with myself, told myself that my aloneness was no different than it had been on my father's nights out, when I had danced to rock music and indulged in dark, delicious fantasies. But it didn't work. The silence was my knowledge that my father would not come home, would never come home. The silence was grief.

I wondered why I did not cry for my father, weep for myself, but I felt dry and shrivelled and weary. It surprised me. Although I was capable of controlling my tears, I was not controlling them. They simply weren't there. I know now that I had 'gone blind', an old trick I had devised to escape from my own helplessness. I knew my father was dying. I admitted it, and then went blind, which denied it.

He was not dying. It was a dream, and eventually I would wake. But it was a strange dream. It veered between nightmare and nightmarish bliss; perverse, wicked bliss, spiked with guilt and ecstatic fantasy. At night, my aloneness was lonely and painful, but by day it was independence. Freedom. I spent every morning busying myself with details, being responsible, playing at being grown up. The house must be kept clean, food bought and eaten, relatives (we had very few) informed of what had happened. I based these mornings on multiple influences from Jane Austen, Anne of Green Gables and Mrs Beeton. I was calm, cheerful, efficient. Mrs Lear came in to show me how to use the washing machine. She looked around the spotless kitchen and said, 'Well, miss!' – which I accepted as a compliment. When she had gone I realised it had been a nasty backhander, realised too that I was afraid of Mrs Lear. I took stock of all my father's friends and recognised that they all frightened me. A strong man, he had surrounded himself with strong people, every one of whom threw my weaknesses into cruel relief. I decided that after the funeral I would sever all connections and be a sad, neat little hermit.

I was very confused. My life – which I had always believed would end when my father died – now seemed to be opening up in a series of tantalising corridors. I was to go to university in October. The college was a mere ten miles away, not far from the hospital where my father lay dying. I had seen this next stage in my life not as a development but a continuance, like changing from one school to another. I would still live at home, still be subject to my father's rule. Now I began to see myself as an independent career woman, an intellectual, a racy little beauty. I entertained myself with plans for literary soirées, romantic love affairs. I dressed myself from the pages of *Vogue* and redecorated the house from *Homes and Gardens*.

Then, in the afternoons, I sat at my father's bedside and repented my sinful imaginings, praying for him to live and be my Daddy again. But growing up, once begun, was an irreversible process, and the hospital staff allowed me no room for backtracking. The stroke had been massive. There was little chance – if he lived – that my father would ever be the same again. 'But we don't know.'

I was amazed at how little they did know, how little they could explain, what little hope they offered. If my father lived he could be anything, beginning at imbecile and working up to invalid. I gave it little thought. I was convinced he would die. On the third day, when he rose from the dead, I was disappointed.

That disappointment – the work of a moment – was quickly over and quickly forgotten; but it explained, at least to my subconscious, a great deal. In that moment I knew that my father was a trap from which only death – his or mine – could release me. A stab of awareness, swift to come, swifter to go, and then my father smiled and wept, and I was enslaved again.

Chapter Five

Myra tells me I am a self-pitying brute and that it is time to forget my manifold woes and think of Anna.

'Do you realise,' she says, stabbing her forefinger into my knee, 'that your daughter is one in a million?'

Yes, miss. I smile smugly. That's how I made her.

'Oh, and don't think *you* can take all the credit!'

I keep forgetting that Myra, by dint of professional necessity, is a mind-reader. I am unaccustomed to having my mind read. It is not an entirely comfortable experience.

'Anna is eighteen,' Myra informs me sternly. 'A young woman with a mind of her own, a life of her own to live. You may be content to see that mind of hers go down the drain, her life wasted in dedication to your selfish needs: but I am not. Indeed, I won't allow it, and have told her so.'

Have you, indeed? Watch out, Myra, my dear. You are going too far. No one speaks to Max Knighton like this and gets away with . . . *Spoke!* Max Knighton is in the past tense. Speak away! I cannot defend myself.

Oh, shit upon shit! What have I come to, to sit humbly, gagged and tied, while some jumped-up bitch tells me how to behave? Anna is mine. Is mine. You cannot tell me to relinquish her. She does not want to be relinquished. You say that I have been here for five weeks and that Anna has visited me, talked to me, read to me, walked with me every single day. So what? Why not? She is my daughter.

I can only sniff and put my nose in the air. It means, shut your mouth, Myra. It means . . . ah, yes: 'Bugger!'

She laughs. I am furious, but my emotions are very biddable and I cannot help laughing too. Then I remember I am in despair and I weep. Then I realise I am weeping and am furious again.

'Pah!' I sweep my left hand, which is getting fantastically strong, past the end of Myra's nose. Anna would have flinched. Myra merely catches my hand and presses it between both of hers. Oh, I hate you, you beautiful, beautiful woman. I hate you. How can a woman – and not Emma – possess me as you possess me, enslave me as you enslave me, nag me, beat me, without even knowing who I am? I am the great

29

tormentor! I am the slave master! I am the one who calls the tune, and you do not even know!

'You're going home next week, Max,' Myra says quietly.

Yes, thank the Lord, I'm going home. God only knows what I shall do then, but at least I shall be my own master, and Anna –

'And the following week,' Myra continues slowly, 'Anna is going to college.'

No! No! I wrench my hand from Myra's grasp. My lips draw back from my teeth; my left hand makes a fist to knock her across the room. She looks a little wary, then angry. All right, if you want to fight with fallen angels, Myra my lass, I'll show you!

Something passes the side of my face and I turn sharply to see my useless right arm gradually climbing the air as if pulled on a puppeteer's string. That arm is my humiliation, my cross. A dead weight, pale, soft and shameful, it rises up, in the moments of my greatest grief, to haunt me. That arm, the one which has stroked so many women, created so many things, breaks me.

I sit down again and the arm falls at my side.

'Bu. Bu.' I am sobbing, chopping at the arm with my left hand, sawing at it. Cut it off! Take it away! I have to sleep with this corpse! It lies dead at my side and I feel it, without it feeling me, and I wake up screaming. But even my screams are silent. God, oh God, you devil-spawned devil, what have I done to deserve this?

'Max. Max.' Myra's arm circles my shoulder.

I am no longer angry. Touch me, touch me, hold me in your arms. I'm so afraid!

'Max, I'm so sorry. It's cruel, I know. But the arm will improve. You mustn't lose hope.'

Hope? It is a word I no longer acknowledge. Shut up, Myra. Destroy a little more of me while you're at it. Tell me about Anna, and of how she will desert me.

'All right, now?'

'Bu.' Yes, fine. Simply wonderful, my dear. Please don't concern yourself with my feelings when yours are of so much greater importance.

'Anna?' she begins cautiously. I nod. Get on with it.

'She deserves her own life, Max, doesn't she? College? A career? Your wife had her own career, didn't she?'

She grins. I give her a sardonic look.

Emma had a career, all right. The damn girl wouldn't marry me,

30

that's why. I met her when I was sixteen, married her when I was thirty, straight from a German prison camp. She took pity on me. Poor Emma. She wanted a gentle, helpless fellow, one she could nurse and mother. She was a woman who enjoyed a woman's power. The power of love was not enough to satisfy her.

'You admired your wife, didn't you?' Myra goes on. 'You respected her. Don't you want someone – some nice young man – one day to feel the same for Anna?'

What? What nice young man? Dear God, I've never even thought of it! Yes, I have, of course, but not in the sense you mean. A single father with a young daughter thinks constantly of young men: nice ones, nasty ones – they're all the same. They're festooned with red lights which scream, 'Danger!' and make one reach automatically for the chastity belt, the padlocks and chains. I have never in my life thought of a young man, in pleasant terms, for Anna, my Anna, my budding little Emily. Anna married? Anna pregnant? Jesus, she's only eighteen, and I – I am forty-nine. I don't want to be a grandfather just yet, thanks. I have a lot to – Oh God. Oh *God*! I am weeping again.

I am weeping again, but Myra is pitiless. 'You don't seem to realise, Max, that Anna is a woman now. You don't expect her to give her whole life to you, surely? Become an embittered old spinster who hates you for destroying her chances in life? You must let her go to college, Max, and let her go gracefully. Don't make her feel guilty. She hasn't enough confidence to cope with it.'

I rest my head on my hand and contrive to look bored. I am not bored. I am terrified. Somehow, between them, without so much as a by-your-leave, these women have made their decisions. Anna is to go to college. All right. What is to become of me? I suppose I am too selfish and self-pitying to be considered?

I wonder how magnanimous you would feel, Myra, my darling, with a gag in your mouth and a leprous corpse where your right arm used to be. Are you afraid of spiders, Myra? Are you afraid of rats? Are you afraid of dirt, cold and loneliness? Imagine yourself, you, clean and white in your hospital coat, your Chanel No. 5, locked naked in a tiny, freezing cell, tied down, up to your elbows in your own shit, with spiders on your face, rats gnawing at your strong right arm. Go on. Imagine it, and tell me, my clever darling, if there were one person who could help you, would you care that she would hate you, just as long as she let you out? You are not talking to a reasonable, kindly father, my dear. You are talking to a man in hell.

31

And I am talking to myself.

'Bu! Bu-bu-bu-bu?' What will become of me? What dreadful fate have you planned for me, you bitch?

'It will be quite easy, quite painless,' Myra says cheerfully, 'and, what is more, very good for both of you.'

Oh, I see. That's all right, then. I take it you mean to give me a private beach in the south of France, a bevy of gorgeous nurses and a jet to bring me home at weekends? That will be fine. Lay on a bevy of hatchet-faced chaperones for Anna while you're about it, and everything will be just perfect.

'While Anna goes to college,' Myra smiles, 'you will attend the day centre, here at the hospital. You will be taught to take care of yourself, to live efficiently with one hand while strengthening the other. You will have physiotherapy, occupational therapy, speech therapy. It will keep you busy, be company for you, aid your recovery. By the time Anna sits her first-year exams, you will be ready to . . .' Myra swallows and looks away.

Kill myself?

'To climb Mount Everest!' she concludes with a smile.

Quite easy. Quite painless. My, oh my, what a liar you are, Myra. I hope you're not teaching Anna any of your nasty habits. Perhaps you do not realise that I've seen your wretched day centre? The physio took me there yesterday, for a 'little visit'. It is a dreadful place, its walls pale green and lined with ugly leather-cloth chairs. It stinks of urine and Chloros bleach and is strewn with raffia, laminate off-cuts and string.

Company!

A raddled-looking crone, who, upon closer inspection, proved to be scarcely older than myself, pointed to the bird's-nest tangle which lay in her lap. 'This is my basket,' she moaned, and a syrup of saliva fell in glistening threads to the wet bib of her dress. Three old ladies sat in a row, staring mutely at the wall while they crocheted white string into dish rags. Red in the face and only barely keeping her temper, a therapist taught a legless torso with a mouth the finer points of operating a wheelchair. 'Fucking stupid cow!' the mouth bawled. 'Get out of my fucking way, will you?' *Company?* If he were the last man on earth I would still kick him in the balls and laugh that he had no legs to kick back!

There was a single man of my class in that day-centre bedlam. I smiled at him, shrugged, pointed ruefully to the hanging corpse at my side. I said, 'Bu-bu-bu.'

And he gave me courteous answer, 'Be-laddle-de-la.'

I was envious. Such articulate gibberish! He might regain his speech one day. Myra, oh, cruel, deceitful Myra, I know I will not!

Chapter Six

My father's tears seemed to complete my lessons in growing up. It was as though I stood beside a railway line and saw the points change. The points changed – *da-dum* – and suddenly the train was travelling on another line to a new destination whose name I did not know. There was no way back.

All my life I had feared my father's death, yet now I realised that his death was a mercy we had both been denied. I pitied him. I had never loved him so much, for I had never known him before. His life of grief, danger and romantic torment had, until now, been only the trappings of a hero, bloody wounds bound with silken scarves. Now I saw his life as it had really been, a desert of loneliness and longing, without joy or substance.

What do people do when every point of reference is destroyed and life must begin again? They scuttle, they hide, they pretend it isn't happening. That was what I did for a while, hating the pretence but knowing that my shattered world was too great a problem to solve all at once.

Jenny and I had left school and now awaited our A-level results. We pretended to enjoy the agony of waiting, especially the bits where we groaned and said our lives would be ruined if we failed. My life was in ruins anyway, but it was part of the pretence that I did not mention it, for we had shared everything in the past, and I was too lonely to claim my differences now and stand aloof, suffering a separate pain. Yet I had always been different, and I had never understood why Jenny clung to me when there were so many easier friendships she could have made. Perhaps it was merely that she liked being needed, that I gave her a sense of power. I knew that power was essential to one's personal dignity. I had thought myself without it, but my sudden loss of direction was also a loss of power, bringing confusion and humiliation on the heels of grief. Having worked so hard for my exams it was shattering to find that I no longer cared whether I passed or failed, and Jenny's nail-biting groans and sighs struck me as being faintly ridiculous. I could not share her anxiety and she could not share my grief. It was an unbridgeable gap. My father had done all he could to part me from Jenny and his efforts had achieved nothing except to push us closer together. Now he had stopped trying, we were sundered; and, while I knew we would never be joined again, I pretended it wasn't happening.

But we passed our exams and I pretended to be relieved. Chez, Jenny's brother, picked me up and whirled me around in his arms, a heady experience which made me blush for an hour afterwards. Chez was twenty, a student at Oxford. I had thought him very romantic and mysterious until he picked me up, when I discovered that he had bad breath. I like to think that I blushed for his bad breath, but I suppose really it was for his mystery. He laughed, anyway, and apparently exhilarated by my confusion, he snapped his fingers under his father's nose and said, 'Pa! The champagne!'

Mr Cole grumbled something to the effect that he wished Chez would not call him that, and produced a bottle of Asti Spumante, saying that it was quite good enough to celebrate our little triumphs.

Having virtually no experience of wine (my father drank claret occasionally but rarely gave me any) I thought the champagne very nice, and could not wholly believe in its alcoholic properties. I drank two glassfuls of it. We were celebrating on the narrow strip of paving which Mrs Cole called The Terrace (my father had been on it once, and hadn't stopped laughing for a week afterwards) and suddenly I felt myself crushed by the congratulations, the hopes, the ambitions. 'Aren't the roses pretty,' I murmured in a distant voice which I did not recognise as my own, and wandered down the garden to inspect them, hanging on to my glass as to the last – which it was – hold on the shaky support of my pretence.

I heard Mr Cole say, 'Poor kid. She must still be wondering what's hit her.' Which was all that was needed to complete the work the wine had begun. I cried.

A hand touched my shoulder, and hoping it was Jenny, certain it was Jenny, I sobbed, 'I don't care! I don't care! It doesn't mean anything!'

But it was Chez. 'Buck up, kid,' he murmured in a slightly disapproving tone. 'It's not the end of the world.'

I was amazed, infuriated. It was the end of the world! That was the whole point! I wanted to scream at him, kick him, demand what right he had to judge me, when his life was still clearly drawn on a map, with roses and champagne as his landmarks! Instead, very politely, I said, 'Of course. I'm sorry.' And sniffed.

34

'Good girl.' He patted my shoulder and left me staring at the roses, which were pink and red and labelled: Fellemberg, Sirsa Nurseries, Exeter.

When I returned to the terrace a few minutes later, Jenny was smoothing sun oil on her legs; Mrs Cole was singing, *I'm as Corny as Kansas in August* at the kitchen sink; and Chez and his father were playing clock golf. They were pretending it wasn't happening, which was good of them, because it made me see how futile a pretence it was.

My father was a broken, sick man. My future was wrecked. That was reality. That was what had to be faced – without tears, without self-pity, without . . . anything.

'See you tomorrow,' I said.

'Yes. Bring your swim things if it's sunny.'

'Thank you for my champagne, Mr Cole.'

He looked at his watch and pretended to be surprised. 'Oh! Going, are you? Regards to your father, my dear.'

'Oh, are you going, Anna?' Mrs Cole emerged from the kitchen with an onion in her hand. 'See you tomorrow, poppet. Love to your father.'

I smiled, being realistic. They were glad I was going. After all, people who cried during a celebration were rather a pain. I could see that. Having to send 'love and regards' to a man they disliked must have been a pain too, but I did not allow myself to be hurt by their hypocrisy. They were being kind, which was more than my father would have done had the positions been reversed. My father disapproved of Jenny, thought Mr Cole 'jumped-up' and Mrs Cole 'depraved' – chiefly because she had allowed Jenny to have her ears pierced at the tender age of eleven. 'Why didn't she drive a ring through her nose while she was about it?' he had demanded angrily. 'People who mutilate their children should be shot!'

I forebore to tell him that Mrs Cole felt the same about people who slap their children and refuse to allow them to go to parties.

I felt quite tough and cheerful as I waved goodbye and set off to meet the cold world on equal terms. Huh, I thought, I can take it! And then I stepped out of the garden gate and almost collapsed with terror as soon as I realised I was alone.

I am alone!

I almost howled it out loud; almost ran back to Mrs Cole to beg her to adopt me. Then I remembered that she did not want me, had been glad to see me go. I remembered too that I had grown up, and that this was what it meant.

'I am alone, and there is no one to help me.' My father had been saying something similar for years, and I had been continually wounded to think that I did not relieve his aloneness. How could he be alone, I wondered, when he had me? Now I understood. His aloneness *was* me.

Once, when we were on holiday in the Lake District with my mother's cousin, I had come close to understanding this, but the nervous strain of the occasion had confused me too much to fully grasp the idea.

Aunty Mary, my mother's cousin, was fond of me, but her relationship with my father left a lot to be desired. They bickered in low voices and their silences were deafening. Mary's three children were all older than I, friendly and cheerful with a tendency to make me, in my father's words, 'disgustingly over-excited'. They went to boarding schools and in the holidays 'played native', a delightful arrangement which included camping in the garden and avoiding hot water, good manners and adults except when absolutely necessary. Mary's chief object in life was to persuade my father to let me play native too, but he wouldn't hear of it. He said that having spent ten good years of his life teaching me how to behave, he had no intention of letting me forget it.

In spite of a searing desire to sleep in the tent, get filthy and swear, I privately endorsed his point of view. In three weeks of unrestrained low-life I knew I was capable of forgetting everything, and the idea of being taught it all over again made my hair stand on end.

I was, though, typically delighted when two of my cousins appeared in my room one night with the whispered news that they had come to spring me from clink – via the window. It was scarcely more than a ten-foot drop, but the gap which existed between Jane and Sarah's arms above and Robin's arms below, seemed like the helter-skelter into hell's maw. Excited half out of my wits and three parts out of my nightie, I screamed. Robin clapped his hand over my mouth, while I, moaning, and almost wetting myself with terror, clapped mine over my modesty.

'Shut up, you twit! Don't you want to sleep in the tent?'

'Yes, but what if Daddy . . . ?'

With the authority which is natural to all thirteen-year-old natives, Robin said, 'He won't!'

He did. I was filthy, and as high as a kite on adrenalin and burned sausages by the time he found me. He didn't say a word. He picked me up as if I were a roll of verminous old carpet and carried me back to the house.

Aunty Mary met us in the hall. 'Oh, Max! Why couldn't you leave her alone?'

My father put me down and held my hand very tightly. 'Why don't you leave her alone?' he said in a low voice. 'She is mine, Mary. She is my responsibility, subject to my authority. I will not stand by while you and your brood teach her the finer points of deception and disobedience.'

'Oh, don't be so silly!' Mary spluttered furiously. 'If you had the least idea of what a normal child looks like, sounds like –'

'Like this?' my father demanded, jerking me forward to exhibit my filthy nightdress and smutty face. 'It might have escaped your notice, of course, but the welfare state was created just so that normal children need not look like this. Your children do, but that is your affair. Anna is mine!' Aunty Mary was shaking with rage, but she still did not raise her voice.

'She is Emma's!' she said. 'Have you forgotten that?'

My father lifted me up again, properly this time. I knew he had every intention of smacking me silly before, during or after my bath, but there was something in the way he held me which made me suspect that he was using me as a shield to protect himself. I was already trembling, but a glance at his face terrified me. He looked like a cornered animal, his eyes smouldering with killing malevolence.

'Emma is dead!' he snarled. 'I am alone!'

The pity I felt for him then did not survive my bath, and when I was left to cry myself to sleep in a clean nightdress, my thoughts turned again to the idea that if only he could love me, I could be his friend, his wife, his companion, and he need never be lonely again. But I *was* his loneliness, and the loneliness was so much worse for being incomplete, as I saw now only too well. As a child, I was part of his wife yet not his wife. As an invalid, he was a part of my father yet not my father. The agony was in continually being reminded of what had been and would never be again.

But as my father's condition improved, I began to hope. Having never had any certainty that he loved me, I was not certain now; but now he smiled when he saw me, touching my face tenderly with the tips of his fingers, saying, 'Bu, bu,' in a voice which, if he could speak, might well have articulated words of love. I allowed myself to believe that he loved me and became unreasonably, almost hysterically happy. If he loved me, everything would be all right. If he loved me, nothing else

37

mattered. I could abandon my future, abandon the compulsive need I had felt to meet my mother's legend on my father's terms; for if he loved me I had achieved my heart's desire, and could now spend my life with him, for him, forsaking all else, all others, for as long as we both should live.

I told Myra my decision in a matter-of-fact tone which said nothing of my motives.

'You're mad,' she said. 'That isn't want he wants, Anna. Why do you suppose he's taken such pains with your education? St Lydia's, wasn't it? Any idea how much that has cost over the years?'

I hadn't a clue, and could not see that it mattered. 'It hasn't achieved anything,' I said dully. 'He has to be taken care of, doesn't he?'

Myra smiled. 'Does it occur to you,' she suggested quietly, 'that your father might have educated you in anticipation of just such a catastrophe? Don't you think it possible that he was preparing you for the day when you would need independence, a career, a means of supporting yourself without his aid? If you abandon it all now, Anna, you won't help him at all. He'll spend the rest of his days worrying about you instead of feeling assured of your future. Can't you see that?'

'Yes, I suppose so.' It made good sense, I knew, but it was dead-end sense. If my father had been preparing me for anything, it was his death. He was not dead. He was alive and needing me, in a way I was sure he had never anticipated.

I was fairly certain, anyway, that my education had lacked any motive at all except to make me a less irritating companion for him. When I failed to concentrate during museum visits, concerts and exhibitions, he had always jerked me to his side and hissed in my ear, 'If I draw an ignorant blank the next time I mention Monet [Gibbon/ Alexander Fleming/Copernicus] Anna, I'll cease to speak to you at all!'

It was ironic to think of his speechlessness now. My father's threats had never been idle.

'Anyway,' Myra went on smoothly, 'he's only forty-nine. Failing another stroke, there's nothing to say he won't live another thirty years. Look after him by all means, but how will you support him for thirty years without an income?'

More good sense. I hated it. I had made my decisions, come to terms with them, felt strong and capable in the security of them. Now Myra had confused me again.

'You mean I should go to college? Pretend nothing has happened?'

'I mean you should go to college, yes.'

'Then who will take care of him? I'm all he has in the world!'

Myra grinned. 'First,' she said, wagging her finger at me, 'no one is that indispensable. Who would take care of your father if you didn't exist? Do you imagine we would throw him out on the street?'

'No. You would put him in a home, and my father will go into a home over my dead body. I do exist, Myra, and I love him. Perhaps I am not indispensable to him, but he . . . he . . .' Tears came to my eyes and I swallowed them hastily.

'Quite so,' Myra said. 'He is indispensable to you, which puts things on another footing entirely. It makes your decision a selfish one. But if you are going to be selfish, go a little further – a lot further. For a moment, try to forget your father entirely and imagine what kind of woman you'll be thirty years from now if you take the course you have planned. You'll be forty-eight, dried up, poor, isolated and wondering where the hell your life has gone. No, Anna. That will not do. That is not what the proud Max Knighton has in mind for his little girl. You must never even think of giving up your life, for anyone, ever, because you have only one life, and even in the best of circumstances it's too soon over. All right, I admit that sacrifice is a good and necessary element of human life, but as soon as the sacrifice is more than it's worth, it's wrong! And if it's wrong, there's another solution. Never throw yourself off a cliff just because you happen to find yourself at the edge of one!'

There was a pioneering light in Myra's big, blue eyes, and her words hurt me. But I knew she was right. I knew, too, that I had been longing to hear such words, and that they were saving my life. But I still couldn't save my own life at my father's expense.

'All right,' I said; surprising myself with the hardness of my voice. 'What do you suggest?'

Myra laughed. 'That's more like it!' she said. 'That's who you are, Anna Knighton! You're a tough, capable, intelligent woman, and if you can take a problem by the throat and strangle it, you'll never go under. Understand?'

Yes, I understood. The panic and confusion of the last few weeks melted away and I was calm again, feeling the return of my power, stroking it as if it were a cat which had returned from its wanderings to curl in my lap and purr. I looked at my hands, suppressing a smile.

'Yes,' I said softly, 'I understand. Do you understand that I will take *you* by the throat and strangle you if you don't tell me what I am to do?'

Myra laughed again and told me about the hospital day centre. It solved everything. A few words, just a few words and my life was set back on its course, my father saved, my love for him kept intact with no guilt or grief to mar it.

'Thank you,' I said. But in my heart I said much more.

Myra stood up and pushed her hands into the pockets of her starched white coat. 'How are you off for friends?'

'Er?'

'Friends,' she teased. 'You know. People of your own age. People without responsibilities and furrowed brows.' She pushed the furrow from my brow with a nicely manicured finger.

'Oh, friends. Yes, I have' – I almost said *one* – 'some.'

'Good. Go get 'em. Have a ball. Let your hair down while you have the chance. Life isn't going to be easy for you, kid; so take your opportunities as they come. I want to see you with a sun tan, and sand between your toes. Outside this hospital the sun is shining, and there's a beach ten miles from here. Go!'

I went. I walked slowly at first, and then more quickly, with a skip in my step. I marched past X-ray and danced through Outpatients, and in the doorway an elderly man caught me in his arms and said, 'Hospitals should have girls like you in every ward. That smile of yours could cure anything!'

It was all I could do not to kiss him, and afterwards I wished I had.

The Coles were glad to welcome the new Anna Knighton into their fold, and Chez produced a few of his own friends to give our barbecues and beach parties an extra swing. One of them, a Classics student with the appalling name of Anthony Rogue-Marton, took a shine to me, which made letting my hair down rather more interesting than I had anticipated. Luckily for me, he was too conscious of his name to live up to it, and behaved like a perfect gentleman, retreating five paces every time I blushed.

'So what do you think of our Ant?' Jenny demanded, when we had swum a little way off from the others.

'He's very nice.' I did a nose dive to hide yet another blush. When I came up, Jenny was laughing. 'Don't worry,' she assured me, 'I told him you don't know one end of a boy from another.'

'Thanks!'

'But you were safe anyway,' she giggled. 'He does know one end of a girl from another, but he hasn't a clue what to do about it!'

It was more reassuring than I liked to admit.

Chapter Seven

I am going home today. I feel as excited and scared as a child anticipating his first ride on a roller-coaster. I have been to the lavatory five times in the past hour, not because I particularly wanted to go, but lest, if Anna arrives suddenly, I wet myself with sheer delight. God, you bastard, I have one thing at least to thank you for in your merciful wisdom: I can still control my bladder. So far.

Anna brought me my suit yesterday, the grey, middle-weight one I wear to important meetings. I love that suit and was delighted Anna had chosen it, rather than a pin-stripe or a tweed. Perhaps she is more perceptive of my character than I had imagined. More probably it was a fluke. The light grey sets off my dark skin, outlines my shoulders, emphasises the sleek cut of my waistline. I win arguments in that suit. It is my man-to-man suit, my no-nonsense-I-am-the-boss suit, and I refuse to transpose my worship of its virtues into the past tense. I refuse to admit that it hangs on me now like a shroud, and sags at the seat where my buttocks used to be. If any woman would have me now I would cut her to ribbons with my bones.

Myra has been to see me, to remind me of the words I can say and must keep saying, lest they escape the brain cells which have been re-educated to contain them. Book, paper, bath. Tea, no, Max. Bed, boot, money, me. Bugger, blast. An elegant repertoire. I am unable to fit any of them together to form a sentence. The connecting words – the, and, if, which – all buzz around and fly out through my ears like a cloud of distressed insects. Often, I am unable to recall the meanings of 'my' words, so they aren't much use anyway. But I can read out loud. Anna wrote out an elocution exercise she had learned at school and I read it with great solemnity, not understanding a word, aware only of the occasional accuracy of my pronunciation.

Bobby Bibby bought a bat. Bobby Bibby bought a ball. With that bat Bob bounced his ball, bounced it, bump! against the wall. But so boldly Bobby banged, soon he burst his rubber ball. Boo, sobbed Bobby, goodbye ball! Bad luck, Bobby, bad luck, ball.

I was exhausted by this stage of the game and the words jangled in my head without meaning. Anna, whom Myra has carefully instructed in the peculiarities of my disability, slowly repeated the rhyme, allowing me to understand it and to chide her dirty giggles with one of my sternest frowns.

The verse had a postscript which made me laugh, before its irony made me cry: *Now to solve his many troubles, Bobby Bibby's blowing bubbles.* Anna laughed too, but her eyes filled with tears and she held my hand. Oh, I am so glad she loves me, and I find myself loving her, just for herself. For once in my life, not for Emma. It is agony to think that, had she lived, Emma would have seen me like this. But it is a greater agony to know that she would not have wept so kindly, nor with such a sense of loss, as my Anna weeps for me.

My sins against my child have been great; greater than I knew, though I knew I was sinning. If God had tapped my shoulder and demanded, 'What are you up to, Max Knighton?' I'd have blushed, confessed and apologised on the spot. There was not the slightest chance of any Christly voice interposing, 'Father, forgive him, for he knows not what he does.' I knew. And there was to be no forgiveness, as my present plight makes only too clear. He surpasses me for ruthlessness, anyway. Perhaps I should respect Him for that, but I don't. God should be above such malice. Perhaps I should still have my right hand if God had not taken Emma to sit at His. Anyway, I don't believe in Him. I am an unbeliever. Take that, you bastard.

I feel puckish and merry, and God does not depress me as He intended. I am going home! Ah, here is Anna. She walks like a diminutive duchess, her head poised just so, as if, were she not fully conscious of its balance, it would fall off and roll down the ward to meet me. I paid for her gracefulness: St Lydia's had Posture at the head of the curriculum. At any time, any day, virtually anywhere within a mile's radius of the place, one could hear the awful cry, 'Posture, gels!' I once heard it in Woolworth's.

Anna grows more beautiful every time I see her and my soul is torn with jealousy, green and stinking, like mould on ancient soup. I know what she has been up to. Christ, I hope I know! Has she been seduced by that creeping Anthony fellow and left me in ignorance of the fact? I should try not to consider such possibilities. With madness waiting in the wings for its cue to rush on, screaming, who am I to encourage it with idle speculation? Anna is a virgin, Anthony is a queer. Repeat. Anna is a virgin, Anthony is a queer.

But oh, such a lovely virgin Anna is! She has taken to wearing her hair in a heavy knot, pinned to the crown of her dear little skull. She thinks it makes her look sophisticated. If it did, I'd be inclined to spike her cocoa with Mandrax and shave her head whilst she slept. No, it makes her look as innocent as she did at three years old, when her hair was a bouncing black cap, her eyes like saucers, her speech – unhindered then by nervous inhibition – endlessly gurgling with love for me. She would writhe, and twist her nightie in a knot when Emma attempted to put her to bed: 'My daddy, Daddy do it. Daddy carry me. Daddy lie me down!'

'Hello,' she says now, a little shy, a little scared. 'Are you ready? Have you said goodbye to everyone?'

'Bu.' Yes. I feel shy too, and now the time has come, damn it, I do not want to go. My imbecile babblings are normal here, the corpse at my side just another, ordinary, everyday corpse. I am not a freak on this busy, freak-filled ward where everyone is conditioned to saving my dignity. Of them all, only Myra has presumed to call me Max. The nurses and physios call me Mr Knighton, the doctors call me Sir. Even the visitors, caught up with the fascination of their own pathetic freaks, do not stare at me. I look sadly into my daughter's face.

'Bu-bu-bu?' I ask humbly. How will you lead me home, Anna? Will you punish me with a bus?

Already she has learned which are my rhetorical (by which I mean unguessable) questions.

'Shall we go, Daddy?' she suggests kindly.

Only my new electric shaver (I miss the clean edge of a Wilkinson's Sword) and my night attire are in the suitcase, and Anna can carry it easily. She has removed the rest of my clothes, accessories and invalid doo-dads gradually over the past week. Why? Does it mean a bus? Oh, God, why would I not let her learn to drive? That was a rhetorical question too. Anna, if you take me on a bus I will kill you, the minute we get off it! I will drown you, hold you under the sea with my foot! Both feet! No. She is just a child and I cannot accuse her of thoughtlessness when she has, as Myra has persuaded me, been so very brave and generous during my incarceration here. Oh, but I will die on a bus! What if someone speaks to me? I will die of shame! The words are plain enough in my head, and it is impossible to remember that when I speak I will make only the same burbling, meaningless sounds which have lost their horror – until now.

'Bu! Bu-bu-bu!' Please, Anna! I grab her arm and point frantically at the window.

43

'Yes,' she smiles. 'It's raining, I know. They say it'll clear up, later, but I suppose they're lying again.'

I sag, resigning myself. I suppose I should have realised that a window's resemblance to a bus is too obscure for rapid guesswork. All right, Max, my dear chap. This isn't the first time you've been shit scared. Bluff. That's the way. An *insouciant* smile, chin up, shoulders back, carve a line through the air with that bill-hook you call a nose. Modest Max. This nose is the essence of my charm. It's a sensuous, predatory nose, without which the lopsided smile, the bedroom eyes would seem, well, at best, too far apart. The corpse swings lifelessly, as though from a hangman's noose on a windy hill. My strong left arm snakes around and drags it behind my back. There. The Duke of Edinburgh be praised for making this the royal way to walk. Lead on, Macbus!

My progress through miles of dingy hospital corridors has been undistinguished by anyone's notice. No one has stared at me. No one has asked me to help with a crossword, or to tell them the way to Outpatients, but I am exhausted. My *insouciant* smile is glued on, the heat of my blushes threatening every minute to reduce me to a steaming puddle. Ten miles home. I will be dead of humiliation before we leave the hospital grounds and my smile will slither down my shirt front in a mess of glue and tears. All my life I have been proud of my pride. I wish now I had crawled. A man needs some practice at this game.

'All right, Daddy?' Anna sticks to my side, knowing I am too proud to touch her, guessing that I will pass out if she moves an inch ahead of me or an inch behind. We are bound more closely together now than we have ever been, yet – look at this, God – not a single scale of my skin is touching a single scale of hers. We are not joined but we are inseparable. Many women, through the years, have crawled into my arms, and I have thrust my body into theirs, boring and tunnelling past teeth and tongue and throat, past thighs and fur, tensing muscles, with such need, such violence that I have often been surprised, desire spent, to see that they are still whole and that I have not torn a bloody gash from swollen lips to shuddering groin. Yet never have I felt as close to any woman – no, not Emma, not even my Emily – as I feel now to this fragile child.

She has spent her life crawling into my arms, wresting from them warmth, protection and, more often, forgiveness. Now she is crawling into my mind. I feel her small hand probing through my terror, gently searching for the strings of understanding that will make me whole again. Yet, if ever I am whole again, I will not forgive her. If ever I am whole again I will beat her senseless for her temerity in touching, so intimately, the secrets I have withheld from her all her life.

We reach the great door and pause. She smiles up anxiously, her smile a whole foot nearer the ground than mine. Don't worry, little girl. I shall never be whole again. You will not be punished. Touch my mind, understand me, I beg you – *and do not take me on a bus*.

Chapter Eight

My father had a clique of friends with whom he regularly dined, danced, drank and talked politics at the Watersmeet Hotel: the Townsends, the Brands, the Hurleys. They were all married couples. He seemed to have no bachelors among his acquaintance, although when people came for drinks or for dinner at our house there was often a woman friend – usually one I had not met before. It never occurred to me that maybe she was my father's 'girlfriend', but I suppose she must have been. His discretion, in keeping me ignorant of this side of his life, was absolute. His women friends never came to our house without the chaperonage of other guests, and if they accompanied us to the beach or on Sunday afternoon outings, someone else always came too. I am quite certain my father remained celibate after my mother's death. He rarely stayed out late enough, or went out often enough to conduct an affair, and he almost always told me where he was going. But I knew his friends loved him, and it gave me a feeling of possessive pride to see it, for even if he did not love me, he was mine.

I never became inured to my father's good looks, his elegance and style. When he smiled at me – usually by accident – with his black eyes dancing and his mouth tilted to one side, my heart always missed a beat. He had the same effect on everyone. When he was with them, women forgot their husbands to talk with my father, to hold his arm, to look into his eyes and smile. And when their wives were not with them, the men deferred to my father and asked his opinion. It came as something of a shock, therefore, to find so few of his friends in evidence when he fell ill. Most of the men visited him once and never came again. The women disappeared. Even Mrs Lear did nothing more than to ask me how he was, her face pinched and her eyes evasive, as though she blamed me for his predicament and was too polite to say so.

Curiously, the most generous friend of all was a man who – he confessed to me quite early on – had never much liked my father. Mr Grant, one of the directors of the firm where Daddy worked, was big and bashful, with a naturally deep voice which he suppressed to a hum, just in case one should get the wrong idea and think him fierce. His bashfulness was rather irritating, but I liked him very much, chiefly because he talked to me honestly, accepting that I was a responsible adult with a mind of my own. Immediately he had told me he did not like my father, he was sorry.

'Now don't misunderstand me,' he said hurriedly, snatching off his glasses to wipe away the steam. 'He's a clever man, a valuable man! But, you know . . .'

He looked at me pleadingly, and I smiled to encourage him. Now that I had lost all hope of hearing my father's secrets from his own lips, I wanted to hear them from others, and I did not care how much it hurt.

'He was hard,' Mr Grant moaned apologetically, apparently not noticing that he had put my father into the dead tense. 'He had no give. Not that it did any harm, I'm not saying it did, my dear; but . . .'

Mr Grant sighed, giving himself time to be tactful. 'People never seemed to matter much to him. I like people, Anna.'

He smiled and reared back in his chair, clapping his hands together softly to give notice that he was going to tell a story. 'There's a funny old chap – odd-job-man really – makes the tea, sweeps the floor; been with us for years. He's a poet, Anna. A good one too, though he's never made a living from it. You'll find one or two of his poems in modern anthologies under the name of Alexander Marley. I mentioned him to your father once, and he shrugged and changed the subject. Alexander Marley, as far as your father was concerned, was not a poet. He was not even a man. He was simply an extension of the broom he pushes to earn his bread. Now your father was no philistine, was he? He loved music, art, architecture. He cared for the things men create. But he didn't give a damn for the men who created them. I can't understand that, Anna.'

Mr Grant smiled again, to comfort me. 'There,' he said. 'Perhaps it was that detachment which made him such a fine engineer. But it didn't make him popular, my dear.'

This was not news to me, but it was shocking to hear it expressed with such sadness. It was as if Mr Grant thought my father deficient, somehow pitiable for his lack of 'give'.

I had visited my father's office only once, and had seen that side of him with the same sense of shock. But it had certainly not prompted any feelings of pity – except perhaps for the men who worked under him. I had sensed that he was greatly respected by them, but not greatly liked. I had sensed too that he enjoyed not being liked. My visit was mercifully brief, but it disturbed me for days afterwards.

Later, when I had recovered, I asked my father if he enjoyed working there.

'Yes, why?'

'It doesn't seem . . . very friendly.'

'Friendly?' He seemed surprised. 'I work to make money, not friends.'

'Then how do you make friends?'

'I don't. They make me.'

I must have looked shocked at the contempt in his voice, because he laughed and went on, 'If I had to make any effort, I wouldn't have a friend in the world, Anna. And what is more, I wouldn't care.'

I took it personally, of course. 'But I'm your friend,' I began, meaning to ask, as soon as I could get my breath back, if he cared as little about me.

'That's quite different,' he interrupted quietly. 'Friends have the advantage of choosing or of being chosen. You and I are stuck with one another, whether we like it or not.'

The unmistakable inference was that he did not like it, and I staggered inwardly, feeling my heart shrink away from him. I must have turned pale, too, because he smiled quite kindly before going on, 'You are my little girl, Anna, not my friend. The word friendship implies a measure of equality, and equality is something we do not possess. I am a man, you are a child. I am big and you are small. I have experience and you have not. We are not friends because we are not equals. Do you understand that?'

'Yes,' I said, choking on it. 'But if you and all my friends were drowning, I'd save you first!'

My father bit his lip on a smile. 'So would I,' he said, the deliberate ambiguity leaving me with the sensation of having dashed my head against a rock. He must have known what I wanted from him, but he would not give it. He never gave it. Mr Grant was right. My father had no give at all.

Now, denying it, I said, 'Perhaps he felt it was wrong to mix business and pleasure.'

'Perhaps,' Mr Grant said feebly, but he wasn't convinced. I didn't blame him. I knew my father did not care about people. In his whole

47

life he had cared for only two: himself and his wife.

'He loved my mother,' I said wistfully. 'I don't think he cared about anyone else after she died.'

Mr Grant smiled and looked at his hands. 'Except you,' he said; and I could not bring myself to correct him.

It was Mr Grant who offered the company Daimler to bring us home from the hospital. I thanked God for the chauffeur's inscrutability when, recognising the car and the man who stood saluting at the door, my father burst into tears and wept until the city was behind us, the sea gathering us to its mist-cold shore. I held his hand and said nothing. People or no people, his work was an essential part of his life, his pride, his strength. He must have realised, though we had not told him, that he would never work again. How could he not weep, knowing that this would be the last time he would be saluted, the last time any man would look at him and recognise Max Knighton, Senior Engineer?

But even after two months, I was still not hardened to seeing my father's tears; and the bewildered innocence in his eyes still had the power to wring my heart. Myra had explained that the brain damage which had destroyed my father's facility for language had also destroyed the barriers which kept his emotions subdued.

'He isn't feeling any more emotion than he did before the stroke,' she had said, looking at me sternly to make sure I believed her, 'but now he can't hide the emotion he feels. You'll have to get used to it; and learn to ignore it.'

It wasn't easy. When one has spent one's life with a man as controlled as my father was, watching him cry is rather like watching him defecate. Now it was my turn to be cool and controlled. There was no sense in both of us bawling our eyes out, and from now on, Myra had warned me, my father would cry at anything which moved him: from the cloying sentiment of romantic songs to the sight of a child in its mother's arms.

His temper, too, would be equally beyond his control, and Myra said that he might become violent when the frustrations of his disability became intolerable. I already had some experience of this. Once, when I had been helping him to walk, he had slung me clear across the ward, managing, to my amazement, to keep his own balance in the process. It was the first time he had humiliated me so publicly. If I misbehaved on the beach, in town, anywhere where there were witnesses, the worst he ever did was to make a quiet promise of what would happen to me 'later'. So when I fetched up in a heap against the foot of Mr Hamnet's bed, I was more embarrassed than hurt. All the other men in the ward turned their heads, like dancers in a chorus line, to look at me. The Staff Nurse trilled, 'Pick yourself up, dust yourself off, and start all over again!' and did a tap dance to go with it, as though my father's violence were nothing more than a pre-arranged cue for a song. I knew I had to laugh it off, but laughing at my father's rage was like swearing at a priest: an unspeakable heresy. I managed it, but it shook me badly, and I was not looking forward to a repeat performance (minus the tap dance) in the privacy of our own home.

I was still telling myself that he loved me. It was something I had to believe in order to make the thought of the next thirty years endurable. If I was wrong about his love, how would I survive the violence of his uncontrolled rage? It did not bear thinking about, and when, against my better judgment, I did think about it, I comforted myself with the nasty consolation that he could do rather less damage with one hand than he had been capable of with two.

Our homecoming was strange and quiet and I saw our house through my father's eyes, contrasting it with his warm, cluttered hospital ward and finding it curiously wanting. Built by a minor romantic painter called Roland Embridge, the house had an air of martyred sadness which made it resemble, more than anything else I can think of, a church without a tower. It had two revoltingly ugly gargoyles at each end of the ridgepole, mullioned windows which I had recently discovered were murder to clean, and a porch which, during sudden summer showers, could contain two deckchairs, a tricycle and a lawnmower without seeming especially crowded. I always felt it was a house which should correctly accommodate two sweet old spinsters and a little dog, be filled with the scent of roses, lavender and pot-pourri.

If my grandmother had ever allowed the house its romantic way – and I do not remember her well enough to know that she did – my father had soon put an end to such nonsense. He had a passion for cleanliness and order which would have made a hospital matron feel ashamed of her slatternly ways, and in his pursuit of these virtues he had stripped the house of its ornaments with a ruthlessness which must have turned poor Roland Embridge in his grave. To be fair, I suppose my father's real reason for reducing things to their basics was the knowledge that he would have to do most of the housework himself. After my grandmother's death he employed several dailies, but I don't remember any of them. I remember, though, my father's face, his teeth bared and his jaw muscles standing out like conkers, when he found dust on the banisters or fluff under the beds on the very day the current daily had had 'a good clean down through'. When the last of these unfortunate women had been ignominiously sacked, he polished everything in sight and kept it polished for ever afterwards. And I wore my sleeves pulled down over my hands for fear of getting fingermarks on the door knobs.

It was not a homely place, and until I was fourteen and discovered that much of the furniture was antique (until then I had thought it merely old-fashioned), I was bitterly ashamed of it. My father had excellent taste and his love of comfort was equal to any man's, but somehow, in providing us with warmth, order and cleanliness, he gave the house a spartan starkness which might have been more appropriate in a monastery. The walls were a flat, creamy white, the doors and windowsills plainly varnished. Board floors, stripped with turps every quarter and repolished with a vigour which sent me scooting to my room, were covered with, I realise now, very fine oriental rugs. Once a week I watched those rugs having their backsides beaten on the clothes line in the garden, my father, looking much happier than usual, thrashing dust to the winds with a demonic glint in his eye. Sometimes, overwhelmed by the violence of his cleanliness, I prayed for fitted carpets and a vacuum cleaner.

I was not a tidy child and, of all my faults, this was the hardest to bear, mainly because it was the one my father seemed most to despise. He told me that my mother had been a neat, fastidious woman and I believed him, knowing that if my mother had been slapped as often as I was for leaving toys on the floor and the cap off the toothpaste, she would never have lived long enough to die at thirty-five. My father's determination to cure me of untidiness never flagged, but it was my only real claim to original sin, and I clung to it with suicidal stubbornness, a kind of malice, aimed not at him but at my mother, for being so inimitably perfect.

Guilt and terror caused me to undergo frequent periods of reform, the most prolonged of which followed the burning of my beloved doll Miranda, whom my father martyred in the kitchen boiler for her heresy in being left on the stairs. He made me watch. She had red hair and bandy legs and a heart of gold, and she melted and dripped, sending up a noxious smoke which tainted the air for days afterwards. I thought I would never, ever stop crying. I certainly never forgot it; but my untidiness endured, scourging me endlessly, both with guilt and with the weary consciousness of doing things against my nature.

Guilt was one of my most urgent feelings when I brought my father home from the hospital. Having begun like Jane Austen, Anne of Green Gables and Mrs Beeton all rolled into one, I had gradually degenerated, during my seven weeks of freedom, into an over-acted portrayal of Maggie Tulliver. The charm of living in a house which resembled an abandoned gipsy encampment had, fortunately, worn off fairly regularly, but my sudden bouts of houseproud zeal never lasted long enough to get the whole house tidy; just bits of it. In the end, with only three days still to go, I cleaned from rafters to cellar with the narrowed eyes and gritted teeth of a hired assassin – and still wasn't sure, when I had finished, whether it would survive my father's inspection.

He wandered from room to room like a child in a fairy grotto, his eyes wide with wonderment. He patted the clock and his chair by the fireplace, ran his finger along the bookshelves, looking for old friends. There were tears in his eyes and straining in my throat.

'Bu,' he said softly. 'Tea?' And he smiled.

I could not move. He had fought off his tears, but mine were blinding me. He cupped my face with his hand and stooped to kiss me. Then, 'Tea!' he said, and pushed me away. I laughed. When we went to the kitchen my father ran his finger over the door lintel and held it out to me, grinning from ear to ear. It was filthy.

Chapter Nine

I am so lonely. All my life, save for those sweet few years of marriage, I have been lonely, but never like this. Always, before, there has been me. Nail a man alive in a coffin and hear him go mad. He goes mad in the attempt to keep himself sane, and he does it by talking to himself.

'Okay, Basil,' he says firmly. 'Okay, old chap. So you are nailed down in a coffin, is that it? So what? It's not the end of the world, is it? Think of all the millions of people who've been nailed down in coffins before you!'

'Yes,' Basil replies irritably, 'but they were dead, you stupid bastard!'

It is so lonely, being lonely without even the sound of my own voice to comfort me.

I'm being foolish. Anna has merely gone to the shops and has promised to be back at three. Do I trust her to be back at three? I don't know. This is only my second day at home, but already she is feeling her power, learning it step by step; and she has years of revenge to work out on me.

Throughout her fifteenth year – looking back, it's all been hell, but her fifteenth year was the worst – we fought the Battle of Time. Her time, my time, her friends' time, all out of synchronism. Anna's vocabulary narrowed down to five words, which she practised, on average, fifteen times a week: 'But Daddy! You don't *understand.*'

I understood something which she stubbornly failed to grasp – that there was only one time; and it was mine.

'But Daddy, there's no point in my *going* if I have to be back at eight!'

'Don't go, then.'

'But I want to go! I promised to go! I must go!'

'Go, then. Be back at eight.'

'Ohhh, you don't *understand.*'

The truth was that I did not want her to go. I wanted to spoil all her fun, make it sour and empty until she tired of it to stay at home with me. Why? Was I lonely then? Yes; but not for Anna's company. I've never enjoyed her company. At least, not since she was very small. Anna the Adolescent was a beast of a girl, and my only comfort was the realisation that Emily must have been an adolescent too, before I met her in the loveliness of her sixteenth year. It came as something of a shock to find, when Anna turned sixteen, not a sweet, lovely girl in a white dress and a hat trimmed with roses, but a goddamned teenager in a sloppy sweater, a tight skirt, black stockings and mascara an inch thick. If it had not been so utterly appalling it would have been hilarious.

Afraid to give her an allowance in case she used the money to run away, I had opened an account for her at the local department store. She knew about budgeting, and the account, though not over generous, was certainly adequate to her needs. Why then, I wondered, had she chosen to buy the cheapest, nastiest clothes she could lay her hands on? She looked down at them in frank bewilderment.

'They're the fashion,' she whispered.

Under my attacks, Anna had utterly failed to grow up. She still shook, her eyes still performed their trick of widening to meet the puzzled quirk of her eyebrows and she still had to bite her lip to keep it from trembling.

'Do you intend to waste any more of my money on such trash?'

'But it's the fashion, Daddy!'

'Anna, I have known many fashionable women in my time, and I can assure you that none of them looked like dockside whores. You, on the other hand, do!'

This was not, by any means, true. Anna had worked very hard to look like a whore, but she had failed by miles. She looked like a guilty five-year old, caught in the act of playing with her mother's lipstick. But I was too angry to be charmed. 'If I see you dressed in such "fashionable" garb again,' I snapped, 'I'll strip you to the bone, Anna, and take off your paint with wire wool! That's a promise!'

Anna knew it was. She turned white with rage. She tensed as though to hurl herself at me — and then thought better of it. She submitted. But she had learned how to submit, and although she did it in silence, it had all the grace of an outright victory. I much preferred a fight, for then I knew I had won. But I suppose I won, because she never tried to be fashionable again, poor child.

It was hard for Anna to steer a straight course between the demands of her friends (who all looked like whores: it was the fashion) and the demands of her father. But I wanted it to be hard. I wanted it to hurt. I wanted her friends, who were so callously leading her away from me, to reject her inability to conform and send her running back to Daddy, with tears washing the last illicit trace of mascara from her dark, bewildered eyes. Given my own way, I'd have kept her locked in her room, tied to the bed-post for preference; but I was also governed by the need to conform. A lone father could be permitted a little strictness, a little possessiveness, but not too much. I had to give her a breath of freedom if only to keep the social workers at bay. For the same reason I fed her, clothed, washed and housed her to a standard which no interfering bitch could ever fault — unless she asked why. Why? I'm not answering. It is Anna's task in life now to read my mind, and she must never read what is written here.

Yet, listen to me, God. Listen, Emma, and put in a good word for me with that bearded louse whose right hand you sit upon. Listen to me, will you? My motives were clear to me all along. I am not blind, and although an obsession is a blindness, and I was obsessed, the mind has many parts and I could observe the blinded part with the parts that still could see. I overruled the blindness, disciplined it, tied it down. I forced it to accept that my wife was dead, that Anna was my child and I her father. Grant me that. Grant me that!

Ah, but . . .

Oh, shut up. It's ten minutes to three. I go to the window, holding the corpse behind my back. It is raining again. Odd. It matters now, the rain. Hospitals are brutal, ugly places, but they are weather-proof, even-temperatured, and the windows are too high to see out of. I forgot, even with all my terrors, how dangerous a place the world is, how wet the rain. I trembled when I saw the sea, grey, endless and cold, and when we turned from the shore road it broke my heart to see the town. Were the streets so dirty, the buildings so mean when I was a man? Anna pointed things out to me as though I were a tourist from the African bush. Myra has told her to talk to me, perhaps not realising that Anna has never talked to me, except in moments of crisis and during their forgiving aftermath.

It is five minutes to three and there is no sign of her hurrying through the rain. My heart is beating so violently it is lifting my shirt front. What if she has been run over? What would my life become without Anna in it? What happens to people like me when they are quite alone? I'm only forty-nine! Do they put men of my age in old people's homes? Max, Max, for Pete's sake, don't cry! Wait until the clock strikes at least! Bobby Bibby , . . can't remember. In Debtor's Yard the stones are hard. Sod that! Anna, Anna, Anna! Oh, blue! Blue, everything. And I'm dying; drowning in fifty shades of cold blue sea.

Hissss! A snake? No, the bloody clock. It always hisses before it strikes. Strikes, evil and malevolent like an old, impatient reptile. That clock – must be dirt in it somewhere. I wonder if it's possible to clean it now. One-handed. Left-handed. It's amazing how strong my left hand has become, but it acquires no dexterity. It is as sensitive as a sledge hammer. You don't realise how stupid your left hand is until it is let loose without its master. Anna! Where are you? You too are stupid, strong and blundering, let loose without your master. Are you lurking in Josie's Coffee Shop, with a line of froth on your lip, making eyes at Anthony the Queer whilst I seethe in agony? Have you no imagination? Don't you know what I am suffering?

You deserve it.

I do not! No one deserves this!

She has been late before. Later than this. It is – the minute hand has scarcely moved from the zenith – three o'clock and a bit.

One evening, soon after her sixteenth birthday, Anna lifted her head from the gloomy interior of a geography text book and gasped, 'When?'

54

It is not a word which makes much sense when it is isolated at the end of a two-hour silence, and I glanced up to hear the rest. Anna blushed, coughed and asked something about the rainfall in India.

Later, she said, 'When?' and pretended she hadn't with another diversionary cough. I picked up a newspaper and gave half my mind to the crossword. The other half concentrated on Anna. Something nasty was in the air, and I aimed to have all my wits about me when it broke. A few minutes later, humming tunelessly, Anna trailed disconsolately across the room to warm her bottom by the fire.

'Don't do that, Anna. If you go up in flames you'll have to buy a new dressing gown.'

'Sorry.' She trailed away again, running her finger along the back of the sofa.

'When?'

'When what?' I snapped. The suspense was killing me.

Anna blushed and looked at the floor. In a moment, I knew, she would pluck up courage, stand to attention and face me eye to eye. And her courage in such a conflict was terrifying. Emily had been able to turn my bones to jelly with the direct glance of her eyes, and the only reason Anna failed, usually by a whisker, to do the same thing was because I kept telling myself she was a little girl: not Emily, not Emma.

Anna's head went up. She turned pale, blushed again and then, to my astonishment, burst into tears and ran from the room. Ten seconds later she was back, sobbing and trying to peel my fingers from her wrist.

'Do you want me to slap you?'

'No, no, but I don't want to tell you, it doesn't matter, it isn't . . .'

I shook her and she gasped and stood quite still, biting her lip. Stubborn little cat. We were in for a fight, and I was not at all sure I would win.

'When what?' I demanded. 'Out with it. Secrets are as bad as lies, Anna. And you know what happens to liars, Anna, don't you?'

She was still crying and her eyes were flitting all over the place, panicky and scared. 'When . . . When . . . people, girls,' she spluttered; 'when girls grow . . . grow up, when they're six-six-six —'

'Sixteen,' I supplied, feeling my heart sink to my boots: she thought sixteen was her passport to paradise. My fault. It had seemed such a long way to go when I first told her she'd be grown up at sixteen, but she had clamped on to it like a vampire to a jugular vein.

'Yes! Well, when they are six-sixteen, they have, they have . . .

Mummy did, I know she did, and you can't . . . can't . . .'

'Mummy did what?'

But I did not need to ask. I knew, and was already turning cold.

'She had a *boyfriend*!' Anna wailed.

I knew I would kill her if I moved a muscle. Anna knew it too. She stopped crying as if her tears had been turned off at the mains, and together we watched while our healthy complexions drained away with the sweat under our fingernails. I have always, I *was* always able to master my rage; and I mastered it now, releasing her from my grasp, and trying to keep my eyes averted from the fire-irons with which I would have beaten her to shreds if I were not the master of my rage.

'We'll talk about it at the weekend, Anna,' I said quietly. 'When I have had time to think, and you have had time to calm yourself. Go to bed, now, there's a good girl.'

Scarcely believing her luck, Anna kissed my frozen cheek and crept away to bed. I mastered my rage for another ten minutes and then fled to the garden, where I punched steam out of a perfectly harmless apple tree, under the crazed impression that it was Hitler, who was also Anna's boyfriend. He won.

His name was Eric. I hated him, and terrified him with courtesy. He was a flabby youth with green eyes, yellow teeth and freckles. His father, whom I knew vaguely, was a schoolmaster; a degenerate, woman-voiced toady, worthy of my whole-hearted contempt. Eric received his father's due and his own – for any flabby youth with his eye on my daughter deserved all the contempt he could get. Yes, deserved it; and I mean that in a charitable sense, for contempt is an easier thing to bear than loss of life – the only other alternative I could think of for him. But Eric was quite safe. It was Anna whose heart I planned to tear out by the roots. They went out together four times, so laden with conditions and warnings that I was surprised Eric bothered to pursue his suit. My soul spent these evenings on its knees, praying for them to miss their curfew, praying for them to be ten minutes late.

They did it at the fourth attempt, bless their hearts. The porch fluttered with their apologies, colliding in mid-air like sparrows, trapped, squawking, feathers flying.

'Awfully sorry, Mr Knighton. My fault!'

'The bus was early, Daddy! We ran –'

It was difficult not to laugh, but self-control is – was – one of my greatest strengths, and the plan was clear, waiting only to be executed. 'Saying nothing' was also my strength. How vicious of God to make it now my most bitter weakness! I said nothing. I hauled my child to me by the scruff of her neck, and grimly stooping, in full view of her flaccid lover, I slapped her legs raw.

Eric's romance, his courage, even his feeble outrage, drained out through his greasy pores, dripped from his sagging mouth. And I smiled and closed the door.

Anna wept. Anna stormed. She said that she had never been so humiliated – as though I were quite in ignorance of the fact. She said that Eric *loved* her – ha! – and that I did not. Again – ha! And that I had ruined her life. I laughed, a dry, sarcastic laugh which I knew would incite her to rage. I wanted her rage, because in rage she invariably said and did things she would afterwards regret. I did not enjoy these sayings and doings for they were always too near the truth, too inescapably just; but she did not know it, and remorse was their inevitable consequence. How pitiful was Anna's remorse, how sweet her broken pleas for forgiveness, and when, eventually, I gave it, what joy to hear her whisper, 'I love you, Daddy.'

'But I thought you loved Eric.'

One could almost hear her shriek, 'Who the hell is Eric?' 'No, not very much. Not as much as I love you.'

I never told her how much I loved her. Oh, I wish I had! I meant to, and now it is too late.

Late! It's five past three! When she comes home – if she comes home – I will slap her legs and she will punch me in the mouth. She will knock me down. I can't keep my balance in a fight. This corpse pulls me sideways, swings me off my feet. When she comes home. If she comes home. Oh, Anna, Anna, forgive me all my wrongs, I beg you. *Mea culpa. Mea culpa, mea maxima culpa.* How's that, God? Already you are turning me to the glories of Rome. I don't believe in you. I don't, I don't, I don't believe in you. I am an unbeliever. Oh God, please God, please, please God, bring my Anna home!

Must I live the rest of my days like this, dependent upon your infinitely finite mercy? How long will be the rest of my days? They will be long. Oh, I know they will be long, long days, for even if I have another stroke and die tomorrow, these last ten minutes have been eternity to me, and every minute until she comes – if she comes – will be ten centuries of pain beyond endurance.

Oh! Oh! 'Bu-bu-bu! Bu-bu!' Anna, Anna! All I see are her black wellingtons, her darling, glistening-wet knees, my black umbrella. But she is hurrying, hurrying, splashing the puddles, the umbrella flapping like a greedy bat, eager for her blood. I too want blood!

'Bu! Bu-bu-bu!' I am weeping, stamping up and down, hammering the face of the clock with a hooked finger. You are ten minutes late, you heartless bitch!

She smiles, damn her. 'No,' she says sweetly, dripping water all over the polished floor, 'it's fast, Daddy. Why didn't you look at your watch? It's only ten to three.'

'*Bu?*'

I look at my watch. It's been there on my wrist all the time, and I knew, I knew there was something wrong with the clock! I knew!

Ten to three.

I fall into a chair and cover my face with my hand. I feel so humiliated, so helpless and stupid. Anna kneels beside me and strokes my hair.

'Don't be afraid, Daddy,' she whispers. 'I'll never leave you. I never will. Surely you know that?'

I lean back in my chair and look at her sadly. Yes, yes, my darling, I think I know it, now that you are here. Why should I doubt it? But I do.

There are no certainties any more. The only certainties are those we grab for ourselves and hold; hold in a strong right hand. I no longer have a right hand. I am no longer a man, no longer at the centre of the world. You have escaped, and hold me now in your right hand, more tightly, more cruelly than I ever held you.

Don't crush me, Anna! Please don't crush me.

Chapter Ten

It was three days before anyone came, and then it was Mr Grant. He had been to the hospital several times, and although he had done his best, he did not know what to say to a man who did not talk back. I had thought it would be easier at home. In fact it was much more difficult. At the hospital, when you ran out of things to say, you could crack jokes about the nurses, admire the flowers, criticise another visitor's hat. In the stark purity of our sitting room, what was there to say?

'Hello, Max,' Mr Grant smiled self-consciously and shook my father's left hand. My father's mouth quivered with the trace of a smile, and then he turned his head abruptly, pressing his lips together as though to bite back a scream of humiliation. I nodded frantically to Mr Grant. Go on! Help him!

'Home at last, eh, Max? How's it feel? Good to be your own man? Independ —' Mr Grant screwed up his face and bit his lip.

'Will you have a drink, Mr Grant?' I said hurriedly. I had completely forgotten to offer him a chair and he swayed helplessly in the middle of the room, like a bullock tethered for tiger bait.

'Er, yes. No, I don't . . .'

'Bu, bu.' My father waved a weary finger at the whisky decanter.

'Yes, all right. Thank you, Max.'

I was ridiculously pleased that he had thanked my father, and not me, although a few months earlier it would have wounded me to the heart.

'Do sit down, Mr Grant.' I gave him a beam of approval, and he sat down, responding to my smile with a determination which was almost funny. He was brave. One had to give him that. Stupid, but brave.

'You know, Max,' he said, 'this girl of yours is a trooper, a real trooper. You're a lucky . . .' He coughed and stared at the carpet. My father closed his eyes and touched trembling fingers to his lips. If he had believed in God I'd have said he was praying, if only for words enough to call Mr Grant a tactless idiot.

There was a long silence. Mr Grant squeezed his fingers together until the knuckles cracked. My father looked deeply shocked. My mind had gone blank, and the silence was a cesspool in which we must drown simply because we could not bear the stench of swimming. I tried to think of a safe topic of conversation, but every subject seemed spiked with cruelty. When I gave Mr Grant his whisky he sat up very straight and said loudly, 'Oh!' – as if it had come as a complete surprise. 'Thank you, my dear! Thank you!' The ooze sloshed noisomely, dragging us down.

To my amazement, it was my father who swam clear and pulled us spluttering to the side. He raised his eyebrows, rubbed his fingers together in the manner of separating banknotes and said, in his thin, hollow voice, 'Bu. Mon-ey. Money.'

As a conversation opener it wasn't too successful. Mr Grant looked stunned.

'Money?' he repeated stupidly.

My father screwed up his mouth and took a deep, offended breath. 'Pen,' he said. 'Pen?'

Mr Grant leapt in his seat as if the horse he had bet his shirt on had won the Grand National. 'Pen!' he said excitedly. 'He wants a pen!'

'Bu! No!' A violent shake of the head. 'Bu-bu; mon-ey. Bu-bu-pen. Pen; *pen*!'

'Pen; pen,' Mr Grant frowned studiously and looked again at the carpet.

'Money,' my father repeated. Then, 'Pen?' and a wildly exaggerated look of enquiry.

I thought it was only half a word which he wanted finished for him, but even so pen remained a complete word in its own right, and I could not detach it from its meaning.

'Cheque book!' I ventured, too keenly.

'Pah! Money! Pen!'

'The bank?'

'Pah! No-no-no-no! Money. Money.' He began to look bewildered, as though the whole idea of the pen (whatever it was) was becoming lost amidst the problems of expressing it. He leaned his elbow on the arm of the chair and rested his chin on his hand, a frail, defeated gesture, eyes down-cast to shut us out. I do not know if it was my awareness of being shut out, or my horror at seeing him so hopelessly shut in, but suddenly I was furious; though exactly with whom or with what, I could not say.

'Daddy,' I said, surprising us both with the sternness of my voice. 'Daddy, you mustn't give up now. Mr Grant and I will try to think of everything to do with money and you must tell us when we're getting warm, like in I-Spy. Er, salary?'

'Bu! Bu!' My father jumped excitedly, his finger raised. You're getting there!

'Salary. Salary,' Mr Grant murmured. 'Sick pay?'

'Ah.' A smile, a nod, the finger raised again.

'*Pen*sion!'

'Bu. Bu-bu-bu. Pensh; pensh . . .' Tears poured down his face. 'Pensh, pensh . . .'

We were not to notice his tears, not to embarrass him with our embarrassment. I knew I felt only a tenth of his frustration at our stupidity in failing to connect 'money' with 'pension' when it was so obvious, but I think I felt all his relief that we had guessed it at last, and it was hard not to weep with him.

'Right,' I said briskly. 'Tell us about pensions, Mr Grant!'

I sounded like someone else. I felt like someone else. I'm sure that if Mr Grant had mumbled that he knew nothing about pensions, I would have shaken him by the lapels and snapped, 'Pull yourself together, man!' Luckily for him, he knew it all, and he sat with my father at the desk, explaining it in careful detail, leaving me to a trembling, but still purposeful relief.

I did not, still do not know what my purpose was at that moment, but I suppose it had little to do with love or with kindness. It was, almost certainly, a simple determination to survive. In reviewing the events of my father's thwarted life, I knew there would be no easy way out for him, that he must take the longest, darkest road to reach the light. And on that road, every step of the way, I would be with him. Even though I still saw my father as a hero, I knew that he had sinned somehow, and a phrase from the Bible came into my mind, a stab of horror, of sheer evil: 'The sins of the fathers . . .' Was I to be visited with my father's sins for the next thirty years? I looked at him. He was clutching his paralysed hand, nursing it like a kitten in his lap, and his eyes were huge, the effort of understanding Mr Grant's explanations stripping his soul with all its cruel, cruel wounds, naked for a stranger to see. No, my father was carrying the whole burden of his sins, and my burden was the same as it had always been – that I could not come close enough to help him. But for pity alone I must try. I could not foresee a time when I might leave him, but I think I saw the bitterness and the frustration of years spent at our desperate guessing game. I must learn to play it, and play it well, before both of us, with all our friends, went mad.

All our friends? How many were there? I had sent Mr Hurley away. Mr Lear had been once to the hospital and never visited again. Mrs Lear was pretending to have emigrated. Where was Mrs Townsend, who had loved him? Where was Mr Townsend, who had called him 'My dear Maximum'? Where were Mr and Mrs Brand, whom he had known since they were all children climbing trees together? Why didn't they come, now, when surely they knew how much he needed them, how lonely he must be? I was torn between anger at their neglect and relief that they were leaving me alone. I liked being independent. I did not want their advice or their companionship, but I felt my father's hurt as if it were my own. Had they all, like stupid Mr Hurley, written him off as a vegetable? I wanted to pound on their doors, to scream at them, 'No! He still thinks, he still feels, he still cares!' And it is one of my most lasting griefs that I had not courage enough, generosity enough, to do it.

During that week we received a visitor whom neither of us wanted yet could not turn away. Aunty Dorothy (she was not the sort one could shorten to Dot) was my father's sister, a stunningly beautiful woman who, at forty-eight, looked scarcely a day over thirty. She was dark, slender, with all my father's grace and fastidious cleanliness, his sense of style. But they were different. He was quick and she was somnolent. He was warm, cooling it; she cold, and incapable of warming. The incisive tones in his voice were soft and weary in hers, and although for both of them laughter was a rare thing, my father's laughter was a generous, embracing sound. Aunty Dorothy, when she laughed, seemed to suck you in and choke on you. They loathed one another, making polite gestures for the world's sake which said 'blood is thicker than water'. But as my father informed me when talking of her, for some reason, in the midst of one of his spates about God, 'Water slips down the throat very pleasantly. Blood can make one sick.'

She had never married and lived with a short, burly woman of apparently unlimited wealth whom my father loathed (to the detriment of his blood-and-water theory) even more than he loathed Aunty Dorothy. Her name was Constance Read, but my father had another name for her. I heard it only once, yet even having no idea what it meant, I knew it was something very insulting. 'Put the kettle on, Anna,' he growled when he saw Mrs Read's Jaguar draw up outside. 'Here's Dorothy and little Connie Candlepower.'

Aunty Dorothy had taken care of me for a short time after my mother's death. I remember nothing about it, but I sensed that it had been a disaster and that somehow – even as young as four – I had disgraced myself for ever in her eyes. She certainly didn't like me. Admiring her beauty, her perfumed *hauteur*, I had often wished she did, but her distant acknowledgements of my attempts at conversation soon brought me out in solidarity with my father. We loathed her together, but I did it more politely than he did. 'You again?' he would say irritably, as if she visited every day, although we were, in fact, rarely troubled by her comings and goings. 'I suppose you want tea?'

'How nice.' She had a way of tossing her head in slow motion. 'You are too good, Max.'

She never looked at my father. Her gaze would travel frostily over everything else in sight, but it always skidded past him. She would sit down, cross her legs, and very deliberately light a cigarette. When Mrs Read had lit her own cigarette (a different brand which smelled like Bonfire Night) my father would give each woman a narrow look and open the window. The atmosphere was larded with smoke, cold air, spite and tension. I always felt curiously excited, curiously safe, as if I were watching them through plate glass. They were like people waiting in a dentist's office, strangers politely discussing the weather – except that their courtesy was only a veneer covering great depths of rotten wood. I can remember very few of these 'conversations', but the essence was always the same.

'How tired you look, Dorothy,' my father would say solicitously when the tea and Dundee cake had been brought in. 'Helena Rubenstein isn't quite up to our time of life, I'm afraid.'

Then, his alligator smile turning swiftly to Mrs Read, 'And how is Constance? Is Jesus still bidding you shine, Connie?'

At this point – I always supposed it was because she was devoutly religious – Mrs Read would turn brick red and say in a poisonous little voice, 'I don't know why you bother, Dorothy.'

'Don't you, Connie? Dorothy comes in hope, my dear, but as you see, we do very well without her. Do have some cake. I don't think you need worry about it spoiling your figure.'

My aunt sat in silence, but I always felt she was working up to saying something important. Eventually she would dart her eyes towards me, scan me from head to toe and say, 'How are *you*?'

Spoken in this accusing tone, her question always shocked me, and my reply tended to stick to my tongue as if the words were coated with glue.

'She stammers, Max.'

'Only when she's frightened, Dorothy.' He would smile so broadly, and his eyes sparkle so wickedly at this, that I was surprised when Aunty Dorothy did not smile with him. It was obviously a joke, because I wasn't really frightened of her, just fascinated.

Although my aunt did nothing to parry the thrusts of my father's spite, I never felt he was winning or making the slightest dent upon her sleepy composure; but Mrs Read seemed very slowly to fill with air, her stomach and eyes growing rounder by the minute until at last she snapped, 'Well, I've had quite enough of this! Come on, Dorothy!'

Aunty Dorothy never failed to thank my father for the enormous pains he had taken in making the tea and opening the cake tin, and he invariably told her that no effort was too great. I was made to kiss her. She turned her head at right angles, and when my lips touched her ear I experienced the full force of her perfume, which was lovely, French, and worth – my father informed me – two years' pocket money.

Even when I was very small I knew that Aunty Dorothy's visits were in the nature of a game, like Oranges and Lemons, where, even though we had our heads chopped off, and our blood curdled at the words, 'Chipper-chopper, chipper-chopper, last man's dead', it was still only a game. Mrs Read seemed not to appreciate this, and she often made some vicious parting shot, usually about our garden, which, though never left to run wild, often looked suspiciously natural. 'That lilac's too near the house. You'll be sorry. It'll have the foundations up before you know it.'

'You and your green thumbs,' my father would tease gently. 'Had much joy with your cucumbers this year?'

I was surprised to find that my aunt (minus Mrs Read) visited my father regularly when he was in hospital. She looked completely out of place there, and apparently felt it, for she kept her nostrils pinched as though she could not stand the smell. She showed my father no affection, no compassion. She said, 'How are you?' as if holding him entirely to blame for his predicament. And then, after several minutes' silence, with a faint smile, 'It seems they've put you in a geriatric ward, Max.'

She did the crossword and absently ate a grape before turning to me. 'Are you managing?' I did not notice it then, but I remember that her eyes skidded past me as once they had skidded past my father, as if she denied my existence. 'Do you need any help?'

'I'm fine, thank you.'

'Hmm.' This was evidently quite hard to believe, but her doubts seemed to incense my father, and when she left – exactly half an hour after she had arrived – he would almost explode with fury, flapping his hand at her gracefully departing rear view.

'Bu! Bah!' Ill health had changed none of his feelings towards her.

She came into our house now with a proprietory air, looking like someone who has been away for a month and left the servants in charge. I felt as if I were the visitor, she the woman of the house, and my offer of tea, which seemed rather presumptuous, stuck to my tongue in the old manner, making me blush.

She gave me a pained look. 'Yes. How kind. Do remember to warm the teapot.'

This insult made me quiver with fury. I was still not a very good cook, but I knew all the basics, like being gentle with pastry and warming the pot! No wonder we hated her. When I think of all the awful, cruel things my father did to me when I was a child, I can't think of a single one which hurt me as deeply as that little dig. I was still fuming when I took in the tray. Aunty Dorothy was smoking in her usual chair, and I noticed with a spiteful surge of pleasure that my father had opened the window.

In the past, my father had always given his sister the privilege of pouring the tea. She did it very elegantly and put the milk in last. Now I ignored her and kept the tray on my side of the table, pouring without a trace of elegance and putting the milk in first, a statement of independence which made me blush for ten minutes when I realised how puerile it had been.

Aunty Dorothy said, 'Thank you,' and looked into her cup for signs of arsenic. 'Do you still intend going to college, Anna?'

'Yes. I begin on Monday.'

'Studying – what was it?'

'History.'

She smiled. 'How perfectly useless,' she said softly. 'Don't you think you should try something with more earning potential?'

'Earning potential?' I meant: why shouldn't a history degree get me a job? But she misinterpreted – deliberately, I suspect – and smiled frostily.

'Really,' she said, lifting her hands palm upwards in a delicate shrug. 'Daddy is no longer in a position to support you whilst you pursue the . . . academic life, Anna. There is an unpleasant chance that you will have to work for your living – and his. I would have thought a secretarial course would have been more . . . realistic.'

'I can teach. Teachers earn more than secretaries.'

'Teach?' She shrugged again, her eyes travelling over me slowly, taking in my navy blue jersey, grey skirt and flat-heeled shoes with as much contempt as if they had been rags. I knew precisely what she was saying: I had no more style, no more confidence, no more authority at eighteen than I had had at twelve, and could rarely string more than three words together without saying 'er' while I searched for the fourth.

'Mummy was a teacher,' I muttered, hoping this would solve everything. Even Aunty Dorothy had admitted how like my mother I was.

But she denied it now, pinching her nostrils in the awful expression of distaste I had come to hate. 'Your mother was quite a different kettle of fish,' she murmured, packing a whole world of abuse into the last word.

My father glowered at Aunty Dorothy and raised his eyebrows at me. I was uncertain of his meaning, but the old feeling of being his ally against a common foe stiffened my spine. He could no longer fight her. It was up to me.

'I can teach,' I said sharply. 'From now on, I can do anything I have to do. Have some cake.'

'Hmm.' She arched her brows, twirled her fingers over the soggy sponge cake I offered and declined with a little smile. 'Hmm,' she said again. 'I suppose you can bake cakes, too?'

It was more than enough to undermine my feeble show of strength, and I had neither courage nor wit enough to laugh and turn the joke against her. To my surprise, my father reached out and patted my arm, saying, 'Bu, bu,' like a very young child comforting a teddy bear. Then, turning lethally narrowed eyes upon Aunty Dorothy, 'Bu!' he said sternly. His meaning, the juxtaposition of the two moods, was as clear as day, but my aunt chose not to grasp it.

'What?' Her ability to invest a single word with so much malice made my blood run cold. Protective rage surged, stopping my heart, making me gulp. My father had trained my temper, at least partially, and now I felt crippled by it; afraid to let rip, incapable of doing anything else.

'How on earth does one understand him?' Aunty Dorothy asked sweetly. 'What on earth is he trying to say?'

'Bu!' my father roared, and his right arm climbed the air, a frail spectre of its ancient strength. It seemed the only message strong enough to move it was all-out fury. I pushed it down, holding it; holding his left hand too in case he lost his temper completely and knocked my aunt flying. I did not much care if he did, but my own rage was approaching a state verging on the primitive, and I did not like the idea of my father and I spending the rest of our lives incarcerated in separate prisons.

'It is very easy to understand him if one has any sense,' I lied, feeling my heart, like a small boat at a very choppy mooring, jumping for its release. 'He said, we are doing the best we can. He said, if . . . if all you can do is crit- criticise, perhaps it would be . . . be better for you to . . . to go – and say nothing more.'

'Bu!' my father agreed stalwartly, and his right hand escaped my grasp to climb the ghostly stair of his rage.

I half expected Aunty Dorothy to get up and walk out with an offended gasp, but she didn't move. I had a nightmarish feeling that she hadn't even heard me. She looked up slowly, staring into my father's eyes, saying hard, hard things to him which he understood, though no words were spoken. Then, to my horror, he looked away, turning his shoulders defensively against her. I had been teaching my grandmother to suck eggs. Aunty Dorothy knew more about silent communication than I would learn if I lived to be ninety.

'You are quite right, Anna,' she said at last. 'But I am afraid your best is unlikely to be good enough.' She stood up and carefully pulled on one glove. The left one. It was black kid. 'Your father has brought you up to be useless,' she went on. 'And unless you are made of stronger stuff than you seem, you will remain useless, and have nothing more than this,' she slapped the loose glove contemptuously against my father's still hunched shoulder, 'to save you from yourself.'

She had turned me to stone. I couldn't move. I couldn't speak. She went to the door, turned, smiled; but she still did not look into my eyes.

'Let me know if you need anything,' she said.

Chapter Eleven

This happened to the Prodigal Son, of course. He spent all his substance and his friends left him. In the end, there was nothing to do but to go home to his father, or starve. I always had a brotherly fondness for the Prodigal – until he went home to that sanctimonious, calf-killing old man of his. Wipe that smirk off your face, God. I'm not coming home. I'll starve, thanks, and keep my pride.

Mary Lear walks past the house and turns her face the other way. Joan Townsend, Margaret Hurley, pretty little Muriel Brand – where are they now? Thanking God for their husbands, I suppose. It's all right. I don't want to see them. I don't want them to see me like this. But what of their husbands, my friends? I never cheated them. My friends' wives were special and I loved them; not quite chastely, not quite innocently, but without deceit. I filled the gaps their husbands generously left for me. I talked, teased, flattered: brought piquancy and challenge into the humdrum of their long-term marriages, the dreary selflessness of housekeeping and motherhood. I loved them, but I did not want them; and if they wanted me, it was in the secure knowledge that I was unattainable, like a Leonardo which one covets without regret, knowing that it is of more value left on public display in the Louvre.

But I am angry. I know why they do not come. Jack Lear, who dashes in occasionally, blushing and avoiding my eyes, has told me quite clearly – though without words – that he cares too much, that they all care too much and cannot bear to see me broken. It must afford them great satisfaction to talk about me with tears in their eyes, describing my affliction in horrified whispers; saying, 'No, no we love him too much! We cannot bear to see him like that!'

Love me hell!

If they loved me they would be here, worrying not for the things they cannot bear, but for the things I must bear. And cannot.

No, I am the Prodigal, loved for my riches, abandoned now that my substance is spent. And my riches? Not money. Anna's school fees and my fastidious tastes have put paid to any capital I might have accumulated. No, my riches were my eyes, my smile, my voice. My riches were intelligence, humour and courtesy. And they are lost, squandered. I have nothing left but pride and starvation to sustain me, while the swine still eat, doing obeisance to God, the swine. But I still have Anna. Anna still loves me.

Poor Anna. She is making pastry and I cannot bear to watch. The end result will be fine. She cooks very well, give or take the odd disaster – but oh, the mess! Give her anything practical to do and she has all the grace of a three-legged bison. On the other hand, although I know it will set my teeth on edge, I am too lonely not to watch.

'Oh, hello.' She's embarrassed. She has flour on her face, up to her armpits and all over her shoes. Her pinafore is still clean but there are dusty handprints all over the seat of her skirt. Two eggshells on the floor and a mound of apple peelings on the chair complete the picture of domestic industry.

'Bu?' I smile, and indicate that I will help with the clearing up.

'Oh, thanks.' She blushes and bangs the rolling pin accidentally against her knuckles. Tears flood her eyes. I will not notice. The poor child has been cooking all day, laying in provisions for our first working week. It won't do, Anna, and I am as frightened as you are. You are shy, inept. Going to university, even with your father in good health, was bound to be an ordeal for you. But you are also very, very stubborn, and your teeth are gritted.

There is only one way I know to ungrit your teeth, and I am no longer capable of it. You will never be humiliated again. Not by me; not by anyone. You are coming into your own, and if the fight is hard, although I am wholly to blame for it, you will blame no one but yourself. It is the way of women to blame themselves. Caught in the grip of cataclysmic forces, swallowed by earthquakes, raped by armies, one hears them muttering, 'It's my fault. If I hadn't married Gilbert and moved to Picton Street . . . If I had learned typing and shorthand while

I still had the chance . . . If I had had the simple common sense to realise . . .'

Anna has wiped her tears on her sleeve and is beating hell out of the pastry. She is probably thinking, 'It's my fault. If I had had the simple common sense to be born a boy, none of this would have happened.' She could be right. I often wished she had been a boy. If Anna had been a boy, made in my image, not Emma's, things would indeed have worked out differently. But if Anna had been a boy I might well have been locked up in a home by now.

Removing a mound of apple peelings from a chair with only one hand – the wrong hand – is incredibly difficult. And washing dishes is a nightmare. They slosh around in the bowl, resisting all efforts to catch them. It is impossible to work up any elbow grease for removing baked-on bits of cake and pastry. The strength of my left arm is quite wasted without the dexterity of my right. Damn! Damn it! My shirt sleeve is wet and there is no way of pushing it up. Oh, God, I can't stand this!

'Bu!' I turn to Anna, demanding help. We make a pathetic pair: me dripping, Anna covered with flour. She closes her eyes, her shadowy lids fluttering down with exhaustion; but in that moment she finds her strength, and what passes, after years of suppression, for her native sense of mischief.

'With a dash of salt,' she grins, looking us both up and down speculatively, 'we could get together and make pancakes.' She rolls up my sleeve. 'Oh, I'm sick of this. Let's have some tea.'

'Tea!' It cheers me to say a word which makes sense and I smile and say it again, for the hell of it. 'Tea!'

I fill the kettle. This, too, is difficult, but done in easy stages, not too frustrating. Lighting the gas is more hazardous, and I curse myself for taking such care of my mother's stove, which has never, as a result, needed to be replaced with something safer. I take a match from the box. Trap the box between my knees. Turn on the gas. Strike the match. If it fails to light first time, too much gas escapes and there is a bang, a singeing of eyebrows. Anna has already noticed this and is buying a safety lighter tomorrow. I am surprised, however, that she does not attempt to stop me doing it the dangerous way in the meantime. I am glad she does not, but I wish I knew why. Does she think, kindly, that I will be humiliated if she cossets me, or is she hoping I'll blow myself to smithereens?

While I make tea, Anna grits her teeth harder and summons a new burst of energy; putting the apple pie in the oven and clearing up in a wild rush of activity which leaves the kitchen tidy, but smeared. I know she cannot see the smears. She doesn't know it, but Emma suffered the same blindness. She thought housework a bore, but she understood its importance and her own importance in meeting its endless challenge. Anna is frightened by it, sees herself as its victim, though in this, as in everything else, she is my victim; for although I taught her to be ashamed of slatternliness, I never gave her an opportunity to be proud of domestic creativity. She could not boil an egg until she was fifteen, and bedmaking is an art which still eludes her. Now she cleans the kitchen, puts everything away, sighs as if to say, 'Got you, you brute!' and then almost shrieks with surprise to realise that our cups of tea, our slices of cake, have produced more dirty dishes, more crumbs. It is constantly sneaking up on her.

I understand. Yes, I understand and sympathise, but I still want to wring her neck, to yell, 'It's easy, damn you!' It takes only a little planning, a little energy, a little time. It infuriates me that men, with their stupid ideas of the natural order, have allowed women to become enslaved, and to see themselves as slaves, to domestic drudgery. With planning, energy and only a little time, I have maintained this house in good repair, with the highest standards of hygiene and good taste, for thirteen years. I have brought up a child, kept a responsible job, a reasonable social life, and never felt that my home was my master. True, I had help with the cooking and the mending, but most women have help – if only they would shelve their stupid, ancestral guilt to claim it – in their husbands.

I have never thought domestic work demeaning for a man, and I despise the attitudes of men like Bob Hurley, who think that to wash dishes while there's a perfectly capable woman in the house is the equivalent of volunteering for castration. Castration is being married to a woman whose love is soured by resentment, whose mind is fettered by grocery lists. Hmmm. Bob Hurley doesn't know what he is missing, doesn't know that a happy man is one whose wife bathes and perfumes herself, secure in the knowledge that her lover is scrubbing the kitchen floor, and will soon come for his reward.

Oh what did I do, God? What did I do? I loved her, served her, made her happy. What did I do? And why do I persist in asking such questions of the non-hearing, non-seeing Nonexistent? I must be going mad. And why not? I am a powerful man. Was. And every time I have lost my power, to the Germans, to death, to this, I have turned to you, hating you, rejecting you, abusing you because I am no longer in control. Control is necessary, and I don't have it, Anna doesn't have it. It's my fault, all my fault, my most grievous fault. If I had controlled her less, taught her more, she would not now be standing at the sink as if she were manacled to it. She would be whistling and singing and planning our lives as I once did, with a sheet of graph paper and a gleam in her eye. Anna, Anna, it's so easy! It doesn't have to kill you, if only you think it out!

Anna was not quite six when her grandmother died and left me, trembling slightly, to my own devices. I sat down then with my sheet of graph paper and planned our lives in a single evening. In thirteen years the plan faltered only once – when Mrs Barkworth, my cook/mender, died suddenly when Anna was fifteen. It was – save for the horrible realisation that I had loved the sour-faced wretch – a minor spanner in the works. I encouraged Anna to darn the socks, and with another sheet of graph paper and an extra half-hour's work each day, I managed the catering quite easily.

Joan Townsend did not believe in my half hour. 'What are you living on?' she demanded. 'Bread and cheese?' She was more furious with me for denying her frail claims to sweated labour than for her suspicion that I might be lying.

'Boeuf à la Bourguignonne and Crêpes Suzette,' I smirked.

'But Anna helps!' she spluttered, poor woman.

I agreed. It seemed more gentlemanly to lie cheerfully about it, though in fact Anna merely lit the oven when she came home from school, and laid the table.

Housekeeping is not an art. The placing of a vase, the choice of a painting, are pleasant enough activities in the arrangement of a home, but women take such things to extremes. One vase is not enough. They have to have six, plus a collection of china ornaments, silver jugs and antique brasses. It makes a cosy enough clutter – and it makes work, takes time which would be far better spent elsewhere in developing real talents. I had thought that by never making a drudge of Anna I would give her time to develop such talents and allow her to see housekeeping in its proper context, not as a way of life but as a means of living. Instead, although she draws and paints, embroiders, collects flowers and plays the piano, like one of those gracious eighteenth-century women to whom suffrage was not yet a gleam in the eye, she is useless; totally unfitted to grasp the responsibilities which have so unexpectedly been thrown at her.

I foresee that we will, before long, be living in chaos. Anna tires easily and is easily discouraged. How will she cope with full-time study while she struggles with our domestic burdens and an invalid father? When she was a child I merely waited until she was tired enough to do something stupid, and then sent her to bed early for a week to punish her. By the end of the week she was rosy-cheeked again, bursting with energy and accusing me of cruelty.

Now I am helpless to control anything. Both cruelty and kindness are beyond my scope. If chaos comes, if Anna exhausts herself, goes astray, I must simply watch and hope that we both survive. Gritted teeth are no substitute for strength. It would help if my friends had compassion enough to become Anna's friends, to help and to guide her. I don't care if they abandon me, but Anna has no one to turn to. All her life she has been echoing her baby chant: 'Daddy do it, Daddy carry me!'

Now Daddy, though still here, still at her elbow, is as good as dead, crying, 'Anna do it, Anna carry me!'

And she can't.

What, in God's name, is to become of us?

Chapter Twelve

I was rarely ill, but when I was fifteen I had a serious throat infection which lasted for weeks and almost landed me in hospital. For several days, until the penicillin began its work, I could neither speak nor swallow, and every breath was torture. My father took me into his bed, and slept beside me between the bedspread and the eiderdown, wearing his dressing gown and a pair of sea-boot socks. Every time I woke, he woke too, and fed me drops of iced barley water from an egg spoon. I sweated terribly and he changed my nightie three times in one night, washing me, drying me very gently with talcum powder and cotton wool. He smiled at my shyness and whispered, 'Close your eyes so I can't see you.' When he lifted me up to put a clean nightdress over my head, I opened them again, and for the first time in my life I saw fear in his eyes.

The second time was when I began to talk of going to university. Our relationship had mellowed by then. We had reached an uneasy compromise. Sometimes I thought he had beaten me into submission and sometimes I thought I had won a moral victory. I knew the precise measure of his patience and became too proud to goad him beyond it, imagining that if only I could maintain my dignity he would ultimately recognise it and give me a free rein out of simple respect.

One of the advantages was that he took to attaching questions marks to orders: 'You'll be home at nine?'

This allowed me the spurious privilege of replying, 'Yes, I think so,' as if I had a choice. We both knew that if I were not home at nine he would kill me.

One of the disadvantages was an acute loneliness. Because we did not quarrel we did not need to be reconciled, which dispensed with virtually all verbal and physical contact between us. Once, when I had been sunbathing in the garden, he caught me by the ear and said sharply, 'Is that dirt on your neck?' He rubbed my neck with his finger, 'Good Lord, it's sunburn,' and let me go. I was angry, but in a secret place of my soul I wished that it had been dirt, for then he would not have let me go, would not have stopped speaking – even if his touch and his words had hurt me. We could survive for days saying little more than goodbye, hello, please, thank you and goodnight. If he came home from work with the information that the roads were icy, or that he was cold, I counted it as conversation.

I had, by the time I was sixteen, largely overcome the peculiar speech impediment which had glued my tongue into knots, but panic could still render me speechless, not because I could not say the words, but because I could not remember them. Forgetting words like 'abdicate' and 'omnipotent' was nothing remarkable. I could just as easily lose 'sock', 'pin' and, even more embarrassing, 'dictionary'. Most people managed to deal quite tactfully with my frantic substitutions – 'the book which tells you the meanings of words' – but my father was unfailingly irritated by them and behaved as if my agonised hesitations were designed to spite him. When he deigned to inform me that the roads were icy, my brain teemed with suitable responses – Yes, treacherous! A car skidded on Elmhurst Road, and if the kerb hadn't stopped it, it would have annihilated the bus queue! Instead, losing my grasp on the words at the last moment, I said, 'Yes,' and kept 'treacherous' and 'annihilated' for my English essays.

Applying for a university place made speaking to him a necessity, but I sat for the best part of an hour before I could pluck up courage to begin.

'Daddy?'

My father was reading and did not hear me. I tried again.

'Mph!' He shook off my interruption like a fly from the end of his nose and went on reading, his brow creased in a frown. He had become increasingly morose as I grew up, and I sensed that he liked me less than ever.

'Daddy, I'm, er, supposed to discuss my university application . . .'

My father pressed his lips together and took a very deep breath. 'What?'

He spat the word, and his eyes, when they met mine, were glittering with impatience. I hunched my shoulders defensively and a chill wind shivered through my mind, blowing all the words away. I held out the list of colleges at arm's length.

'I'm . . . I . . . Miss Rowles said . . . that we should talk to our – parents about this.'

He ignored the piece of paper and frowned. 'Well?'

'We have to decide which . . . where . . . which colleges to . . . apply for.'

'And?'

'I thought,' I halted, feeling myself shrivelling under his contempt. Why bother to be tactful? It was obvious he would be glad to get rid of me. 'I thought I'd go to London,' I went on, suddenly calm. 'Jenny's going to be nursing there, and it'll be nice to be able to see her occasionally.'

That was when I saw the fear in his eyes, a leaping spark which was hidden as he took the list and read it.

'London,' he said quietly, at last. 'And when you get lost, do you suppose you'll manage to ask your way to Piccadilly? Come to that, can you say Piccadilly?'

I would have greatly preferred a punch in the teeth. I felt my colour draining away and the old disbelief at his cruelty turned my limbs to water.

'Well, Anna?'

'I can say – it.'

I couldn't. I was too close to tears, but I suppose it was what he had intended because he smiled quite kindly before going on, 'You are still very young, Anna.'

'I'll be eighteen when I go. It's almost – almost two years, Daddy.'

'Then why must we decide now?'

'I suppose they have to have time to, er, process everything. And I have to send for the p-p-pros-'

'Prospectus,' my father supplied grimly. 'Very well, we'll decide.'

74

His eyes narrowed, and after another perusal of the list, he stared at me as if trying to assess what price I might fetch on the secondhand market. He stared into my eyes and I lowered them. He stared at my hands and I hid them behind my back. His scrutiny was like a rope, winding round me, tying me down, and his decision, when he pronounced it, was merely the finishing knot.

'You will not go to London,' he said. 'You will stay at home and go to college in Exeter.'

He opened his book. I almost accepted my dismissal, but then a devil – one I had frequent struggles with – whispered, 'To hell with dignity! Fight it out!'

'Daddy, we were . . . we were supposed to discuss it!'

'We did.'

'But I didn't say anything!'

'You said you wanted to go to London. I said you were too young. I considered your point of view and my own, and decided in favour of mine.' He moved his lips in the parody of a smile, and turned a page.

The devil gave me a sharp dig in the ribs. 'Why?' I croaked.

'Why what, Anna?' He looked quite astonished.

'Why do you want me to stay at home? You don't – don't need me. You don't even like me!'

'Oh?' My father laid down his book and patted its cover as though to give it some assurance that it would have his attention again soon. 'Would it make you any older if I said that I like you? Would it enable you to speak more clearly, or to remember where you left your latch key? Where *is* your latch key, Anna?'

I flushed, more with rage than embarrassment. It was an old trick, and he caught me with it every time, giving me a few yards of rope with which I might hang him, and then dropping the noose neatly around my own gullible neck.

'I don't know,' I muttered. 'But Daddy, I *will* be older! I'll be eighteen!'

My father shrugged. 'You said much the same thing about being sixteen,' he said. 'Yet here you are, still stumbling over your words, still losing your possessions, still asking me what day it is; and I have little faith in your being more competent when you are eighteen. The question of whether or not I like you has no bearing on the matter.'

I was very angry, very frightened. I knew that if I lost my temper he would win the battle without giving me an inch, but my heart was trying to break out through my ribs and there was an ache in my throat which only a full-bodied scream could relieve. I swallowed, and twisted my hands in a cold, sweaty knot.

'Perhaps I would be-be-become more competent,' I began.

'If you had any grasp of practical matters,' my father continued smoothly, 'like money, for instance. I've paid for your education so far, Anna, and will of course continue to do so, but there are limits. In London, you would have rent to pay, food to buy, travel expenses, clothes, books – and you won't get much of a grant. If you stay at home you will save me the bulk of those expenses. If you go away, you'll make a pauper of me before you get your degree. Do you understand?'

My rage died, leaving me feeling sick and beaten. 'Yes.' I looked at my shoes, remembering the fear in his eyes, realising, now that the hope was gone, that I had hoped it was fear of losing me.

'Now, have we discussed it?'

'Yes . . .'

'Is our discussion over? May I read my book, now?'

'Yes. I'm sorry I, er . . . sorry.'

I had not thought much about going to London, having learned that wanting something inevitably meant that I did not get it. But I knew now that I had wanted it badly. Later, when my father brought in the coffee tray, I murmured, 'Perhaps I'll be a nurse, instead. You wouldn't have to pay for that.'

He laughed.

'I mean it.'

'Oh, I'm sure you do, darling; which only confirms what I said earlier – that you are totally impractical. Wasn't it you who cried for a week when Jenny's dog was run over? Do correct me if I'm wrong. One wouldn't have minded if it had died, or had been maimed for life, or even if it had had a decent pedigree . . .'

'It screamed!'

'So do *people* who have been run over, and people who are dying from unpleasant diseases. You're being ridiculous, Anna.'

'I am not! I'm trying to be con- con-'

'Contumacious?'

'Constructive,' I sighed, being unsure of what contumacious meant; although I was fairly certain it was something unpleasant.

'You failed,' my father said, snatching away the plate of biscuits as I reached absentmindedly for a third one. 'You are not going to London, Anna, and even at the risk of boring you as you are boring me, I will repeat it. You are not going to London, Anna. You are not going to London.'

I accepted it, but did not cease to regret it until my father fell ill. Then I thought again of God, and of God's plan, which could have such nasty repercussions if one attempted to change it. If He – in my father's shape – had agreed to let me go away, I would have been in serious trouble, torn between my need to care for my father and my need to shape a life of my own. Now I could have both. God had arranged everything, and if I could remember to trust Him with my fate, I would survive.

But God was not much help on my first day at college. I was scared. Jenny had gone away and I knew I was too shy to make new friends. My father, spending his first day at the hospital day centre, had left home in a worse state of nerves than my own, and if things went badly for me I would get no help from that quarter. I remembered my first day at St Lydia's, when he had dressed me because I was shaking too much to do up my buttons, and then – when it was over – sat with me while I did my prep, gentling me through it, assuring me that only the big girls got punished for making mistakes. Now we had changed places. At the end of the day, he would weep and I would dispense comfort, even if I wanted to weep on my own account. Being alone was hurting more than ever, and I felt tired even before the day had begun.

I knew most of my fellow students had come straight from the sixth form, like myself, but it was difficult to believe. They seemed so much older. Anthony Rogue-Marton, for all his gentlemanly behaviour, had done little to overcome my terror of boys, and I had been quite relieved when he went back to Oxford; but there was no escaping the fact that I was now surrounded by boys – men! – with deep voices, predatory eyes and a general air of worldliness which made Anthony, in retrospect, seem almost girlish. By accident, I made eye-contact with a tall, golden-haired youth whose thumbs were jammed into the waistband of his jeans. He smiled at me, and with the nightmarish feeling that I had no clothes on, I turned away and went to the back of the lecture room, trembling and wishing I could go home.

The girls frightened me even more. Most of them – or perhaps only the ones I chose to notice – were dressed to kill; cool, sexy creatures with bouncy breasts, supple hips, cheeks glowing with excitement and self-confidence. That the glow was largely due to make-up made it all the more threatening, emphasising my drabness, accentuating my shyness. I watched them covertly, choosing the one I would have for a friend, knowing that whoever I chose would never know it, never care. Being alone had grown on me like a skin, and with Jenny gone, I had resigned myself to eternal solitude. The girl I chose was the one I wanted to be. She was tall and healthy, with red hair and eyes which, even at a distance, were bright and blue and generous. When she smiled, she lifted her chin, and her humour spilled out in a wide crescent instead of dripping shyly into her collar, as mine was apt to do. She was warm and relaxed and already had a circle of people around her, though she was not especially beautiful. I knew (one does not bother to be modest whilst talking to oneself) that I was prettier than she was. My hair, which my father called black, had chestnut lights and a sheen like silk. I had good skin, a dainty bone structure and eyes 'like peat bogs' to use my father's description, though he had also admitted, to my astonishment, that they were finer than my mother's. So why was I stuck all alone at the back of the room while she held court at the front? It had nothing to do with beauty. It was the smile, the confidence, the way she had of sharing herself, as if she thought it would be unkind to do otherwise. It was the first time I had seen my shyness as a selfish, rather than as a self-denying fault; and I took it very much to heart, forcing myself to relax so that if anyone turned to look at me I would seem as generous and kindly as my distant 'friend'.

When the lecturer coughed for our attention, I gave him (without his notice) a mellow smile, stretching out my legs so that my knees no longer touched, stretching out my arms and letting my hands hang loose. The effect was amazing. I felt wonderful – for a little while. I found that relaxing was very like having a friendly conversation with my father. As soon as I realised how good it felt I was scared it would end, which it immediately did, forcing my stomach into the familiar knot of weary panic.

At the end of the lecture we were given directions for reaching the cafeteria, and my panic developed into outright terror. Sitting alone in a lecture hall might easily be considered wise. Sitting alone in a cafeteria would immediately brand me an outcast. I stood up, attempting to look vague and dreamy, as though I hadn't noticed I was alone; but my eyes must have widened to twice their normal size, and my shoulders ached with tension. I felt like an invalid out of bed for the first time: weak, wobbly and ominously close to tears. A group of students rushed past, ignoring me.

Then the girl with the friendly face stopped and smiled straight at me. 'Coming?'

'Oh! Yes. Sorry, I was dreaming.' I blushed and bent down to reach for my bag. When I straightened up, I was surrounded.

'Who's this, Lib?'

'I don't know,' she laughed. 'I'm Libby and this is Dave.'

'No, you idiot. I'm Chris.' He was dark, with nice teeth and cynical eyes. 'This is Dave.' Dave was the golden-haired one who had taken my clothes off an hour before. I flashed a smile at his Adam's apple and avoided his eyes like the plague. 'And this is Ian.' Ian was short and spotty and he seemed to hate me on sight, which, perversely, made him less threatening than the other two.

'She's Libby,' Dave poked his finger into Libby's midriff. 'Who are you?'

'Anna.' I pretended the boys weren't there, and gave my name into Libby's keeping, hoping she would be kind to it.

It was a long walk to the cafeteria and by the time we sat down together I had four friends. A few minutes later, to my amazement, I had six. Two other girls joined us, elbowing their way into our group with smiles and shoves.

'I'm Cathy!'

'I'm Jane!'

They announced themselves as if they assumed we had been waiting for their company and thought ourselves incomplete without them. Jane was actressy and obvious, summing up the boys with her eyes and then lighting a cigarette as if she were raping it. Cathy was very short, which made me like her immediately, and plump, with crusty traces of acne under her make-up and a suggestion of prominent teeth. But she thought herself beautiful. She was projecting beauty, demanding that we recognise it. I learned more from Cathy in five minutes than I had learned in a lifetime of self-effacing shyness.

She and Chris were Londoners, Jane was from Gloucester, Ian from Huddersfield and Libby from Manchester. Dave was Welsh. They all had regional accents but seemed oblivious to any differences – until I spoke. Dave asked if I knew where the Union building was.

'It's at the end of Bath Street, by the river.'

There was a very noticeable silence. I blushed. Had I said something stupid? Surely he had meant the Students' Union, not the Transport and General Workers'?

Dave grinned. 'There's posh,' he teased. 'Your jaw almost touched your knees when you said Bath Street. *Baahth*.' He dropped his jaw dramatically and brought his knee up to meet it.

'Don't!' Cathy leaned across the table to thump him. 'You're making her blush, you creep!'

'Roedean?' Chris enquired sarcastically.

'No.' I smiled, but it was my nervous good-girl smile, and I got rid of it hastily. 'It's natural. I was, er, born with it.' This was so ridiculous that I decided, in a moment of unprecedented rashness, to risk everything on a joke. 'Soaked it up with the *baahth* water.'

They laughed, and I met Libby's eyes, which were glowing appreciatively. She liked me. It was a miracle. I felt as if someone had lit the fuse of my suppressed longings and that at any moment I might be blown sky high.

It was a dangerous sensation and one I knew very well. My father called it 'over-excitement' and it was a cardinal sin; almost as bad as losing my temper, three times worse than being untidy. I did my best to stay calm, but when Libby asked me to go with them to the Freshers' Dance, three emotions hit me at once: delight at having been invited; disappointment that I could not accept; and then, shame, at my reasons for declining. Was I ashamed of my father? The idea appalled me, and it was little comfort to realise, after a moment's reflection, that I was not ashamed of him, but of myself – for being dutiful enough, devoted enough to want to care for him.

'I can't. Thanks.'

'Why not?' Chris glared at me as if I had said something rude.

'I, er, can't,' I repeated stupidly. 'I'd like to, but . . .'

'She caahn't,' Dave finished, his eyes twinkling so pleasantly that it was impossible to take offence. 'And if she caahn't, she caahn't.'

I blushed and looked at my fingers which were writhing like a brood of elvers in my lap. I was losing, and I could not lose so much so soon. I lifted my chin and grinned. 'Don't be daahft.'

Dave threw back his head and laughed: a deep, beautiful laugh which infected all the others. Chris clapped me fondly on the back and Cathy patted my hand as if she were, in spirit, hugging me. Another sizzling inch of fuse burned towards my heart, and I thought I would weep for joy. Oh, they liked me! And if I lost them because of my father . . .

For a moment I hated him, that speechless, weeping, helpless burden, and could feel the weight of him dragging me down into the lonely void in which he had kept me all my life. He had not lost his power after all. He was more powerful than ever, for now I was denied even the conviction that I was right to want to escape him.

We were told we could have the afternoon off and Libby arranged a visit to the pub across the road. Wrenching a smile to my face I said, 'Yes, I'll meet you there!'

This was a lie, but much easier than explanations. I had promised to call at the day centre at lunchtime to tell my father what time I would be home. I set off jauntily with my shoulders well back and my collar turned up for the most dashing effect. For a few minutes I was a carefree student, an armour-plated college girl with friends, ambitions, soaring hopes. Then I saw my father eating mince and chopped carrots at a laminate table with a dozen broken old people who dribbled and drooled. I saw the shame in his eyes, a beaten hopelessness which pierced my armour as if it were no harder than the skin on a blancmange; and my friends, ambitions and hopes were swept away on a tide of grief and pity.

In June, my father had given a dinner – ostensibly to celebrate his birthday, though really to square his conscience for eating so many of his friends' dinners and giving them so few of his. As usual when he entertained, I was not invited, an exclusion which hurt all the more because I was seventeen and thought myself perfectly capable of playing hostess. But I was allowed to help with the preparations: the bits I couldn't ruin, like picking strawberries and cleaning the silver. I arranged flowers for the hall, the dining room and the sitting room in three elegant glass vases with narrow necks. My father, when I wasn't looking, shoved all three arrangements into a big willow-pattern jug and stood it on the piano. I was hurt again, largely because it looked so much better. He seemed to do everything without making any effort. He had cooked a leg of pork the day before, and the potatoes for the salad were boiled in their skins. He spent a few minutes seiving carrots for the soup. All of a sudden there was an elegant, four-course meal, the wine cooling in the fridge, the brandy, cheese and port set ready on the sideboard, the table laid with crystal, silver and my grandmother's ecru lace napery.

My father seemed very happy, and while he shaved I sat on the edge of the bath and asked, not for the first time, 'Can't I come, Daddy? I could help.'

'No.' He turned his head at right angles, stretched his skin with his fingertips and shaved a brown, satiny track from his ear to the point of his jaw. 'Look,' he said, pointing to a few grey hairs at his temple. 'You're turning my hair white.'

'I won't say anything: I'll just help.'

'You've arranged to go to Jenny's. Anyway, I refuse to censor my conversation for your ears. You can't come. I don't need help.'

'Can I stay for sherry?'

My father shaved his upper lip with a thin, rasping sound, moving his mouth so that his bottom teeth showed. He liked shaving, and he always seemed nicer when he was doing it. He looked at me in the mirror and smiled. 'Yes,' he said. 'You can stay all evening. In bed. With a sore behind. Now, if you want to do something useful, go and find my cuff links.'

'I'm seventeen!' I protested, and he flipped me with the towel.

'You'll find them in the same place they were in when you were twelve.' He grinned, deliberately misunderstanding. I gave up.

While he dressed, I sat on the windowsill in his room, alternately watching him and the martins which were nesting in the eaves. My father was not at all shy, and I often watched while he dressed, though he kept the secret of his masculinity until the night of his stroke. I had little idea what it was that made him a man but I knew it was inside his white cotton shorts. Black hairs made a dark triangle on his chest and ran in silky ridges down his thighs. His tummy went in at the waist and his shoulders were smoothly tanned. The only flaws on his body were large, ugly vaccination marks on each upper arm, which he had acquired during his years in the Navy.

He dressed methodically, enjoying it, half smiling at his reflection in the mirror. His shirt was sea-island cotton, silkier than silk. His black suit, which had been tailored almost thirty years earlier, was still in superb condition and still, miraculously, in fashion. He was very careful with our clothes, and he pressed my school gymslip into knife-edged pleats twice a week. It took me three years to grow into my gymslips and four years to grow out of them, so I never had a new one from my first year to the upper sixth. My father put on a pale grey tie with diagonal black stripes, a gold stud, gold cuff links. He pushed a white silk handkerchief into his breast pocket and stood very straight, grinning at me. 'Am I gorgeous?' he demanded.

'Not unless you let me stay.' I blushed, but he really was in a good mood and I knew I could tease him.

'Grrrr!' he said, and stretched out his hands to strangle me.

He hadn't been so nice to me for ages; but I knew he wasn't being nice for my sake. He was simply excited because his friends were coming to dinner. He hooked his arm around my neck and squeezed.

'Give in?'

'Yes, yes! You're gorgeous!'

'In that case, you can stay for sherry.'

He laughed and kissed my ear, and suddenly I was crushed with shyness. I knew I would not stay. He didn't want me.

Mr and Mrs Townsend arrived just as I was leaving for Jenny's, and I watched my father greeting them, his smile radiant. He was graceful and strong and his warmth tore at my heart. I was jealous of his friends. I felt small and shabby, like a poor relation at a wedding, wishing the bridegroom would notice me.

'Have a nice time, Daddy.'

He cupped my face in the palm of his hand, frowning and smiling at the same time. 'Next year,' he promised softly. 'When you're a grown-up college girl.'

Four months later my father gave his grown-up college girl a tremulous smile and pointed to some chairs by the window. He stood up, fumbling for his handkerchief, and shuffled to the window, his shoulders stooped, his feet barely clearing the floor. He looked like a man of eighty. I was screaming inside, 'Myra, you bitch! You lying, wicked, black-hearted bitch!' but I smiled and said, 'Have you seen Myra?'

'Bu.' He shook his head very slowly, sitting down with a squelch in one of the nasty, leather-cloth chairs, pulling his crippled hand on to his knee and kneading it miserably. I couldn't think what to say. 'Nice place'? It stank of unspeakable things: stale urine, boiled meat, Dettol and cabbage. An old lady in the chair beside mine farted wetly and the stench of cabbage was suddenly much stronger.

'Bu! Bu-bu-bu!' My father was pleading with me, begging me to get him out, his tear-brimmed eyes enormous, like a new-born calf's. I held him in my arms, rocking him.

'There, there, Daddy. There, my daddy, my darling. It's all right. I'll make it all right, I promise.'

He stiffened and pushed me away, turning his head abruptly to stare out of the window. Within the space of a second he had changed. His spine straightened, his chin lifted bravely; but I could still see the side of his face and the large, glittering tear which rolled, proudly ignored, to his lapel. He was dying of shame.

I spent the afternoon with Aunty Dorothy. I had no alternative. I knew that, set against my father's suffering, my pride was unimportant. I stood there like a carving in granite on the doorstep and said grimly, 'You said to let you know if I needed help.'

'Come in,' Aunty Dorothy said. She was trying to hide her smile of triumph, but it escaped through her eyes, and I stepped inside, certain that I was leaving my independence behind.

Chapter Thirteen

My God, my God, why hast thou forsaken me? Oh, don't answer. I can't bear it though. I can't, can't bear it. Don't you realise that this is coercion, and that coercion's illegal? You should know. You made the laws. It just goes to prove what was known all along, that the law is a ass, and you a arse-hole of great and stinking magnitude.

All right. One sees some sense – though not much – in the rich man having no more chance of entering heaven than a camel has of passing through the eye of a needle. Yes, yes. If love and charity are the passports to heaven, then I agree: the rich man must give all he has to the poor. It was very good of Christ to advise him so. The poor sod obviously wanted heaven, believed it existed. I don't. After death there is nothing. Nothing exists after death. It is dark and silent. You are not there.

It isn't as if I condemn those who believe otherwise. Anna, for instance. She believes in God. She believes her mother is in heaven, keeping an eye on her from God's right hand. Fair enough. And if she wants to join her mother, no doubt Anna will give all she has to the poor, when she has anything to give. But me? Are you listening? I couldn't give a damn for the poor, and if I gave Anna's outgrown clothes to Oxfam it was not for the good of my soul, but because I can't tolerate waste. Waste! Waste! I don't believe in heaven. I don't believe in you; and I did not want to give away my riches! You took them!

Is it any wonder that so much evil has been spawned by the Church? The Crusades, the Inquisition, witch-hunters, Jew-baiters. It's no bloody wonder, is it? God is the Mafia. God is a Nazi. God is a Stalinist bully-boy, a lout who eats babies and kicks pregnant women in the belly. Yes, you! I wouldn't give. I held my riches in my strong right hand and you took them; took my right hand, too. Took my speech. Took my pride. You held a gun to my head, blasted my brain into bloody fragments and took! So. Now I am stripped of my wealth and have a passport to heaven, do I? Thanks. Keep it. I'd rather burn in hell.

84

But on my own. I won't burn with others like myself. I cannot bear to be with those disgusting inbeciles who show me what I have become. I can't bear it! Oh, forgive me!

No! I will not crawl! I have done nothing to deserve this!

Anna . . . A few months after Emily died, she took my hand and said, 'Daddy, where is dead?'

'Where is what?'

'Where my mummy is. I want her to come home now.'

I was still prone to weeping at night for Emily to come home, and I can't have explained it terribly well.

My mother died soon afterwards. Anna scarcely knew her. She had cancer, and spent the last few weeks of her life in a nursing home. I must have told Anna she was dead, but I don't recall that she took much interest. A short while after the funeral, whilst walking with Anna in the park, I met an elderly woman who had known my mother. She said, 'I hear poor Mrs Knighton's gone home,' and offered her sympathy in the conventional manner. Before she had finished, Anna went berserk.

'Mummy?' she screamed. 'My mummy's come home?' She tore her hand from my grasp and ran away, hell-bent for home, no doubt, to lay out the welcome mat. She howled blue murder when I caught her, and before I managed to restrain her she drew blood from my face with her fingernails and landed a paralysing kick in my groin. I threw her down on the frozen grass and sat on her; and there, before a fascinated crowd of onlookers, I told her about heaven. I told her it was full of ice cream, bluebells and budgerigars.

'And fairies?' she wailed.

'Yes, and angels with golden wings.' That impressed her. 'And when people go to heaven, God gives them their own wings, like the angels'.'

'They can fly?'

'Yes, so you see it's very nice there, and one wouldn't want to leave it once one had learned to fly, Anna. Mummy and Grandma live there now, and that is their home. They won't come back.'

Having spent a significant proportion of her life flapping around in the garden in an attempt to take off like a fairy, a butterfly or a budgerigar (her favourite among the winged species), Anna could understand that no one of sound intellect would wish to leave a place which permitted unlimited flying *and* ice cream; but her eyes filled with tears again.

'Can I go too?' she whispered miserably.

85

The pain in my groin having subsided to a tolerable level, I picked her up, straightened her hat and kissed her. 'Yes, of course, darling. We'll all go. But we have to wait until God calls us.'

Call me! Call me, you bastard! I can't stand it here much longer!

'Bugger! *Bu!* Bugger, bugger!'

. Now I'll put the kettle on. Anna will be home soon. I'm a bloody fool. There's no use in fighting, pleading. I'm stuck, and must stick it out. One can't tunnel out of this kind of prison, and He hasn't had the decency to erect an electric fence I can throw myself on.

Memory has failed me, and there is only one thing on my mind. That fucking day centre. Think of something else, think of something else, think of something else! Anna! Emily, oh, Emily!

Now come on, Mr Knighton, dear. You can do it. Look at this lovely picture. We're going to weave a pretty little gallery all around the edge, and then you'll have a lovely tea-tray for your daughter's kitchen. Won't that be nice?

My kitchen. And I wouldn't give the goddamned thing house room.

Oh my God, I'm crying, and here's Anna, and I don't want her to know! I am sobbing like a baby. She flies in at the door and throws her arms around me, rubbing her hands over my quivering back. She kisses my neck; warm little kisses to comfort me.

'Come on,' she says firmly, and with a new despair I see that she is smiling.

So much for my grief. So much for my ruin. She doesn't care. She has her own life to live, and I am the living dead, buried alive in God's own shit.

'Come on. Sit down and cheer up. We won't be beaten, Daddy. I've told you that before, and I meant it. You don't need to go to the day centre again. I've sorted it out.'

'Bu?'

I sit down very suddenly and stare at her. Is Anna capable of working miracles, or is this a new disaster creeping up on me in disguise? She lights the gas under the potatoes. The beef casserole is already heating in the oven; I attended to it before I started weeping.

'Let's have a drink,' she says crisply. 'You do it. I'll have a sherry.'

Will you, by heck? I've just made some tea. Still, who am I to argue? You're eighteen, I suppose, and no doubt Anthony the Queer has led you off the straight and narrow before this. Thank God he's gone back to Oxford. As time goes on, my queer theory carries less conviction. She is so beautiful, my Anna. How could anyone resist her?

I give her a small glass, half filled. She laughs, and I am afraid she will defy me and fill the glass to the brim; but she is too kind. She is much kinder than she should be. It frightens me. It can't last. Anna is no saint.

'Bu?' What have you been up to, little madam?

'I went to see Aunty Dorothy,' Anna says chirpily, as though Dorothy were our most dearly beloved kin, with a heart of gold to boot. I frown, and Anna, showing a cynical edge which I have never seen before, grins. 'Well, she said she'd help,' she says. 'And after all the rotten digs she's made at us, she deserves to.'

I manage a tremulous smile. What's going on? I don't want help from that po-faced bitch. I am scared. I feel like a Hebrew of Polish extraction being offered first aid by a member of the Gestapo. Anna, this is your daddy! What are you doing to me?

'Bu-bu-bu?'

'I was scared,' Anna smiles, and then pulls a face at the sherry, which is too dry for her taste. 'But I brazened it out. I asked if she knew someone who would come and sit with you while I'm at college. She could come herself, of course, but I didn't ask that, obviously. She'd be worse than the day centre.'

She grins again and I love her so much I could eat her. My face is tearing itself apart as I attempt to keep it from crying again. How does she understand about the day centre? She was there less than ten minutes, and I was being brave at the time.

'Anyway, she did know someone. A Mrs Underwood. She used to be Mrs Read's daily, but she got old, and has rheumatism.'

'Bu?' I don't wish to appear ungrateful, but . . .

'About seventy, apparently.' Bless her heart. I can read her mind, pretending to read mine. 'But she's quite lively, and she'd like something to do as long as it isn't housework. Aunty Dorothy 'phoned her and she's coming to see us after dinner, and if she likes us, she'll start tomorrow.'

Anna heaves a big, smiling sigh which suddenly becomes a bated breath as she realises how unpleased I am.

'Well,' she says defensively, 'if you like her, of course.'

No, my clever little mind reader, that isn't what I meant. How are we to pay this Mrs Underhand? Have you any idea how much other people's time costs?

I reach for my wallet and slap it once against my knee. 'Mon-ey,' I say, in the awful voice which seems to have its own built-in echo.

Anna blushes, and there is a spark of resentment in her eyes. 'I've thought of that,' she says loftily. 'And, of course, we can't afford to have her permanently. Not full time, anyway. But she doesn't want to work full time. I thought, if you agree of course, she could stay all day for a week or two and then gradually taper off until she just comes for your lunch, a few hours either side. Sort of.'

I am thinking about it.

Anna swallows. 'If you can't cope, of course, we'll have to think again.'

She stands up and goes to the kitchen to attend to our meal. I recognise the gesture. I've done it to her countless times and it means: that is my decision, like it or lump it.

'Anyway,' she shouts in over a clatter of plates, 'you'll still have to go to the day centre twice a week to see Myra and the physio.'

Aha! I thought it was too good to be true. Still, twice a week is better than a full-time sentence, and I must be grateful and pray that this Mrs Undergrowth likes me. It can't be guaranteed any more. My eyes used to say the things women wanted to know. Now they simply expose my feelings, and my feelings are mostly pitiful.

The casserole is good, with herbs in it and bits of orange peel. Anna's sensitivity surprises me. So far she has cooked nothing which needs cutting up before I can eat it, but neither has she prepared any invalid mush. It shows thoughtfulness and ingenuity, and all for the spurious purpose of saving my pride. It is very difficult to eat cleanly even so, and my pride falls a little further every time I push some messy morsel off the side of my plate. She pretends not to notice, though when I was doing the laundry she did not dare make a mess. Anna's perfect table manners earned me more acclaim for fatherhood than I deserved. Her manners were of minor importance. I was cutting down on the ironing.

I have been so unkind to her. If God had turned Anna against me I could not have borne it, but I could have understood it. She loves me, and for the first time since Emily died I love Anna as I should always have loved her, and take my first joy from my daughter without a trace of guilt. If Emma had lived I might have had a normal family life, and Anna would wear mascara and have a boyfriend. She doesn't need mascara. Her eyelashes are like the wings of minuscule ravens, flying sunset shadows across her cheekbones. But perhaps she needs a boyfriend, and someone is bound to fall in love with her before long. What will I do then? I'll be jealous as hell. But Michael Grant once informed me very kindly, and not at all suspiciously, that all fathers are jealous. Apparently we get over it in time. But do all fathers love their daughters as I have loved Anna? If they do, they've kept very quiet about it and have left me to suffer alone.

I have suffered; but Anna has suffered more, for she never knew why. Sometimes I would see her looking at me as one might look at a creature from another planet, her eyebrows making a v, her eyes two huge os as she tried to puzzle me out. The puzzle, I knew very well, was that I was entirely predictable. Given factors A and B, consequences C and D would inevitably follow. There was no give, no room for excuse or appeal. Anna's doubt was that there was no doubt; her fallibility was that I was infallible. Such rigid discipline is essential on a battle cruiser, which is where I learned it; but in a home? It verges upon inhumanity, and I knew it. It was deliberate; a manic, obscene plot which, like all such, failed with a puff of smoke and the stench of self-immolation. Tyrants, take note. God always has the mastery of us and we never win through to the end.

Look at her. I could imagine she was eight again. The little frown, the air of mustn't-do-it-wrong concentration, the slight tremor of nervous hands serving the apple pie.

'Custard?'

But her eyes have changed. As big as ever, they are older, harder, wiser – and all in the space of a few months. Perhaps she is not irrevocably harmed. Perhaps all my wrongs have been turned against me, leaving her quite intact – but so vulnerable! Or is she? Is she? For it was her very innocence which beat me, though at the time I could not admit my defeat. She was mine, and now? Whose little girl are you now, Anna? Your own? Or have you, today, sold your soul to Dorothy, who will crunch it up like an apple and spit the pips in my eye?

Thank Jesus and all the angels for custard. The pastry's like leather. Anna knows it and her face is red. 'I'll wash up while you make the coffee,' she says sharply. Little devil. I notice no question mark, no 'please, Daddy', and I greatly appreciate it. The rules have changed, but I can attempt a show of protest lest they change too much, too soon.

I frown at her and then realise that the word I need begins with a b and that with a bit of effort it might be possible. 'Boss-sy.' I sound like a fog horn and feel like a king.

'Daddy!' Anna whirls on me, her face alight. 'Did you learn that today?'

'No.' I am grinning. Two words in a row!

'You mean you just said it? You found it all by yourself?'

89

'Bu-bu!' Well, well, well! Ain't I the clever one?

Anna smiles, a dinner plate in one hand, a pastry slice in the other. She looks like Boadicea after the razing of Colchester (not that I was there).

'It's going to be all right!' she says, almost convincing me. 'When you start saying your own words, it must be a sign that there's something worth working on!'

I am going to cry, and feel I must stop myself somehow.

'Bu!' I turn her back to her duties. Get on with the dishes, madam brain-surgeon. I can do without cheerful prophecies which will come to nothing. God is not on my side, and my only comfort is that He will not let me die until I repent, meekly, and upon my knees. This renders me immortal, and it's killing me.

While we drink coffee, Anna reads to me: a biography of William Cobbett. She reads well, her voice clear and lively, but I do not understand very much. Speech, when it is prolonged like this, is as difficult to grasp as the written word. I can read the newspaper headlines and understand them, but beyond the first line all meaning blurs. It is like playing a concerto in reverse, a cacophony without rhythm or harmony. Conversation is a different matter. It comes in short, sharp bursts, like headlines. If modern conversation were inclined to soliloquy I would be as good as deaf. I wish I could explain this to Anna. Perhaps if she left a few seconds' silence between sentences I would be able to grasp what is happening.

I must do without books. I can't listen to the radio – except to music, of course. Music still sounds good to me, and opera is best in Italian anyway. But what am I to do with the rest of my immortal life? I can't spend every minute listening to opera. What if there's a war, an invasion, a general strike? I have to know what's going on, if only to keep myself from going mad with boredom.

Oh-oh. Mrs Dunderhead is here. Anna goes to the door, throwing me an encouraging wink over her shoulder; something she would not have presumed to do a few months ago. Her confidence amazes me, and I am further amazed to hear how she receives the old woman, her voice firm and kind, with a smile in it. Did I teach her that? Was I a better father than I thought?

'Shake his left hand,' she whispers confidentially, and I blush like a virgin bride.

'Daddy, this is Mrs Underwood. My father, Max Knighton.'

'Howja do.' Mrs Underwood shakes my left hand very firmly. She is small, thin, healthy and rather common. I like common old ladies. They are easy going, and have a mild sense of inferiority which makes them determined to be in awe of no one. Mrs Underwood is as bold as brass. She dumps herself into a chair, picks up my book and surveys the title with a frown. She looks searchingly into every corner of the room and gasps, 'Good 'eavens! Haven't you got a telly?'

A what? A telly! Behold, the light of the world!

'Bu! Bu!' I laugh, pat her knee, jump up and grab the gin bottle, waving it at her.

'Ooh!' She rubs her hands. 'Don't mind if I do.'

Anna is confused, wondering at my sudden animation. I pour Mrs Wonderhead a double pink, thrust it into her hand and rush for the evening paper, where I know there is a half-page advertisement which will explain what I want. After much bumbling and blundering I find it and slap it a few times with the back of my hand. 'Bu! Bu!' Anna, for God's sake, look!

Mrs Wonderful says, 'Cheers, then,' swallows a stiff slug of gin and informs my astonished daughter: 'He wants a telly, love. I'm surprised you didn't think of it before.'

Chapter Fourteen

I told Libby my problems hurriedly, and in a shamefaced monotone, merely to explain why I could not share a flat, go to the college dance or take part in the dozens of extra-curricular activities to which I was invited. Libby had a very expressive face. She was tactful and careful with words but she could not hide her feelings, and I knew she had thought badly of my excuses to date. Eventually, giving the wall the benefit of one of my boldest stares and Libby a view of my left ear, I said, 'Actually, Lib, the truth is that my father's an invalid, and I'm all he's got, and I can't leave him. Sorry.'

Libby laughed. 'Oh, that's all right,' she said. 'We thought you had a heavy romance going.'

By lunchtime she had told everyone the truth about my heavy romance, and Dave, who had appointed himself universal Dutch Uncle, told me sternly that I could manage things better if I tried.

'What do you mean?' I was shocked to be finding no sympathy for my misfortunes.

'Couldn't you get someone to give you a hand occasionally? If you leave yourself out of everything here you'll get only half an education; the other half is the social life. You're eighteen, not forty. How do you expect to grow up if you stay at home with – Daddy? I bet you call him Daddy; if you stay at home with Daddy all your life?'

I blushed and then turned white. I was very angry, and deeply hurt. Chris, who had been listening attentively with all the others said, 'Lay off, Dave,' but in a half-hearted tone which suggested that he agreed with every word. Cathy was ominously silent, picking off her nail varnish with her teeth.

'It's true,' Dave said callously. 'If she put her mind to it, she could find a better way to cope.'

'Corp?' I said, sarcastically mimicking his Welsh accent, but no one laughed, and Libby, tactful as always, changed the subject.

But I knew he was right. I was getting only half an education, being left out of things just as I had been at school. Then, as now, my father had been to blame, but now I had the power to change things, to claim my proper position. The responsibility was mine, and I was too scared to accept it, still too scared to grow up. It was a terrible thing to admit that after all my years of wanting to be grown up, I now wanted to be a little girl again; but almost as soon as I admitted it, I realised it was not quite true. I wanted to be grown up as my friends were grown up – without any responsibility except to themselves. I felt that I had been catapulted from adolescence into middle age without having had any fun in between, without realising any of my dreams. Dreams. I wanted to be tall and sophisticated like Libby; to be respected like Dave; to be crazy and cheerful and daring like Cathy; and to have people say, 'Let's hear what Anna thinks about it!' as though my opinion mattered.

I sensed that I would have to make my mark socially before I would be accepted as someone with a mind and a voice, and Dave's advice gained weight every time I thought about it. I decided that I must go to the college dance just once, to say that I had been, to prove that I could do it; and there were so many other things too. The theatre, the film society, the debating club – all were passing me by, leaving me only half educated.

From their first meeting, my father and Mrs Underwood had been the best of friends, which was odd, because before his illness my father would not have given her the time of day. She had been one of Mrs Read's charladies, and, although she was now too old for housework, there was nothing elderly either in her eye or in her tongue. She seemed completely undismayed by my father's inability to speak, and swept him along on a calm tide of assumptions which I now realise revealed a devastating talent for character assessment.

She arrived every morning by a short cut through the fields, bringing big white horse-mushrooms when she could find them. My father showed her the correct way to make an omelette, and to sprinkle nutmeg on the mushrooms to bring out their best flavour. In the afternoons they drank copious quantities of tea and played pontoon for ha'pennies. Sometimes when I came home I would find my father laughing, or so serene that one would think he hadn't a care in the world. And although I called myself every kind of fool, I was jealous.

Oh, and there was the television! I could scarcely believe it when my father did a war dance on the evening paper, pointing at the advertisement and saying, 'Melly! Melly!'

'He wants a telly,' Mrs Underwood announced smugly, as if it weren't quite obvious.

I stared at my father in disbelief, feeling unreasonably angry. At various times throughout my childhood I had attempted to explain to him that television was one of the necessities of life, like milk and electricity, and that any child forced to live without it could not be expected to grow up properly, or to begin to grasp what life was about. Nothing he had denied me had made me feel so deprived. And brave.

I reasoned with him. I nagged him. Later, when desperation set in, I begged and wept – all to no avail. As I grew older, and a little more confident, I tried reasoning again. I explained how educational, how sensible, how well-mannered television was (although in truth I simply wanted to fall in love with the rock singers and film stars who peopled my friends' fantasies). 'No,' my father said, and slapped me. I threw one of my tantrums, said my life wasn't worth living. How could anyone be so cruel to his own flesh and blood?

'It's perfectly easy,' my father retorted pleasantly. 'And at times like these, Anna, eminently satisfying.'

I was furious, and used the most dreadful language I knew at the time, 'Damn you! Bloody damn and blast you!' – while he hauled me to my room and slapped me until I was reduced to helpless, sobbing apologies.

The argument was suspended for several years and I did not broach the subject again until my sixth-form teachers began to demand that we watch plays, documentaries and discussions in the conviction that we all had the wherewithal to do so.

'No,' my father said. 'Television is an evil, time-wasting vehicle for propaganda and corruption. Ask me again, Anna, and I will ensure that you regret it.'

Now here he was, less than a year later, demanding that we buy a television set. For ninety pounds. At a time when we had very little money and no hope of ever replacing our capital. I couldn't believe it.

'But they cost ninety pounds.' I told him faintly.

'Bu! Bu!' He fetched his cheque book and slapped it into my hand.

'Better than reading this old tripe,' Mrs Underwood said, banging my father's *William Cobbett* down on the table with a contemptuous thud. 'I don't know how he can read all that rubbish, I'm sure.'

'It isn't rubbish,' I said, becoming quite exasperated. 'And anyway, he can't read. I read it to him.'

Mrs Underwood gave me a narrow look. 'Oh,' she said, 'that's nice for him, then.' I saw what she meant, of course.

'But ninety pounds!' I gasped. 'Daddy, how can we afford it?'

He frowned horribly, snatched the cheque book back and slapped it again into my nerveless palm. 'Bu!'

'Unless, of course, you want a madman on your hands,' Mrs Underwood said, getting smugger by the minute. 'If he can't talk, can't read, can't do anything to occupy his mind, a clever man like him, he'll go crackers. I'm telling you. The telly's just what he needs, and if it takes your last penny, it's worth it.'

I asked Mr Lear to choose one for us, and that weekend it was installed with due ceremony in a corner of the sitting room. My father changed the station from horse racing to rugby, and for the next two hours watched in a frenzy of excitement, gripping the arm of his chair with his left hand while his independent right arm writhed and stretched in mid air, the fingers curled like claws. As an experiment, I went out to the garden to plant daffodil bulbs, without telling him where I was going. I stayed out for an hour. He did not notice my departure and failed to notice my return. I was piqued, delighted, charmed and disgusted all at once. I knew it represented a release for both of us, but again, to my fury, I was jealous.

Of course, I was glad my father was so much happier. But it was galling to realise that it was no thanks to me. Somehow, just when I thought I had come into my own and become the apple of his eye at last, I had been given the elbow again. I felt like everybody's outcast. Libby, Cathy and Jane now had a flat and spoke a special language concerning it which left me bewildered – and terribly impressed. Dave,

Chris and Ian Collard did not share the flat, but they knew its language; for they spent a good deal of their time there, drinking, playing records, unblocking the sink and helping Cathy, who was brighter than all of them, with her essays.

I wanted very much to join in, but I wanted even more to know that my father still needed me. I rushed home every evening to cook his meals and tell him about my day, to exercise his hand and do his speech-therapy homework. He seemed bored by my attentions and was irritable until I had finished and he could switch on the television again. Then he drifted far away, living out every detail of the programmes he watched with smiles, frowns and tears. He cried even when the Persil Mum forgave her little boy for getting his shorts muddy.

In the end, about a month after Mrs Underwood's arrival, I conceded defeat and asked her to do a late Friday. She said, why didn't she stay the night and save herself the worry of walking home in the dark? It was agreed. All I needed then was the courage to tell my father that I was going to the college dance. I had never in my life told him any such thing. Before his stroke I had never stayed out later than ten, never been anywhere he did not approve, never gone past our garden gate after dark without asking, 'May I?'

There was no question of asking his permission this time. I was determined. 'I'm going to the college dance and won't be back until midnight.'

The words came to my lips and died there several times before I actually spoke, but my father was leading a wagon train to Utah at the time, and he looked up irritably, said, 'Bu?' and then shrugged the whole thing off as being too trivial for his attention.

Chapter Fifteen

I'm getting accustomed to it, making the best of it; and now that I have my 'telly', I quite frequently forget all about it. And I seem to have lost interest, for the first time since Emma died, in Anna, my daughter. It is a relief, but also a sadness, for in losing interest I lose the last of my power over her, which is the last of my power over anyone, anything.

Mrs Underwood is a gift. She talks endlessly, sweeping me along like an unresisting leaf on an autumn breeze; but miraculously, as if God (in a brief moment of compassion) decided that a little indulgence would do me no harm, she has a slight impediment of speech. Or perhaps she has trouble with her dentures. Anyway, although one could safely say that she never stops talking, she pauses frequently to make little sucking noises, like the pretend kisses one gives to dribbling babies who are too disgusting to touch. The pauses, the little kisses which would have irritated me to madness not long ago, are truly a Godsend, allowing me to grasp virtually everything she says.

She gave me her entire life story, all seventy-two years of it, on our first day together. Since then she has gone back to the beginning, expanding the details of her Cockney childhood – 'Twelve of us. In two rooms.' – two marriages, seven children of her own, innumerable funerals, love affairs, catastrophes and disasters, which make my own life seem like plain sailing on a duck pond in June. I can't help thinking there's something odd about her. She lost all five of her brothers and her fiancé in the Great War. She lost a husband in 1940 and another three years ago. Her firstborn was stillborn and her little girl died of TB, aged eleven. And it doesn't seem to have affected her at all. 'Yes,' she says calmly. 'She went thin as a stick, poor little kid.' But it is as if she is talking of someone else's child, and she gives me all the details with a dispassionate air, almost shrugging it off as of no account.

Yet I have never talked of Emily without feeling a lump in my throat. I have never been able to discuss her at length with anyone, not even with Anna. Just the easy bits. 'Your mother was beautiful. Your mother was clever.' I have never reminisced as Mrs Underwood does, giving the details, the truth. No one knows that Emily sometimes wept and stormed, or that she once threw the cheese grater at me. No one knows that when she laughed her eyes filled up with a joy that one could almost catch, like silvery fish which come to the surface of a dark lake. No, I have never been able to say such things, never been able to recreate Emily as a human being whom Anna could love and regret.

Doesn't Mrs Underwood care that she has lost all her loved ones? Didn't she love them? The brothers, the husbands, the sweetheart killed at Passchendaele, the stillborn babe, the wasting child? Or do so many tragedies freeze the soul? No. Mrs Underwood is not frozen. She still has hope and warmth, a delicious sense of fun.

Emma once told me that women were the stronger sex. I laughed and lifted her in my arms, holding her high against my chest until my biceps swelled like shining boulders. It frightened her, delighted her. I could feel her lovely body fluttering with fear of me, desire for me. 'Oh yes?' I teased. 'Prove it.'

And her argument, which, of course, had nothing to do with physical strength, ceased with the onset of laughter and kisses and – more.

But I knew she was right.

I have seen it even in Anna: the instinctive knowledge of her own strength which nothing I could do to her would ever crush. Even in submission and defeat she used my weaknesses against me. She gave me what I wanted, and knew that in doing so she was the victor. She has me where she wants me now. I have lost interest, which is all she has ever asked of me.

Emma and I lived in a village not far from here. We had a ground-floor flat in a converted Victorian manor house; large, high-ceilinged, with enormous bow windows. Emma had superb taste and some money of her own to add to my long-term savings, and when a few strings had been pulled to secure it, I stepped neatly out of the Navy and into my job at Rendell's. We were well off. My mother – a martyr to martyrdom – warned us that marriage was a struggle. We did not find it so. We had fun getting our home together, making plans. I have tried not to think of it since, but I see that flat now as clearly as if I had left it only yesterday. The vermilion carpet in the drawing room, the suite of Waterford crystal, the Coalport, the silver. We had inherited most of it from Emma's mother, who had conveniently died of heart failure during the Bristol blitz – a typical act of kindness, for we could not have managed half so well if she had survived. No, it was not a struggle.

When Emma died, Dorothy and my mother brought Anna here, to escape the violence of my grief. I sold everything. The furniture, the carpets, the china; Emma's clothes, Emma's books. I kept only her gold watch and a pair of shoes. They are tiny – size three – and made of oyster-coloured suede. I have kept them in a shoe box in my wardrobe ever since. I don't know why. I never look at them. But Anna does, sometimes. Anna also wears size three, but she cannot step into her mother's shoes. She has a very high instep. They won't do up.

I did not see Anna for more than a month after Emily died, did not want to. I had decided to leave her here with my mother and go back to sea. I was not capable of suicide, but the sea is dangerous and cold and I thought it might take me if I were lucky enough. I came here to tell my mother my decision, not caring what she thought of it. I remember thinking, just before I arrived: if Anna runs to me, if Anna cries out for her daddy I will kill her; I will hurl her against the wall and smash her to a pulp. I did not want her. I wanted Emily.

I hadn't bargained for the fact that my child would not recognise me. I had been drinking, weeping, not eating or sleeping. I suppose I must have looked like an escaped lunatic temporarily subdued; a somnambulist wearing a nightmare for a mask.

They had had tea in the garden. Anna was sitting on the lawn, quietly undressing her doll. Dorothy said, 'Hello, old boy,' quite kindly.

Anna looked up. Her baby chubbiness had disappeared, perhaps as a result of her own baby grief. Her eyes widened, and then, instead of running to me, she ran to Dorothy and leaned against her, her thumb jammed into her mouth so hard it ought to have choked her. Emma had held strong views about thumb-sucking. Before I knew what I was doing I snapped, 'Take your thumb out of your mouth!'

She did so immediately, her face twisting with fear and bewilderment. Then, only then, I realised that she was Emma. Emma, who had looked just like this, small, thin and bewildered, in the hours before she died. In that moment I took possession, took my daughter hostage, kidnapped her as the instrument of my revenge on God. I ran across the lawn to take her and she shrank against Dorothy's side, clinging to her neck, whimpering.

Dorothy leapt up and pushed the child behind her. 'No!' she said. 'No, Max! She doesn't recognise you!'

I don't know why I didn't punch Dorothy in the mouth. I was crazed with lust for my child. Her fear of me gave me the first moment of pleasure I had known in a month. It was the first pleasure I had ever taken from another's fear of me, the first time I had felt no compunction to disarm myself with laughter and reassurance. I was prepared to tear Dorothy apart rather than allow Anna the sanctuary of her protection.

Dorothy knew it. She dragged Anna forward, saying, 'Anna, it's your father, your daddy!' And somehow Anna knew it was true. She crept from Dorothy's skirts, staring at me, stretching her fingers in a gesture I was to become familiar with, though I never understood it until now. Both her hands were splayed wide, tensing so hard one could almost feel the energy in them, feel the pain in the joints, the stretching of the skin. She was absorbing shock.

I took her up, held her so tightly it is a wonder I did not crush her bones.

'Have some tea,' my mother snapped. 'Sit down, Max. Have some tea.'

I sat, pushing Anna's trembling body into a curve against my hip bone. She gasped once, but she did not attempt to escape me, and she did not cry. Ignoring her, content simply to possess her, I held her on my knee for an hour or more while I discussed our future with my mother. There was room for us both. It was expected that I move in. I did not mention the sea.

The evening was growing dark and the gnats were biting. Anna was asleep, her mouth slightly open, her lashes curving like dark moons.

'I'll put her to bed.' Dorothy reached out to take her.

'No!'

'Max, it's long past her bedtime. She's done in.'

Anna woke momentarily and reached her arms around my neck. Sleep had brought her an illusion of happier times and she croaked, 'Daddy put me,' before sleeping again.

I smiled, for the first time since Emily's death, and kissed my daughter's face, planting the first seeds of a deadly love which is now quite dead. I have lost interest.

Chapter Sixteen

I was so excited I could scarcely sit still, and I heard nothing of the morning's lecture. I took notes, but afterwards had no idea what they meant. At lunchtime, Libby and Cathy came with me to help choose my dress for the dance. I was terrified of buying the wrong thing, scared of being less fashionable than everyone else, afraid to buy anything too extreme in case my father went mad and burned it. Cathy said I should throw caution to the winds and buy something short, red and whoreish. Libby said my legs weren't long enough. Cathy said whores didn't need long legs, she was the proof of it. Libby and the boutique assistant had hysterics while Cathy, producing more proof, hitched her skirt to show fat, lumpy thighs to innocent passers-by. I blushed and pretended I wasn't with her. In the end I chose a plain black dress with a heavily studded belt; largely because, without the belt, it looked like something Aunty Dorothy might wear to a cocktail party. Libby liked it. Cathy hauled it up on one side to show my leg and the edge of my knickers.

Afterwards, too excited to care, I accompanied them to the Queen's Head, a rather sordid pub which was very popular as a student meeting place. I went blind, deliberately not noticing the smell, the noise, the leering men, in case I should run out again; but it was hard not to hold

Libby's hand. I had never been in a pub before. Jenny and Chez always went to the Yacht Club bar; quite a different proposition, and wicked enough for me. I heard Chris shout my name, and I sat down with the others, grinning, pretending I had been frequenting such dives all my life.

That evening I paid my first visit to Libby's flat. I had expected a neat, modern little council flat like Mrs Underwood's, and was surprised to arrive at a seedy terraced house with brimming dustbins on the pavement outside. The flat was on the ground floor. It was filthy and it smelled worse than the Queen's Head. The wallpaper was peeling off, and when I walked on the dirty orange carpet in the living room, it squelched, and a froth of tiny bubbles squeezed up around my shoes. Libby laughed and explained that they had had a party and someone had left the tap of the beer keg turned on.

'It'll dry out eventually,' she assured me kindly. 'Want some coffee?'

'Thank you,' I said, very nicely, as if I were taking tea at the rectory. Everyone laughed. I was paralysed with embarrassment.

The boys arrived, looking sleek, smelling good and shouting at the tops of their voices. Libby went off to have a bath in the primitive lean-to at the rear of the house. It smelled strongly of drains and mushrooms. When she emerged ten minutes later, she swept through the living room with her nylon housecoat wide open and not a stitch on under it. She seemed not to notice that we all looked at her as she passed. The silence went on for ages.

Then Dave, coughing into the side of his fist, said, 'That's that, then. She's not a natural red-head.'

Everyone laughed except Ian, who still had his mouth open. 'That's bloody disgusting,' he said in an awed voice. 'That's bloody disgusting, that is. Christ, I've never been so bloody disgusted.' And everyone laughed again. But I was scared. I wasn't sure if he meant it.

When I joined Libby in her room I was shaking. Libby was applying her make-up at a dusty, cluttered dressing table. The room looked sordid, with two unmade beds, the sheets rather grubby. I had never seen so much dirt all at once, but Libby was very clean, and her dress, hanging behind the door, was freshly pressed. The way she put on her make-up, her graceful fingers stroking and smoothing with ease, spoke of years of practice. But she was only eighteen. Like me. Eighteen!

'How long have you been wearing make-up?' I asked nervously.

'Since I was twelve. I had some for my birthday. Bright blue eye-shadow, puce lipstick and pancake stuff to hide my freckles. *Laugh?*'

At twelve Jenny and I had experimented with her mother's nail varnish. I hadn't realised it wouldn't wash off. When I went home, my father smacked my hands until I was jumping and then stripped off the nail varnish with something poisonous he fetched from the garage. I hadn't the heart to try Mrs Cole's lipstick after that.

'Will you do my face?' I asked Libby humbly.

She did my face and my hair and loaned me a pair of black lace tights with seams. They were miles too long and we pinned the waist to my bra straps. Cathy came in when I was dressed and said I looked terrific, 'Like a red-light district.' I didn't know what a red-light district was, but it sounded pretty and cheerful, like seaside illuminations, so I accepted it as a compliment.

When Dave saw me he laughed and kissed my nose. 'That's my girl,' he said approvingly. 'You look almost human.'

Cathy kicked him, but it was I who was more deeply hurt.

The dance cured everything. During the first nervous hour I drank some beer which went straight to my joints, making them feel warm and loose. The darkness, relieved only by moving coloured lights which made everyone look weird, wild and wonderful, was like a camouflage in which I could hide myself. I stopped being shy, stopped being scared. We danced. I took to it like a duck to water, and then, shedding my feathers, like a fish. I lost myself in the dark, in the light, in a frenzy of movement. I loved it. When the music stopped I could not speak for excitement, for longing to dance again.

The boys got drunk. Dave and Ian became lunatic, nauseous, and then fell asleep. Chris, who was equally drunk, pretended to be quite sober, becoming increasingly stern and solemn as the evening went on. Only the rigidity of his spine and the funereal gait with which he progressed from the table to the bar betrayed him. When 'our' boys were all incapacitated I danced with a literature student called Andrew Hawks, whom Cathy had been eyeing up for weeks. He was blond, venomously cynical, with cold blue eyes and an intense way of speaking which frightened me. After two dances he edged me into a corner and kissed me. I did not want to be kissed. I struggled, laughed, pounded my fists on his shoulders, kicked him – fairly politely. He pinned me against the wall and called me a bitch. I was terrified. His mouth was suffocating me. I thought I was dying.

Then Andrew was staggering across the floor and Chris was holding my hand. 'Silly girl,' he said slowly. 'Silly. Silly.'

For a brief, strange moment, I thought he was my father and I loved him, but the magic of the evening was at an end, and I was in disgrace. Chris walked me to my bus without saying another word.

As I got on the bus he groaned, 'Oh, Jesus!' and vomited neatly into a nearby waste bin.

'Goodnight,' I said. 'Thank you. I'm sorry.'

He looked at me as if he had never seen me before and then walked away, weaving through the ranks of buses with wobbly legs, all pretence at sobriety forgotten.

There was only one other passenger on that last, late bus: an elderly man, who watched me from the corner of his eye and leered at my legs. I felt scared and ashamed and the journey seemed endless. I wanted to be home, sheltered and protected. I wanted to be with my stern, no-nonsense daddy, to be scolded and smacked and sent safely to bed. A great twist of grief caught at my heart to remember that he was not there, would never come back again, would never again rescue me, scold and forgive me. I was out in the world all alone, and I must learn to like it, or die.

Chapter Seventeen

It is all just as I feared. Anna is exhausted and chaos approaches stealthily, getting closer every day in spite of my panicky attempts to stem the flood. I spend hours at the sink trying to wash dishes. Yesterday, enraged at having run out of clean underwear, I braved the washing machine. With success only minutes away, I became excited, then confused, and almost lost my left arm in the spin dryer. Terrified, I had a drink to calm my nerves. I am not supposed to drink. So what?

It was a dry day with a cold, stiff breeze. I could not carry the laundry basket, but deciding that no effort was too great, I attempted to carry the things out to the line one by one. I dropped the first snowy white garment on the path, lost my temper and kicked the damn thing all the way back to the kitchen. When Mrs Underwood came I gibbered furiously at her, doing a war dance in my desperation to get her to hang the washing out. She could not carry the basket either, but we managed it between us, and I watched in an agony of shame while her poor, arthritic hands turned blue in the north-east wind. She gave us tinned soup for lunch. I hate tinned soup, but was too hungry, and grateful, to protest.

When Mrs Underwood went home at three o'clock we had both

forgotten the washing. I turned on the television and watched one of the sillier children's programmes. Some of them are quite good. They tell the stories very slowly, with lots of illustrations. Sometimes they encourage the children to make animal noises, or to repeat a recurring phrase, and I join in, saying, 'Moo!' and 'Baa!' like a bloody idiot, or, 'Be-bi-bo-bum!' I can't say *f*s, but sometimes I prefer to hear my own voice, however pathetic, than to feel so utterly lonely.

After a little while I noticed that the afternoon had grown uncommonly dark and there was an anxiety in my mind which I could not identify. I stood at the window for ages, worrying, wondering why I was worried. I went to the kitchen, my heart pounding. Then I saw the washing hanging lifeless on the line and realised that it was pouring with rain.

'Calm down, Max,' I told myself. 'Make some tea. Forget it. Clean underwear isn't everything.'

But I knew it was. Clean underwear has always been important to me; but when one has lost so much, when cleanliness is the last stronghold and it is disintegrating, it is very, very hard to bear.

I took a cup from the shelf and found that it had a dry crust of sugar inside it, a reminder of my hopelessness at washing up. I hurled the cup against the wall, and when I saw that it had broken into a mere half-dozen pieces, I ground each piece to a powder under my heel. I heard a dog snarling, and only when my rage began to cool did I realise that the dog was me.

Later, I became peckish, and looking at my watch realised that Anna was late again. She is due home at six, but sometimes she does not arrive until seven or eight, white-faced, full of excuses and apologies. If she only knew what I suffer while I wait for her she could not be so cruel. The anxiety nearly kills me. I pace the floor like a mad thing, imagining more catastrophes and disasters than can possibly happen – even to me. But it takes only one catastrophe. Anna needs to be run over only once for my life to be changed from mere nightmare to hell on skates. And I get so hungry! Sometimes I eat dry bread – I can't butter it, it slides all over the place – or sweet biscuits, despairing for my teeth, which I can no longer clean properly.

I had kept patience with Anna until yesterday. I don't know why I kept patience; perhaps the relief of seeing her arrive, however late, wiped the anger from my mind. But yesterday I was too angry. She went into the kitchen, saw the scar on the wall, the broken china, and demanded irritably, 'Whatever is this?' I heard the dog snarling again

103

and the next moment Anna was in a heap on the floor, sobbing and clutching the side of her face where I had struck her. Her sobs made everything worse, somehow. I felt sorry for her, but the noise confused me so that I forgot why I was angry and then was even more angry because I had forgotten. I shook her by the hair. Her hands splaying in that old attempt to absorb my brutality, she screamed and screamed until the noise cut through the shards of my rage, and I released her, and began to weep.

As soon as she was free, Anna made a dive for the pantry and shut herself in. Her sobs were pitiful; deep, racking gasps which shook the pantry door. It seemed to go on for hours. My regret turned to confusion again. Why was Anna weeping in the pantry? I had an idea it was my fault, but I could not, at that moment, recall what I had done. Tentatively, half afraid she would start screaming again, I knocked on the door, begging her to come out and explain what was happening.

'Bu? Bu?'

'H-hang on,' she said. 'I'll be out . . . out in a . . . minute.'

'Bu? Bu-bu-bu?'

She coughed and blew her nose, and then came out, putting her arms around me, weeping quietly.

'I'm sorry, Daddy,' she whispered. 'I'm sorry. I know I'm hopeless, useless. I just don't know, don't know . . .' She coughed again and pushed me away. She was trying to smile.

She moved slowly, as if she were in a dream. But she cleared up the broken china, prepared a meal, fetched the wet laundry and put it back in the spindryer. Then she draped everything over the radiators to dry. Why hadn't I thought of that? I felt humble and ashamed, and after dinner I crept away to hide myself with my television.

This morning when I got up I found a set of clean underwear on the chair and a clean shirt, its sleeves already rolled to save me the difficulty of doing it myself. I bathed and shaved, taking a long time over it to make the morning shorter. My ties are already knotted. I put one over my head like a noose, and then, for minute after frustrating minute, I work the knot higher. It would be easier not to wear a tie, but I have always worn one and feel half naked without it. I have lost enough of my dignity without volunteering to walk around half naked. I wear leather slippers most of the time. When I go to the hospital the ambulance man comes in to tie my shoelaces. Reasonably satisfied with my appearance – except that I can't get a close enough shave with that electric thing – I went downstairs to eat the cornflakes, the bread, butter and marmalade which Anna would have left for my breakfast.

But Anna had not gone to college, and as soon as I appeared in the kitchen – which was cleaner than it had been for weeks – she turned away and began to scramble eggs for me. She was very quiet. I noticed that her eyes were red and swollen and I was deeply sorry for grieving her so. I touched her, turning her face with my hand.

'Bu, bu,' I said. I'm sorry. Don't be angry.

I smoothed her hair back from her cheek, and as my hand moved I saw that there was a bruise on her cheekbone and a swelling as big as an egg. A blood vessel had broken in her eye.

I nearly fainted. Though I had often – especially when she was fifteen – longed to punch Anna's dainty little teeth down her throat, I had never, ever hit her in anger, never caused her real bodily harm. I had been very careful not to – for various reasons. The first reason was self-protection. No one was likely to accuse me of cruelty if Anna complained of being spanked, however hard I spanked her. But a single visible bruise, I knew, would bring the social workers swarming like wasps to a jam pot, perhaps to take her away from me. But I also bore in mind Emma's theories on discipline, a subject upon which she had had much cause to ponder as a school mistress. She always said that training a child was like cooking. You don't, she said, wait until you're hungry before putting the joint in the oven. You anticipate your hunger, and begin to cook in advance of the hour. Likewise, you should never wait until you are angry before chastising a child. If you punish the small errors, even if you are more inclined to laugh at them, the big, dangerous and infuriating errors are much less likely to occur. It makes good sense, but Emma's theory overlooked one very important fact: a meal cooked carefully in advance of one's need is more pleasurable than one snatched in a frenzy of hunger. And it whets the appetite, especially when one is eating not merely to maintain life but to take satisfaction, often of a sensuous nature, from the meal.

It often puzzled me, the satisfaction I derived from punishing Anna. I am not, by nature, a cruel man. I was not even a cruel child, as many boys are. Suffering has always sickened me, especially the suffering of helpless victims. Even as a child I understood that cruelty was weakness – a struggle against one's own fear. Yes, I was afraid of Anna; I admit it. Not of Anna the child, but of Anna the woman. I did not want her to be a woman. I tried to keep her from growing up, to keep her from torturing me with the swell of her breasts, the curve of her hips, the seduction of her eyes. I beat the seduction out of her. It is hard to desire someone who weeps and trembles, who begs and stammers. There is no room for seduction in eyes which are full of tears. I did not want her to grow up, but she did it in spite of me, confounded me at every turn, growing more like Emma every day.

She acquired quite early Emma's nose-in-the-air, though for entirely different reasons. Emma genuinely believed in herself, in her power to take and hold the things she wanted from life, and she refused to put up with the fools who stood in her way. But Anna's aloofness seemed to announce both that she was doomed by fools and that she did not give a damn for them; an attitude which caused me increasing irritation as her technique became more polished.

There was a period of months between her fourteenth and fifteenth birthdays when I felt I had lost my grip on her entirely. Her room was tidy, her fingernails clean, her homework in order and her manners impeccable. She was top of her class in the summer exams and passed her music grade with distinction. I was lost for words.

It could not go on. I told myself it could not go on. No one could be perfect at fourteen: it was too early! She must slide into error soon – perhaps during the summer holidays – and give me my chance to rub that lofty little nose of hers in shit. But she spent the first four days of the holiday weeding the garden, discovering several rose trees behind the summer house which I hadn't seen for years. It looked lovely; and as a piece of manipulative diplomacy it could not have been bettered. She allowed me nothing – except to be grateful.

'It looks very nice,' I said faintly. 'But haven't you any other plans for the holidays? Where's Jenny?'

'She's learning to water-ski.' She hunched her shoulders and a lustful gleam came to her eyes as she imagined it: the speed and the spray, the freedom. 'But I thought you wouldn't let me go, so I didn't ask.'

'How very wise.'

Defeated, I allowed her to go on a picnic with the Hurleys. They did not bring her home until very late. She was flushed with sunshine and excitement, smeared with the dusty evidence of football games, tree climbing and other disreputable activities. I smiled indulgently, largely because Margaret Hurley (equally flushed and dusty) had delivered her to the door.

'I see you had a good time,' I said drily. 'Go straight to bed now, Anna. It's late.'

Margaret, regretfully reminding me that she had children of her own to put to bed, declined my offer of a drink; and after waiting the customary half hour I went upstairs to remove Anna's reading matter and get my goodnight kiss.

'We had fish and chips on the way home!' she said blissfully. They had visited a castle, gone boating, done all manner of delicious things; but for Anna eating fish and chips had eclipsed the lot.

'How nice for you.' I removed her book and the spare pillow, and she wriggled down with a happy little sigh.

'Don't tuck me in,' she said. 'I like to stick out my feet when they get hot.'

She demonstrated the procedure, and as her blackened little foot emerged from the sheets, my eyebrows and my rejoicing heart hit the roof; immediately followed by my astonished daughter.

Somewhere in mid air Anna gasped, 'What?' but the wind was knocked out of her as she landed, and there was an eerie silence until the first blow fell. Then she screamed, her hands scrabbling for a hold on her modesty, her legs pedalling like pistons to be free.

'You filthy, shameless, degenerate little animal!' I roared. 'How dare you go to bed without a bath? How *dare* you?'

Having shot forward with the force of the blow which accompanied 'filthy', Anna endured the rest of the beating with her rump in the air and her face on the rug. She escaped at last by virtue of a forward somersault and lay sobbing dementedly in the corner. She was trying to speak, but no words emerged without first passing through the mincer of her rage.

'You said . . . You said I was to go . . . go straight to bed!' she gasped. 'And I th-thought, thought – it was so *late*!'

I caught her arm and dragged her to the bathroom. 'Thought?' I demanded savagely. 'I'll teach you to think, you lazy little slut!'

She did not realise what form the lesson would take until I locked the bathroom door and put the key in my pocket. Then she screamed, '*No!*' and threw herself at me, clawing and spitting like an enraged sparrow.

The traditional method of child-beating has a great deal to commend it. It offers sensuality, of course; but there is also the comfort of knowing that the backside has no bones to be broken and that no one will see the evidence. It is difficult, too, for a winded, hysterical, humiliated child to retaliate when she is upside down, and even kicking has the disadvantage of unnecessary exposure. Anna stopped kicking. She ceased to claw for my face. She lay like a board, snarling through her teeth, and then suddenly went limp and broke out in a sweat which drenched her nightdress from neck to hem in two seconds flat. I released her. She slithered under the washbasin, unable to breathe for sobbing. I was perfectly calm. I was happy. 'Take off your nightdress, Anna,' I said sweetly. 'Daddy is going to scrub you *raw*.'

She stopped crying and stared at me for a long, long time, her scarlet complexion slowly fading to a defeated pallor. She touched the nightdress tentatively at neck, sleeves and hem, trying to discover the non-existent method of removing it without exposing herself naked to my eyes. Then she sobbed once, closed her eyes tightly – and stripped. Her face was scarlet again. Her nose had taken a permanent dive.

We were both rather tired of the traditional method before that bath was over. Anna behaved like a baby towards the end, sucking her fingers, knuckling her eyes, clutching my hand as she sobbed her way wearily to bed. I smiled down at her as she crawled between the sheets.

'Don't suck your thumb, Anna,' I chided gently. 'You're a big girl now.'

And obediently she removed it, gasping, 'Uh-uh-uh,' into the pillow.

I expected her to cry for hours before becoming desperate enough to ask forgiveness, but when I returned from clearing up the wreckage of the bathroom she was silent and still, lying – understandably enough – on her tummy, with her gaze fixed blankly on the wall. She was breathing normally and, except for her swollen eyes, seemed wholly undistressed. I was rather shocked.

'You were very naughty, Anna,' I said, a trifle desperately. 'I hope you're ashamed of yourself?'

'Yes.'

Under certain circumstances, yes can sound remarkably like no. Anna was not ashamed. I was.

'I know you hate me,' she said calmly. 'But there's nothing I can do about it. I've tried . . .'

She had managed these few words without recourse to stammering, but now her voice fragmented painfully, each word making its exit under violent protest.

'I've tried, tried . . . tried so hard . . . to be good! I've tried, I've tried to be . . . be like Mummy. To please you. But you never, never . . .'

She turned over, exhaling hard, her eyes cold under their burning lids, her voice quite calm despite the panicked flutter of its enunciation. 'And I re-re-realise now that you never . . . never will be pleased, be-because I'm *not* her, and can never be. So it isn't, isn't worth the effort any more. I won't, won't make, won't *make* the effort any more!'

I felt sick. She weighed less than six stone, was not yet five-feet tall – and she had me by the balls. It was Emma's voice I heard. That flat little voice flaying me, accusing me, wielding my love for her like a scourge.

'Oh,' I said distantly, 'in that case . . .' And I walked out; fully aware that of all the brutality a man can inflict upon a woman, walking out on her argument is the worst.

Though my soul paused at the head of the stairs to hear her cry out, my feet did not. And I managed to bluff my way through a half-bottle of whisky before Anna's enduring silence brought me to grief and took me, aching, to my bed. I had gone too far. I had never believed, until then, that love has its own mortal span. My love for Emily had survived death, but Anna's for me had not survived this night, and without it I was bereft, my grief like a malignant ulcer, eating me raw and hollow. I was sick and drunk, and my sick drunkennness yearned toward Anna's room, to her bed, to her arms, to weep there and beg her forgiveness. But a man of my complexity is rarely drunk in all his parts, rarely drunk enough to forget what he would do if he were sober. So I lay there, drunkenly yearning, soberly waiting, and telling myself that I would work something out tomorrow.

I suppose I slept at last, because she came so suddenly, crying, calling me, a white wraith in the doorway. 'It's . . . it's only that I – that I love you so much, Daddy! It . . . it hurts me! Oh, please, please don't hate me any more!'

Relief crucified me. I could not move, could barely speak.

'Come here.' Oh, Anna. My Anna. If you knew! 'Get in beside me.'

She was shivering, and I wrapped her in the dark, between my hands and my heart.

Oh, Anna. I know, I know that the days of holding you in my arms are gone; and my heart is cold, cold, as though the sea, Arctic cold, ran in my veins. I know that you will never again call to me in the night, never again cry out, 'Daddy!' and run to give your soul into my keeping. And yet, you are here. I could touch you now were I not afraid. But fear is like a desert between us, and regret a salt sea in my eyes.

We have worked all day to set the house to rights, and now Anna is curled into a corner of the sofa. A textbook is open at her side, a big, foolscap pad, covered with a wild scrawl of notes, lies on her knee. Her pencil has dropped to the floor and she is fast asleep, her face white, the bruise hidden by a thick loop of black hair. She does not look much like Emily now, but simply like Anna, my sad little girl.

God, why did you do this to us? Couldn't it have waited a little longer? No, no, I am not now asking pity for myself. The bruise on Anna's face is my acceptance, my confession that I deserve no better. But don't you see what you are doing to her? She is so small, so young. She knows nothing, has done no harm. Yes, there is evil in her as there is in all of us, but such small evil; and hasn't she been punished enough? I have punished her! Oh God! Oh, God! What a bastard you are!

I fall into my chair, dragging my hand across my face which has, I feel it, turned pale at the niceness of your justice. Yes, I see. But where does that leave Anna? Is my repentance of more value to you than her survival?

No, I have seen it in her eyes today. You have it all tied up, don't you? All nicely timed, neatly arranged. She has forgiven me. She always does, because she loves me. But today she loves me less than in all her life before. She loves me just a little less, and that little is more than enough. Anna will survive, because Anna will leave me.

God, hear my prayer and let my cry come unto thee! I hate you. I hate you. I HATE YOU!

Chapter Eighteen

About six months after the beginning came the end. At least, it felt like the end. 'The End' kept flashing up in my mind like the last flickering frames of an old and rather pretentious film. Pretentious was not the word I used to describe myself, but 'Fool!' occurred quite often, and pretentious was what I meant. I was remembering my first meeting with Myra, all that heroic nonsense I had fed her about giving myself in dedication to my father's welfare. She had talked me out of that; but afterwards I had impressed her with intelligent questions, ambitious schemes. I was going to be a capable – not to say brilliant – student; an efficient housekeeper, a seductive cook, a patient, kind, generous nurse. 'Oh,' I said with a blithe little laugh, 'I know it won't be easy!' But all the time I was thinking of Florence Nightingale, Elizabeth Fry, Mrs Pankhurst, and, of course, my mother. Heroines, strong women whose ranks I was about to join. Strong women. I thought I was one. But I was still only eighteen; and a young eighteen at that. I didn't have a clue.

Now I was thinking of my mother again, imagining that she was watching me and witnessing my failure, viewing my weaknesses with contempt. Why should she, the perfect woman, have any compassion for me? Her sympathy was all for my father, her husband, the man I was betraying even more than her death had betrayed him. I envied her. She could die and still say, 'I loved him. I did my best.' But there was no excuse for me. I had been brought up to emulate her, had longed to be like her and to take her place in my father's heart; but in this, as in all else, I had failed utterly. I hated her then; not now for her perfection, but simply for leaving me to carry the burdens she should have borne. If she were here . . . I imagined how she would be: a smiling, capable woman, concocting delicious meals to tempt my father's appetite, teasing him, stimulating his mind, making him laugh. If only she had not died! If only I were good enough. I was an imposter, a disgrace. I had spent my life reaching for the sun, imitating the moon; but now my wings were burned and I had fallen to earth.

My father had always told me (I had never believed it before) that I had no stamina. It was not an accusation. It was one of the few things he said with any sympathy, and he said it often, especially when I was doing A-levels and he was still insisting that I go to bed at half past nine on school days.

'You tire easily,' he would say, sadly forbidding the ballet, the film or the concert I wanted to see. 'You haven't enough stamina to burn the candle at both ends.'

I denied it until I was blue in the face, but didn't work up enough courage to fight until, on the eve of Jenny's seventeenth birthday party, he refused to allow me an extension. I called him all the names under the sun. I wouldn't have gone quite so far, but he listened patiently, with a smile which developed, by slow degrees, into a grin. I went mad then. I flew at him with my fists, and when he caught them I kicked him, screaming awful things, telling him, for the first time in my life, that I hated him.

His smile went out, slamming doors in my face. 'I see,' he said grimly. 'Thank you for telling me. That makes everything easier, doesn't it?'

What? I had no idea what he meant. Was he threatening me, or had I hurt him? Did he mean . . . ? What did he mean? The doubt was like iced water running through my bowels. My rage froze, and there was nothing left to do but to plead forgiveness, as on so many occasions before. He did not make it easy. He reminded me that I hated him, quoted the things I had said to him in the heat of my rage, said that I might be better pleased if I left school, left home, found a job and learned to support myself. It must be terrible, he said, to feel so loathsomely dependent upon a 'cruel, selfish beast of a man' whose only object in life was to spoil my fun.

Was he throwing me out? After everything I had done, all the effort I had made to be like Mummy, to please him? Had I spoiled everything? I could not bear it. I cried, begged, grovelled – and at last he forgave me and drew me into his arms, kissing my hair. I was beyond comfort, feeling helpless, betrayed. I was still certain he was wrong, but I was even more certain that I was wrong to give in. I felt stupid, weak, cowardly; and I was aware that I had humiliated myself far more than he had humiliated me. To risk so much, to waste so much, to shame myself so completely for nothing more important than a party! I was despicable. My father was right to have rejected me for so long. Who could blame him?

He sat down and pulled me on to his knee, holding me until I was calm. Then he talked about my mother, how hard she had worked to follow her career, how clever she was, how important she thought it that women should be independent, self-disciplined and strong.

'But how can I be independent,' I asked, 'if you won't let me do anything?'

'You're wrong, Anna,' he said gently. 'I'm giving you an education, which is the key to independence. Without it you can do nothing, gain nothing, be nothing. You've envied the idiots who leave school early and get themselves little jobs, little salaries, small tickets to freedom. But they're not free, Anna. For the sake of a trip to sea they've chained themselves to an oar, and will never again stop rowing. It won't be like that for you, Anna. When your education is complete you will have freedom, and the choice to do with it as you please; but until then . . .'

My eyes were hurting. I had closed them to shut out the light and to luxuriate in the warmth of my father's voice. When he stopped talking I opened my eyes and looked up to see him smiling.

'Until then, sleepy-head,' he said softly, 'I think you would do well to admit that you are tired, and in need of your beauty sleep. Daddy put you to bed?'

He was teasing, because of course I was sixteen and much too old to be put to bed, but the memory of that ancient comfort was like balm to my soul. I wished I was not too old. I wished he would carry me up and undress me with his cool, clever hands, and lie beside me as he used to, holding me until I slept. But the thought made me blush and I kissed him quickly and went to bed on my own. I still knew he was wrong. I still knew I had enough stamina for Jenny's party, but I didn't care any more. What did anything matter as long as there was hope that he loved me?

But he was right! I had no stamina at all, and as the months passed and my exhaustion increased, everything was reduced to an insufferable labour. The best times were when I switched to automatic pilot. The alarm clock, unbearably loud, would rip me out of sleep and out of bed before my dream was over, and I would stagger blindly through the patterns of washing, dressing, eating, preparing my father's breakfast, catching my bus; watching the town, the winter sea, the rain. Then the mechanism switched off and life was hurting again.

I don't know what hurt most: seeing the city in the distance, its teeth bared to chew me into ever smaller pieces; or, at the far end of the day, seeing the lonely, misted lamp posts on the shore road, and the clock tower dome, green as mould against the mould-green twilight sky. The hurts felt the same: a great twisting sensation beginning in my stomach and strangling upwards until it squeezed hard at the back of my throat and was swallowed whole to begin again. The city was blindness, fear, scuttling panic. The shore road was loss, grief and shame. And both were despair. I was too tired to be optimistic.

I could not do anything, was merely feinting, going through the motions. My struggle for understanding, for sight, had failed, and only one glimmer of purpose had penetrated my confusion, a pin-point of light glimpsed through dark shutters. I could not say what it was, but I knew that I wanted it and reached towards it urgently, almost sobbing my need. I know now that the light was myself, and that, set against it, all else, even my father, became mere shadow. The glimpse of myself seen through dark shutters was the source of my pain, as, until then, my father had been. If I could have closed my eyes to it I would have stopped hurting, but that's like saying, if you stop breathing you will stop hurting.

On the bus to the city my answer would come very clearly. Leave him. Forget him. Without him you will be free, with nothing to hold you back. Without him, you would not be fearing your next tutorial or handing in essays with shame for their brevity and confusion. Without him, you could be a brilliant student. On the bus to the shore road my answer was equally clear. Leave college. Forget it. It is too much for you. Without it, you could love him, care for him, live as you have always longed to live, at the centre of his world, as the apple of his eye.

Both answers were true. But the idea of being a brilliant student gave me a sensation of coming into the light. Being the apple of my father's eye . . . It was a dry, tasteless fruit now, bringing, like the first apple, only grief, as though by eating it I knew I should be expelled from the garden. I still loved my father, pitied him. I could not leave him, but neither could I leave the glimpse I had seen of myself unclaimed. I knew that if I abandoned it now I might never see it again.

My friendships at college could not, I knew, be said to have developed. I felt myself accepted – as an orphan is accepted into a happy, bouncing family – with a careless generosity which, for its very carelessness, excluded me. Sometimes, when we met in the pub or the cafeteria, I would stand for a moment in the doorway, looking on, and find myself changing places, seeing myself as they saw me, feeling toward myself as they felt. Standing in the doorway, looking on, I saw them; legs and arms moving without stricture, chins flying up, mouths spreading expansively to laugh and shout and swear. Eyes wide, searching, finding. Arms waving, widening to collect me from my isolation.

'Oy, Anna!'

'Over here!'

And I saw my response: narrowly crossing the floor, wondering what to do with my hands, and wary of every move.

I had never been to a college dance again. I had a vague idea that I was meant to hover on the outside, an envious observer. God's Plan, which had been such a positive source of strength in my adolescence, had changed its name. Now it was Fate, and who was I to argue with Fate and the nasty grudge it was bearing against me? I could only submit. I hadn't the energy for anything else.

I seemed to be dying of exhaustion. Guilt was like a weight on my shoulders which I not only felt but saw, in the sag of my spine, and in the evidence – everywhere – of my failure. I kept making good resolutions, solving my problems on paper with endless lists of things to be done. But I lost the lists, or lost heart after the first completed tasks had brought me closer to despair at the apparent impossibility of ever completing them all. 'Clean the house' became sweep the kitchen. 'Do the ironing' became iron a shirt. 'Get notes up to date' became open the book and fall asleep. The only thing capable of galvanising me into action was when my father, driven by fear and neglect, lost his temper and transformed my guilt, temporarily, into a wild surge of adrenalin. I did not blame him his rage. In his place I knew I would feel the same. But he had so little control over his temper that I began to fear he would kill me. I frequently wished he would. When he knocked me across the room, gave me a black eye, tore my hair out by the roots, I realised with some surprise that he had never really hurt me before. The beatings, smackings and shakings he had administered throughout my childhood had been carefully controlled exercises, designed to inflict the maximum humiliation with the least possible damage. I was glad to have made this discovery, but I preferred having my eyes blacked, a procedure which, though terrifying while it lasted, was forgivable, forgettable. It made its mark outside, not in.

Aunty Dorothy visited us quite regularly now. Her concern astonished me, and the only explanation I could find for it was that her sense of duty towards her brother was greater than her dislike for him. She never brought Mrs Read with her, never said much. She turned up her nose at the mess and made no comment, but sometimes she brought things: a cake, some fruit, or inspired little gifts for my father. The best of these was a game of solitaire which kept him occupied when there was nothing to watch on television. Occasionally she would sit and play draughts with him. (He had always enjoyed chess, but lacked the concentration for it now.) Aunty Dorothy played draughts as if she had a severe headache, hooding her eyes and propping up her chin with a daintily polished thumbnail. She was bored stiff, enduring every minute with an air of martyred patience which seemed wholly at odds with her nature.

After Christmas, when I was wearily preparing to go back to college, she asked me if I would like to meet her for tea in Exeter one day. I was startled, and being too surprised to think of an excuse, I said, 'That would be nice.' I began to wonder if her concern for my father was disguising an even more unlikely concern for me. Her attentions to him certainly gave me some relief, for every hour my father spent alone was a nightmare of guilt for me; yet somehow I could not believe that Aunty Dorothy cared much for either of us, and I was relieved when she did not press her invitation.

But a few days later, I came home to find a note: *Meet you in Blundell's for tea, four o'clock, Thursday. D.* This made me feel even worse than before. I was certain, now, that her only reason for wishing to meet me away from home was to give me a piece of her mind. She would be cynical and sneering, say dreadful things about my neglect of my father. She would tell me that he would be better off in a home, and ask me what sort of daughter I was to treat him like this when he had done so much for me. I dreaded it, because I knew she was right. I dreaded it, because I knew I could change nothing. I was too tired.

She ordered egg and cress sandwiches and chocolate cake.

'You can't cope, can you?' she said distantly.

I looked out of the window and made no reply. I realised that she had another reason for meeting me here: I could not cry in public.

'I'll move in with him,' she said, 'if you'll move out.'

She lit a cigarette, and as a second thought offered me one. I declined it, blushing. A deep hole seemed to have opened at my feet. I understood nothing. The cups and saucers, the linen napkins, the hotel-silver teapot were just so many abstract shapes without meaning. Aunty Dorothy's offer was equally abstract, equally meaningless. It made no sense at all.

'Why? You don't like him. Or me.'

'Blood is thicker than water,' she murmured, and took a long, chin-lifting pull at her cigarette.

'Rubbish.'

I did not realise I had said it until she grinned. 'Thicker than I'd guessed. Have a sandwich.'

Her approval was quite incomprehensible, but it gave me confidence.

'Look,' I said irritably, 'I don't understand. If you want to talk to me, then please talk. Don't expect me to put two and two together to make four, because I can't add up. You don't like Daddy and he doesn't like you. That's all I know.'

She stubbed out her cigarette and tapped the table with her finger. I wondered why she bothered to smoke. She never took more than a few puffs from the same cigarette and was constantly lighting fresh ones.

'All right,' she said quietly, 'cards on the table, if you insist. Your father and I don't get on, it's true. But set against his dislike of me, there are many things he dislikes more: dirt and disorder, loneliness, anxiety, fear – a thousand discomforts which you cannot relieve and which I can. Do you see so far?'

I said yes, not really meaning it. I could see her argument, which was the one I had anticipated, but the unexpected idea of Aunty Dorothy as ministering angel could not take hold in my mind.

'And there's you,' she said, the edge of scorn clearly discernible in her tone. 'College suiting you, is it? Are you getting on well with your studies?'

'No.' I blushed, and again looked out of the window.

'Are you planning to leave it all to take care of your father?'

'No. No, I can't. I keep –' I stopped. I did not want to tell her. I did not know, and could not probe the unknown here, in Blundell's.

'You keep hoping,' she finished, accurately enough. 'Hope is useless without action. If you want to survive you must act.'

'I'm tired,' I said. 'And what does it matter to you? You've never cared.'

Aunty Dorothy made a sort of spitting noise and sat back violently, snatching another Dunhill from the gold case which lay on the table. 'What do you know,' she demanded contemptuously, 'about *my* feelings?'

I fumbled with my knife, pushing it back and forth between my cup and my plate. It had never occurred to me that Aunty Dorothy might have feelings and the thought was not a pleasant one. I did not want her to have feelings. She was easier to deal with without them.

'But no one does anything,' I faltered, 'without a selfish motive. Even saints have motives.'

'Oh?' she said bitingly, guessing, I suppose, that I was not accusing her of saintliness.

'Yes,' I said, 'they want to be angels. What do you want?'

Her eyebrows, neatly plucked and drawn in with a soft pencil, shot up. But she seemed more amused than angry, and my shrewdness, of which I had been rather proud, now seemed silly and presumptuous. It was surprising to realise, a moment later, that she had accepted the challenge, meeting it calmly, as though it were my right to ask such questions.

'I want a home,' she said quietly, tapping the ash from her cigarette with a grave concentration in which I thought I detected a certain embarrassment. 'Connie and I have not,' she swallowed, and tossing her head in the slow, haughty way she had, she turned to gaze from the window, 'been getting on,' she continued smoothly. 'You are, I suppose, clever enough to work out the implications for me?'

I frowned, having no clue of the implications.

Aunty Dorothy made that spitting sound again and her face glowed pink under its smooth layers of cosmetics. 'Oh,' she sighed, 'you're so bloody stupid, Anna! I have no time to explain, no patience.' She took a deep breath and closed her eyes, apparently realising that she would have to find the patience, somehow.

'I need a home. I am more than willing to take care of Max in exchange, and to give you a chance to make your own life. Look, I've spent years looking after other people: your grandma; you for a short while.' She sniffed contemptuously, but I could not work out where her contempt was aimed. 'And Connie, of course. I'm good at it, Anna, and good for nothing else. I could get a job, I imagine. But what sort of job would provide me with a decent home and the standards I'm used to? Good God,' her hands shook slightly as she stubbed out yet another cigarette, 'I've barely enough capital to keep me going into old age, and damn it, you haven't enough gumption to . . . Well, never mind that. You take my point, I'm sure. You are young, Anna. God knows you're foolish enough, but foolishness is one of the privileges of being young.'

She sniffed again, tossing her head as though to shake me off, but then she gazed at me intently, her eyes blazing with something very like desperation. 'Go,' she said in a low, gentle voice. 'Go. Be foolish if you must, Anna. Enjoy it. Use it. But do it where you will do less damage, both to yourself and to your father. Daddy will manage, you will manage, but you will each manage much better apart than together.'

I had never heard Aunty Dorothy say so much all at once and I stared at her blankly, trying to make sense of it all. I gave her full marks for frankness, at least. She hadn't tried to hide anything. I knew she wasn't hard up, but she was only forty-eight, and if she had to pay rent without the means of getting a decent job, she would be broke long before she could draw a pension. She needed a home, and Daddy had one to offer. But that wasn't all. 'Be foolish. Enjoy it. Use it.' There was understanding in those words, concern for my welfare as well as for her own. And if I accepted her advice, my father would be so much better cared for, if not better loved. But how could I accept it? It would be like ringing my leper's bell, admitting once and for all that I was good for nothing, a disgrace to my father's name and my mother's memory.

Aunty Dorothy touched my hand, a tentative pat which she seemed instantly to regret. 'It's a good deal, Anna. A fair deal. None of us need lose anything – much; and we'll all gain some peace of mind.'

She sighed and then said, with more than a hint of exasperation, 'For the love of God, try to be objective for once!'

'He won't agree.'

I was aloof, struggling with my stupidity, determined not to recognise that day had dawned in Blundell's, while outside in the city night was falling frostily with a metallic, February clang.

'As usual,' Aunty Dorothy said, smiling, 'you are wrong.'

Chapter Nineteen

I'm not at all sure. Not sure at all.

Yes, I am sure, but allowing myself to be temporarily soothed so that, temporarily, I may be content. I have not misjudged Dorothy. She is a cold, selfish woman, and I know I am right because we are alike. Substituting only one word – man for woman – I might just as well have described myself. If the house were on fire, we would each smooth our hair before jumping from the window, and neither of us would think of saving the other's life until too late, when we might snap our fingers and say, 'Oh, damn!'

But we would both risk our lives to save Anna's. Is that what we have done? No. As usual we have merely saved ourselves – temporarily.

And to prove it, here we are, together; temporarily happy, temporarily smiling and cheering each other on. Brother and sister, a devoted pair. In a few days she has worked wonders in the house and it looks like home again, clean and shining in brilliant spring sunlight. It smells of beeswax, hyacinths and carbolic soap. Gorgeous. Dorothy has darned my socks, sewn buttons on my shirts, sent my suits to the cleaners. There is a knife-edge crease in my smart grey flannels and my shoes are shining like conkers. Oh! I can't stop smiling and I do not care where Anna is. I do not care what she is doing. Extraordinary! Temporary. Very temporary. Even this sally into thought of her wakens the worm of jealousy, to stretch, and yawn sleepily, 'Anna? Oh, Anna. Yes. Where is she, for crying out loud?'

Go to sleep, worm. We don't care, remember?

'Don't we? But I thought . . .'

Go to sleep. You are tired, little worm. You have worked too hard and need your rest.

Dorothy with her coat on, lipstick gleaming. 'I'm going shopping. Want to come?'

Come? 'Bu?' Me?

She laughs. 'I won't be long. You can wait in the car and then,' she shrugs, 'we could drive to the shore? Walk on the beach? Play ducks and drakes?'

Oh. Oh, that sounds like heaven on earth.

Dorothy has had my car lowered from its blocks, serviced, made road worthy. I gave it to her, shrugging, 'Bu, bu.' Take it. It's no bloody use to me now. Take the damn thing. I hadn't imagined she would take me in it, though. I had not imagined there was anywhere I needed to go. But I need, oh, I need to go to the shore; to throw pebbles on the sea. I shrug and nod coolly. No sense in showing her how I feel. This is, after all, only temporary. Dorothy and I are merely being polite. The fact remains that we loathe one another.

Why? What secrets do we have of mutual wounds inflicted and too dark to mention? A few, but they are not the root of the matter. At the root is a state which most people strive to attain, but which, at its most perfect, is the most rotten thing two people can share: understanding. We are alike. We know one another to the core and are repelled, as if by an unexpectedly ugly reflection of ourselves. Love feeds on un- answered questions. Love is looking at its object and saying 'I wonder . . .' until that day, and beyond it, when the loved one dies. I wonder why she shivers just before she wakes. I wonder what she does when I am not with her. I wonder what she is thinking, what she says about me to her friends; what motivates her; makes her happy. Emily and Anna, although I knew them well, were always posing such questions, always prompting me to search them for unguarded evils, unsuspected virtues. Their mystery kept my love for them new and alive, always unsatisfied and lusting for more. But at heart we are all foul, and when the questions are all answered love must die, leaving contempt in its place.

Dorothy and I learned each other's secrets at a very early age, and the mystery of our separate souls died then, aged five, or perhaps seven. The first time I lied I knew she was equally capable of lying and hated her for it. The first time I masturbated I knew Dorothy was doing, or would do, something very similar in another dark, quiet room – and was revolted. The first time I stole a penny I knew Dorothy would steal it from me, given half a chance – and despised her. I saw little evidence of our common evils, simply knew of them; as did she. To know the depths to which each of us would sink we had only to search ourselves for the answer. We bored one another silly; and boredom is hatred – made boring.

Anna was a little shocked to find me unsurprised at the idea of Dorothy living here, but I had expected it. Like me, Dorothy is incapable of pity, although each of us has a fastidious objection to suffering. We would not nurse a stray, wounded cat back to health, but neither of us would hesitate to take it to a vet – 'Put it out of its misery. I'll pay' – sighing with exasperation.

So why, if not out of pity, did Dorothy visit me so often? Bring gifts? Spend time playing draughts, pontoon, reading the paper to me? Because she wanted something. I knew it. And Constance Read never came with her. Odd, because Connie would have taken a smug satisfaction in seeing malicious Max stripped of his sarcastic wit. Something wrong betwixt the loving pair? What else? And what would become of Dorothy without Connie, Connie's house, Connie's car, Connie's cash? Had Dorothy had enough sense to invest her bit of capital, hang on to it? Unlikely. So what did Dorothy want? The only thing I had to give. A home. I simply waited to be asked.

Nor was I surprised to hear that Anna would move out, and that Dorothy had stipulated the condition. It was logical. Anna could not possibly have stayed. Dorothy and I had never been friends, but without Anna we might have been a little happier with each other. Anna sundered us to the state of strangers passing – for ever, or so we thought. We have affected to forget it, but it is not forgotten, merely sleeping for a while, another exhausted worm. Keep sleeping, little worm. Sleep for a long time; at least until I have walked the shore and thrown pebbles on the sea.

I am so excited! Dorothy laughs at me and helps me into my overcoat. (Made by a frightened tailor named Joel Lubin in the winter of '38: I am conscious of his tears sewn into the seams.) It is too big for me now, but I need its warmth, for I have little flesh left to cover my bones. I possess three newer coats which are warmer, but so heavy they wear my proud shoulders down to an ancient stoop.

Ahhh! My car, a Rover of sleek, police blue, still smells of leather – and is that my going-dancing cologne or a more recent whiff of Dorothy's perfume? The garden is a wilderness, but there are daffodils by the hundred nodding cheerfully above the long grass. It is difficult to imagine Dorothy on her knees in the borders, but we cannot afford to pay a gardener and I think Jack Lear has used up his small store of neighbourly kindness. Why worry? Dorothy won't see us go to the dogs. She'll think of something. I'll bugger the weeds while she damns the lawn mower. But she has a bad back. Why do women always have bad backs? What do they do with them? Too much, I suppose. They heft great lumps of oak from place to place in order to dust behind them. Anna will never have a bad back.

The town looks good today. The slate rooftops reflect the blue sky, and the verdigris on the dome of the clock tower sets up a vibrant hum of brilliance at its edges, competing with the firmament for glory. It is cold, and people still wear their winter coats, their gloves; but there is an elasticity in their movements, a tense readiness which makes them seem like lovers who will soon throw off their clothes in a flurry of abandon. The summer, with bedroom eyes, beckons them to love.

With an irritating disregard for the Highway Code, Dorothy parks my car at a road junction, just outside the main doors of the town's one good department store. To my knowledge, it sells few things which cannot be bought elsewhere in the town, but it has thick carpets, and women with piled-up hair who call out in royal accents, 'Can I help you?' as though, without their constant vigilance, one might forget all moral training and help oneself. It is a place into which men of good sense and timid demeanour do not venture, but it is the only shop which supplies St Lydia's school uniform, so I am familiar with its perfumed halls, and my demeanour, until now, has never been timid.

I took it by storm, marching in with my head thrown back, my nose set at its most commanding angle, and my daughter, attached firmly to me by the wrist, panting along at top speed in my wake. I enjoyed it enormously. The schools department went very quiet when I arrived, and the few mothers who stood dithering over gym knickers and indoor shoes (why do women in shops sound so certain when all they're saying is, 'I'm not sure'?) suddenly lost their confidence and snapped sharply, 'Three pairs!'

'Can I help you, sir?' Well-manicured hands rubbing together, blue-shadowed eyes hooded with lust for my money and my manhood.

'I certainly hope so.' (Shop girls are the last of our ancient race of servants, and should always be treated with a measure of contempt.)

The women shrivelled, blushed and took my typewritten list and my cringing daughter with a whispered, 'Yes, sir.'

I had apprised myself of the prices well in advance and was able to write my cheque – almost the equivalent of a full month's salary – without a tremor; but I was very snappy for a week afterwards, and Anna, nervous and making more punishable mistakes than usual, paid for her school uniform even more painfully than I had done. Much more painfully, since she did not want to go to St Lydia's anyway.

'Won't be long! Don't run away!' Dorothy slams the car door and leaves me. I feel very vulnerable, like a grouse glued to a post on the

Twelfth of August. The people of the town are passing within inches of me, going in, coming out of the shops, rushing by. They all glance at me as they pass. I look down, twirling my coat buttons nervously. What if someone who knows me, without knowing I am speechless, sees me here? What if Margaret Hurley sees me, and blushes, and turns away? Or doesn't turn away? Oh, my God. Shiftily I stretch out my arm and lock the door. They can't get at me now. If they try to open the door I will feign sleep.

I keep glancing up shyly, watching for Dorothy who has probably been gone for half a minute, though it feels like three hours. My heart is thudding, and with the onset of panic my vision fragments, turning people on their heads, hurling the road sideways so that the buses run upside down where the pavement should be. I blink and shrug. Often happens upside down in bits this sight, and thoughts fused condemn me. Pound, pounding in my heart and the temple of my head. Scared! Oh, scared and so alone! Anna!

'There eyes header wood unbelong, Max. Owlets have a locket to see!'

What? What? Oh, Dorothy is back, and we are driving again. How did that come about? Have I been sleeping? Dreaming of a temple with a golden dome in Egypt? No. Perhaps I was reminded . . .

Damn it all! My life cannot last much longer. Why do I feel so sad, so full of grief? I am . . . I am longing, longing. I am longing. I am longing for something, something, but I don't know what. Anna . . .

'Can you afford a new suit, Max?'

What? What is she talking about now? A new suit? The woman's barmy.

'Bu, bu. No. No money.'

'Ooh! Well done! That makes sense! It's just that everything's so big on you. You look rather waifish.'

Yes, a wafer would be nice. No. It's too cold, too early. What is Dorothy talking about? I am sad, and do not care what she is saying.

'We'll go to the far end, shall we?' Dorothy smiles, and I nod. There are advantages in being so alike. She knows I am afraid of meeting people, and while we are being so polite she will read my mind kindly, like this, to cause me no distress. I turn to her, smiling, and come face to face with the Watersmeet, my home from home where I met my friends and danced all night.

Last night I danced with a beautiful woman. Dear God! Was that a dream, or was it real? Oh God, God let it have been a dream, I beg you, or I will have lost – much more than I thought I had lost. I am weeping, and Dorothy pats my hand.

'It looks lovely, doesn't it, the sea?'

The sea. Sea green, sky blue and grey, shushing against the shingly sand. The sun gilds each ripple, warming, beautifying, like Dorothy's rouge. But the sea is cold at heart like she and me; and God, God has no dominion here with us. Oh, I am sad and longing, longing. I want to go home. I do not want to be here, set small and cold against the mighty coldness of the sea. Jesus Christ! We're – they've –

'Come on, sir!'

'I can't get my fucking *boots* on!'

I can't get my fucking boots on! Boots on!

'Shall we walk, Max?'

What? I can't get my boots. Oh, boots? What's wrong with me? I'm wearing shoes. Yes, let's walk if we must.

I inhale the seaweed-stinking air like smoke from a cigar. In, down, up, fluttering the frilly edges of my brain, down, out. Ahh. This is good. Do you know, Max old boy, you haven't been out like this for months? How long? Seven, eight months. I walked with Anna here, long ago, holding her hand, telling her the names of the cliff plants, the rocks and the shells. She wasn't terribly interested, but she listened politely until I paused to gaze out to sea. I felt her fingers wriggling in my palm – 'May I run, Daddy?' – and held them more tightly.

'No. You're getting too much like a tomboy, Anna. Be quiet, for once in your life.'

The life drained out of her. I felt it go. She wanted to run, my poor little girl, and I made her walk a tightrope.

Now I would like to run and am afraid. The corpse, which I hate as much as ever but try to disregard, is very heavy at times like this. Why the hell don't they cut it off? I would feel less mutilated without it. God is holding my hand, forbidding me to run, forcing me to be quiet for once in my life. Ha!

We scrunch down to the sea's edge and a gull cries lonely and wheels above our heads. Piss off, gull, gloating in your freedom.

We went to Newquay on our honeymoon, our beautiful wedding day, and stood at a railing, rubbing noses and laughing. An old lady in button boots and a dead fox said, 'Humph!' as she passed, and Emily blushed and pulled away.

'It's all right,' I said, holding her closer to my heart; 'we're married, darling. Remember?' And as I spoke a gull, passing overhead, unloaded its ballast down my lapel. I smelled of anchovy toast all through our honeymoon. Lord, it was this coat; this very lapel. We thought . . . we thought it was for luck.

Shit. I am weeping again and I want to go home.

'Had enough, old boy?' Dorothy takes my arm. 'Throw just one pebble?' she coaxes softly. 'For luck?'

'Bu! Bu-bu!' No, you stupid bitch. There's no luck in this whole rotten world for me. There never was; and now I've got you, which proves it.

'All right,' she says softly. 'Let's go home.'

Chapter Twenty

My father gave me my freedom with a shrug whilst watching *Panorama*. Later, when I made him listen to explanations, excuses and apologies, he shrugged his assent again, dully, as though to say: I expected nothing better of you; do what the hell you like. It hurt, but I was already becoming numbed to my hurts, blinded to his, and, seeing no other alternative, I told myself I did not care.

I moved into Jane's place at the flat (she had gone to live with her latest boyfriend) and when I had unpacked I sat talking to Libby, feeling an unfamiliar vitality take hold of me.

I said, 'I don't mean to be unkind, but I can't live in this place until it's clean. I'll do it. I don't mean to –'

'No,' she laughed, but this time without the usual embarrassment. I was always embarrassing Libby. I never knew why, but I supposed it was because I was so naïve. She slapped her knees and jumped up, smiling. 'I'll help! Where do we start?'

Apparently it was not naïve to want to clean the flat.

We spent a whole day and quite a lot of money on it. Cathy refused to help in case a mouse or a spider ran up her leg, so we sent her to the laundrette while we scrubbed and polished, sprinkling rodent repellent and DDT in every cranny and corner. I found a Durex under Cathy's bed and asked Libby what it was. She gulped and looked at me with a shocked expression on her face. Then she smiled, and sighed, 'Well, how can I put this? It's a sort of . . . It's a . . . Well, you could say it was, er, diametrically opposed to a gooseberry bush! It's a stork trap.'

When, eventually, I caught on, we laughed until we fell over.

During the next week I worked to bring my notes up to date and up to standard. I altered virtually every garment I possessed, and having a little money and a great deal of energy left over, I made myself a new skirt. There was also time to go to the film society, to whitewash the bathroom and to read *Thérèse Raquin* in bed. I was much too busy to be scared, much too happy to identify the first change which freedom had worked on me, and it was Sunday again before I knew what it was.

Suddenly, as I dressed in readiness for my first visit to my father, a dark wave of exhaustion swept over me. I fell asleep on the bus. My father welcomed me warmly, kissing me, eating me with his eyes, saying, 'Bu, bu?' to ask my news. I did not know what to say to him. There seemed a certain cruelty in recounting all the things I had done that week, especially the bit about cleaning the flat, and when I saw how our house gleamed as a result of my defection, I felt sick with guilt. When I said goodbye to my father he wept and held me tightly, burying his lips in my hair. 'I'll see you next Sunday, Daddy.' I kissed him, licking his tears from my lips and tasting the salt of them like acid on my tongue.

My grief and tiredness endured only until I saw the teeth of the city, no longer snarling, but smiling a welcome. And then there was enlightenment. I was not tired at all, had never in my life lacked stamina, had lacked only the freedom to channel it as I wished, to be in control of events. And the weight I had carried on my shoulders, heaviest since my father's stroke, had been there all my life, dragging me down, wearing me out. The weight *was* my father. Yet why, when I loved him so much, should he have such an effect on me? I didn't have time to analyse it. There was too much to do.

Freedom worked on me like sunshine on a stunted flower: I stretched and expanded, feeling myself grow from the inside out. My spine straightened, my step quickened. I laughed a lot, and sometimes found myself singing under my breath. At college I was moving mountains without feeling the strain. My mind had been swept clean of guilt, and there was plenty of room now for thought and study. I discovered that I had an organised mind, limitless energy and, hardest to believe, a sense of adventure in which fear, if it occurred at all, was so quickly overcome as to be of no account. I dared to express my thoughts, ideas, opinions, but was still too polite to shout people down when discussions developed into arguments.

Learning about myself and about the world was a constant source of astonishment to me, but a lifetime of constraint was a habit too strong to be shaken off entirely. We had parties, and, although I believe I made no conscious decision to do so, I drank very carefully, and at the first sensation of lightheadedness, called a halt. I had been too long without power to surrender it to drink. I had been too long without control to lose it now.

I knew I wasn't ready for many of the things I might have let happen to me. Newly sighted, I wanted to see, not to feel; to question, but not yet to be. Libby often slept with Dave, and occasionally with Chris, and I listened to the sounds of their lovemaking with curiously detached bewilderment. In the next room Cathy's bed creaked rhythmically to the tune of a series of boys whose names I never knew. I thought I understood the mechanics of sex, having learned it from school text-books and school gossip, but the noisiness of it confused me utterly. Why did it take so long? Why did they shout and groan? Was it very painful? It couldn't be, because sometimes they laughed – or were they screaming? I made no attempt to discover the truth of it all. It seemed unnecessary since I had no plans to try it for myself. Again it was a question of control, of power; not of morality. I did not wish to be subjected again to anyone's needs, or to subject myself to the pain – if pain it was – of submission.

I did not have to work very hard to keep my virtue intact, for if I said no, there were dozens of others who would say yes. But I was not often approached. My body lacked Cathy's voluptuousness, Libby's easy grace, and it offered no invitation. I suspect the few offers I was made were rather in the nature of a challenge, and I'm quite certain that this was true of Chris. I had become very fond of him, chiefly, I think, because he bore a vague resemblance to my father. All the details were there: the height, the figure, the grace of movement, the command. His good points were not as good as my father's nor his bad ones as bad, but he made a comfortable substitute and I always felt safer when Chris was near, safe enough to think of him as being as sexless – in regard to myself – as I knew my father to be. I made no attempt to hide my warmth for him, and perhaps because of this a message was conveyed which I had not thought to send.

We were both preparing studies on American History, and I said, quite casually one evening, 'Let's go to America this summer. I've got an uncle in Massachusetts who'd put us up.'

We spent hours working out our finances, planning itineraries, writing to our relatives to beg invitations. I could scarcely believe it was happening; but the invitations came back almost by return, my mother's brother Charles declaring himself almost delirious with joy at the thought of seeing me at last, his only blood relative still living in England. When Chris came to the flat that evening I showed him the letter and he yelled, 'Yippee!' and hugged me. I liked being hugged, but before I knew what was happening, he kissed me. I went rigid.

'Don't mess about, Anna,' Chris said sharply. Then he took my elbow and steered me into the bedroom.

I was trembling, had stopped thinking. I was simply reacting, by habit, to a completely familiar situation. The punishment could not be averted, and fighting only made it worse, so I stood quite still, my teeth chattering, my shoulders hunched submissively, while Chris, repeating almost by rote my father's admonitions – 'You're just being stubborn. There's no point in fighting it, Anna. You know I'm right' – unbuttoned my blouse. The chill air slapped against my shoulders and I shuddered and closed my eyes, forcing myself into the state of blind detachment which had helped me, so many times in the past, to endure such humiliations at my father's hands.

'Come on, Anna.' His voice softened and his hand ran gently across my shoulders. 'I like you, and I know you like me. So come on, eh? I'll make it nice for you, I promise.'

His gentleness broke my trance as his expected violence could never have done. He was not my father. I had done nothing wrong. I did not have to submit; not to him, not to anyone. I shrugged him off.

'No. Please. You've made a mistake.'

There was a long silence. Then, very softly, he laughed. 'Christ,' he said, 'for a minute, I thought I had you. Okay, Anna. Forget it.'

He draped my blouse over my shoulders and tugged teasingly at my hair. 'Sorry.'

Now that it was over I felt curiously disappointed, and rather mean, as though I were guilty of refusing to share a bag of sweets. I grinned at him. 'Cor,' I said cheekily, 'wot a relief!'

Chris laughed, and we ended up giggling on the bed, saying funny things in silly voices and pretending nothing had happened.

But a few days later, Chris informed me that he had done his sums wrong and would not be able to go to America after all. My immediate response was that this too was a punishment and one I could not avoid, for I could not go alone. I asked Libby, but she had no money at all and was living on an overdraft. I asked Cathy and she burst into tears and asked me how I could think of holidays when she had missed a period? I was shocked, and rather tactlessly asked why she had not thought to use contraceptives.

'Thank you, Marie Stopes!' she said bitterly. 'It's too bloody late now, isn't it?'

Her pregnancy turned out to be a false alarm, but she didn't learn much from the experience, and as soon as she knew she was safe, she went to bed with someone to celebrate.

I wondered where I had gone wrong. Had I missed something? Was there any reason why I shouldn't go to America on my own? I was sure there was a reason, but I couldn't think of it. Besides, it was not my place to act, to move, to initiate. I was an observer, one who perched on the cliff edge and watched the gulls take flight. I was unready. My wings were not yet fledged.

That Sunday I told my father that Uncle Charles had asked me to go to America in the summer. I was sure what my father's answer would be: a frown and a clearly pronounced, 'No!' And that would solve the problem once and for all. But he surprised me. He said, 'Bu?' quite mildly, and rubbed his fingers together. 'Money?'

I had a funny idea that the cliff edge was eroding under me.

I swallowed. 'I have enough for the deposit on my flight,' I said stiffly. 'And I can work for the rest. The holidays are quite long enough.'

He nodded. He raised his eyebrows and thrust out his lower lip, apparently racking his brains for an impediment which he could not find.

'What? You?' Aunty Dorothy said, and laughed.

I realised then that there was only one reason why I should not go alone: I was afraid; which was no reason at all. I paid my deposit. I secured a holiday job at Boots. I wrote to Uncle Charles and told him when I would be arriving. Then I told Chris, 'I am going to America on my own.'

He jerked his head up and stared at me as if I had developed an extra nose.

'Well, well,' he said softly. 'Well, well, well.'

Chapter Twenty-One

I am sitting at the table with a large napkin tied around my neck and another in my lap. A bowl of porridge is cooling before me. I am very hungry, but I will not eat. If I look to the left, the room is red, as if seen through a large decanter of port; but on the right of my vision – at least on the furthest periphery, which I see only vaguely – things assume their proper colourings. I am homesick for these muted colours and I turn my eyes quickly to catch them, dodging the port-wine nightmare like a pickpocket dodging a Bobby. If I could be calm the truth would come back to me, I know; but there are no calm places in the turmoil of my mind. Where is Anna? Why doesn't she come? I am lost and drowning in a crimson sea of grief.

I will not eat. I will go back to bed, escape Dorothy's silence, her cold-hearted efficiency and take refuge in sleep or in juicy-sweet chewings of memory. I am old. I am fifty. I am ninety. I have no hope, no future and a present as bitter as gall. My only recourse is to memory, and I hold it to my heart like a hot-water bottle to cold, cold feet. Where is Anna? My imagination is too cowardly to consider the question, though I ask it a thousand times a day. Where is Anna? No answer. Where is Anna? No answer. Where? I will go back to bed.

Dorothy looks silly in an apron. 'Finished already?' she says distantly. (She does not eat with me. My mess disgusts her.) She plucks the napkin from my shirt collar, inspecting it for stains from her grey, invalid pap. What's wrong with toast? I still have teeth, damn it! I look at her with loathing and lay my hand upon the stair rail.

'Where are you going now?'

To shit, to piss, to lie in my bed and fondle my cock. Any more questions? She sighs and tosses her head, heavily, like a stallion in an iron bridle.

She goes to the dining room. 'Max!' She has discovered the porridge, its glistening skin unmarred by any spoon of mine. She is afraid. I smile and continue upwards to my hungry death.

How long will it take? The Mandrax would have been quicker but there were only six left in the bottle and they were not enough. They made me sick, and I slept for three days. Since then she has hidden the supply and doles out *one*, her eyes narrowed. I should have killed her while I had the strength, but I have never had strength enough for Dorothy. She knows me, and knowing me, destroys me. I can only hope to hasten the process. She cannot make me eat and will not find courage to ask for help until it is too late. It humiliated her to call the doctor for my overdose. Why didn't she call Anna? *Where is Anna?* Is Dorothy keeping her away from me, to spite me? No, even Dorothy could not sink so low. Could she?

But she knows what she is doing to me. She knows; and I do not have even the small satisfaction of calling it vengeance. It is not vengeance. It is selfishness, and I know the precise terms under which it operates, having laid down those same terms for Anna. 'It is, because I want it to be so, and damnation take your feelings in the matter.' It is an excellent system if one is not at the receiving end. But I am.

She is treating me like an imbecile. It would not hurt quite so much if she remembered that I was once a man. But no. I cannot list the things she does to me, each one small, innocuous, but in their sum as lethal as cyanide. It would be a comfort if I thought she were doing it for a purpose, driving me to suicide to put me out of my misery. But even such small comforts are denied me. She isn't even doing it for Anna. She just doesn't care – that's the long and the short of it. She doesn't care how I live or how I die, just as long as I don't make a mess on the floor.

I remember with grief what Anna said in jest: 'She would be worse than the day centre.' Oh, she is. The day centre, which I still attend twice a week, now gives me some relief, reminds me of my pride. Myra still has the sense to pretend to seduce me, the physio still calls me Mr Knighton, and the occupational therapist has somehow twigged that I was once a craftsman of sorts and is allowing me to make a strong, sensible chair rather than one of those putrid tea trays. I have found a use, albeit a minor one, for my right hand. I can push with it, hold things steady. While I work on my chair I can think of myself once more as a man. When it is time to come home, I weep, knowing myself a ruin, without any motive save to crumble to dust. Ashes to ashes. I am decomposing before I am dead.

I say it is not vengeance, but I have no doubt that Dorothy gloats over my helplessness and rejoices in it. We have never before fought one another, but now I throw things at her. I bare my teeth and snarl.

She laughs. 'Suit yourself,' she says blithely. 'You'll be the loser.'

And I always am. Her smugness, her confidence and strength crush me to a pulp.

I beat her once, however. It was a very long time ago, but it gave me great pleasure; great enough, if only just, to allow me a little smugness even now, when the only weapon I possess is suicide.

When Anna was born, Dorothy fell in love. With Anna. I have never seen a woman so besotted. She rarely touched or held her – Dorothy hates touching and being touched; it is one of the few ways in which we differ – but she watched her, talked to her, played with rattles, beads and teddy-bears for hours on end. She called herself Aunty Doffy, and rechristened Anna, to Emily's disgusted amusement, Liddle Babytoots.

It was the only time in my life that I came close to liking the woman.

I was just an ordinary father in those days; detached by one remove. I loved Anna because she was my child, Emily's child, created from one of our moments of joy on one of our nights of love. Yes, I loved Anna, my child, but she was a peripheral part of me, absorbing the glow of love which was reflected from my wife. When Emily died there was no glow left for Anna to absorb. I looked at her and felt nothing. It was natural, then, knowing how Dorothy felt, to hand the child over, to sob through my raging tears, 'Take her! Take her! I don't care!'

One is not morally entitled to reclaim gifts, but one cannot, can one, give a child away? Surely that is as morally wrong as selling her would be? Ha! Morality! God, God, are you laughing up there? I hope so. When Saint Peter asks me – about a week from now if I'm lucky – 'What have you done to merit entry at these gates, eh?' I shall say smugly, 'I made God laugh.' Unless God is a Puritan. Which He can't be. Can He? Heaven forbid! So, I reclaimed Anna and did not care how Dorothy felt about it. My first experiments with cruelty were against my sister. Anna did rather well out of it for a while, courted by us both for her fealty; but there was never any question who would win, for I could always say, 'I am her father. She is mine.'

But that was not enough. I wanted Dorothy not merely to withdraw her claim, but to relinquish it utterly. And I knew precisely how to make her do it. I knew her to her bones, and I intended to teach my daughter to spit Dorothy out as I had once taught her to spit toothpaste.

'Say, "Ttt!" darling. Like this. Watch Daddy. Ttt!'

'Tut!'

She was an adorable baby.

She became very quiet and passive after Emily's death and spent a good deal of her time wedged into dark corners. She made houses under the stairs, under the table, under the currant bushes in the garden. She did not play. She merely crouched there, saying, 'There, there,' to her doll, which was almost as big as she was, with stiff arms and legs and a small internal bellows which allowed it to moan, 'Mama!' when it was turned over.

'There, there.'

'Mama!'

'There, there.'

Although she was out of sight most of the time, we always knew where she was.

On the day I moved into my mother's house, Anna looked without interest at my suitcases and turned away, trotting off to hide under the table. Her doll was upside down in her arms and she tripped on its hair and landed in a heap at my feet. I picked her up, to get her out of my way, but she reacted instantly, pressing herself against me as if trying to insinuate herself into my clothes, under my skin. She didn't give a damn who I was. I was large, warm and human and I was holding her. It was then that I remembered Dorothy's aversion to touching, and realised that, but for the maintenance work of being washed and dressed, Anna had not been hugged or held for the best part of two months. Neither had I, so I did not spare her much sympathy, but at least I knew how to teach her to spit.

After that, although Anna spent little more than an hour of each day in my company, she spent every minute of it in my arms. I carried, cradled, bathed her; tickled her, counted her toes. I brushed her hair, blew in her ears, read stories until her eyes drooped down and her thumb, curling sinfully, strayed to her mouth.

'Time for bed, little girl.' She never once protested. Going to bed was the nicest part, for she knew I would lie down with her and hold her in my arms until she slept.

I admit that I occasionally became confused enough to soothe my own aching nerve ends with the warmth of her body, the sweetness of her breath, her soft murmurings of love; but I knew precisely what I was doing. I was giving my lost, bereaved daughter the sustenance she needed more than food and drink, making each day, however good, empty unless I was in it; however bad, endurable because I would end it. Bathtime and bedtime developed into a sacred ritual, a religious rite at which I was High Priest and Dorothy the heretic outcast.

It was a bitter blow to Dorothy. Until my readvent she had been paddling happily in the warm solution to a chilly problem: how to achieve motherhood without men, without suckling, without nappies or any recourse to filthy nature. Now she was floundering at the turn of the tide. She suffered cramps, swallowed water, came face to face – perhaps for the first time in her life – with the idea that she, like me, might drown. I treasured her jealousy like a jewel, anticipated her grief as my rightful inheritance. Why should Dorothy keep the thing she loved most when mine was lost?

She did not suspect me. Her ability to understand me had diminished with Emily's death. Knowing nothing of passion, grief and madness Dorothy kept her eyes averted from them and did not see how I lured her, with me, to taste their bitterness.

'I'll be late tonight, Dorothy. Will you put Anna to bed?'

The poisoned apple. Her eyes gleamed for its rosy beauty.

'Yes, of course. That's why I'm here, Max.'

'I hope you know how . . . grateful I am.'

'Nonsense! Anna's no trouble. Anyway,' she laughed, 'I wasn't doing anything else, Max. I haven't lost much.'

You will. You will. I smiled into her eyes and read them clearly. She thought I had resigned the priesthood. I was three months a widower and she knew enough of my nature to read all manner of prurience into that simple statement, 'I'll be late tonight.'

I wasn't very late. Just late enough. I found Anna in the bathroom, wedged between the lavatory and the wall. She still had her vest on. The rest of her body was pink with hand-shaped weals. Dorothy's hair had come loose in wild tendrils and she was shaking with rage. My mother, almost in tears, was begging Anna, 'Come out now, darling, come out, there's a good girl.' But Anna had taken the lavatory brush as a weapon, and, invested with the strength of hysteria, looked capable of laying out with it anyone who approached. She was screaming; low, growling screams of such dark intensity that they made my hair stand on end. I had not expected her to react quite so wildly. I had depended on her temper, but this was terrifying. She was four years old, three feet tall, and her rage turned my bowels to water.

In my mind's eye I witnessed the playing out of my own rage, saw my fists knocking Dorothy into oblivion. It was a satisfying, calming exercise which allowed me to smile grimly while I heard the account of my daughter's sins, her fiendish temper, to nod sympathetically, to shake my head as though in stunned disbelief. I almost choked on a laugh when Dorothy gasped incredulously, 'She wouldn't let me *touch* her!'

'Anna, come here!' I snapped. She came out, sobbing, looking up at me with an agony of loss in her eyes. She knew adults always stick together and guessed that in rejecting Dorothy she had alienated me. I did not disabuse her of this error.

'You are a very naughty little girl,' I said dreadfully. 'And you must say you are sorry. Now!'

Anna said it, with a multiplicity of ss and gasps which seemed to go on for hours. As she spoke – or perhaps I should say spat – I caught my breath and widened my eyes in a pretence of silent horror as if I had only then noticed the raised welts on her buttocks, legs and arms.

Dorothy turned white. 'She wouldn't let me –'

'Touch her? You seem to have managed it, nevertheless.' I folded my arms, staring murder into Dorothy's eyes. 'Well,' I said. 'Get on with it. I'll supervise, just in case she turns violent again.'

One could have made a horror film of the next five minutes. Dorothy was trembling with shame and exhaustion. Anna shook, whimpered, wept, and shrank from her aunt's repentant gentleness as from the touch of a white-hot iron. At every second she turned to me for comfort, but I was not yet ready to give it. And when the bath was over and she was buttoned, still weeping, into her nightie, I ordered her to bed and went downstairs without saying another word. My hand shook as I poured the whisky, but I had scarcely raised the glass to my lips before Anna howled my victory for the whole town to hear.

I reached her room without having any recollection of climbing the stairs. Dorothy was gripping the bedpost as if it were her last hold on life. 'Max! I didn't touch her! I swear!'

I knew she had not, but she had violated a sacred rite, and Anna, screaming blue murder from under the bed, was letting her know it with piss, vinegar and spit enough to sink a frigate.

'Out!'

Dorothy flew, just as Anna, responding to the same command, crawled out of her stronghold and launched herself into my arms.

'Daddy!' I rocked her, kissed her, soothed and comforted her while she sobbed loudly enough to break the collective stony heart of the KGB.

'Daddy put me! Oh, Daddy, Daddy put me!'

Men and women of ordinary decency are rarely able to forgive themselves the brutality of their own rage. It is something I learned a long time ago. The Navy, and, afterwards, prison camp, taught me the power of controlled rage and taught me to control it, but Dorothy had not had these advantages. Neither did she have the advantage of Anna's love, which would have forgiven her anything. Dorothy could not forgive herself for beating Anna. Worse still, she could not forgive me for having come home early enough to catch her at it. She carried these humiliations with as much dignity as she could muster, but nothing could wipe out her remembrance of Anna's rage, Anna's uncompromising rejection of her love. 'She wouldn't let me *touch* her!'

No, Dorothy would never forget that, never forgive it. Anna was too young to understand what had happened, but she felt Dorothy's tension and became increasingly afraid of her, innocently snubbing every tentative advance with the old (and now more desperate) demand, 'Daddy do it!'

Dorothy could not bear this. It broke her heart.

'I'm not needed here, Max.'

'If you say so, Dorothy.'

She moved out. Anna was all mine.

I was not jealous of my mother. I did not fear her. Like me, she had put the fragile eggs of her devotion all in one basket, and upon my father's death five years earlier, she had become rather vague. I knew she would not guess at my object, and I supposed that, at seventy, she could be depended upon to quit the scene before it was achieved. But I needed her. I did not expect her to die so soon. I did not expect to be ruined in my prime. I did not expect – oh, where is Anna now? After all my work, all my plans to hold her, keep her, I did not expect her to leave me!

Why doesn't she come? I am clean and I do not care. I am fed and I will not eat. I have realised, too late, that Anna made each day, however good, empty unless she was in it; however bad, endurable because she would end it. I have been taken in my own trap, and I want, I want, I want, oh God, I want to die!

I have not eaten for days. It hurts, but I've starved before. During the last few weeks in Germany we ate virtually nothing but swedes and turnips – raw. The pain of hunger gradually diminishes and I depend upon that to keep my resolve going. There are delusions. My memories get mixed up with reality and with dreams. I am constantly sticking my head out from under the covers to see if Emily is really there, or Anna, my father or my mother. They never are. Sometimes Dorothy is there and I have hardly enough strength left to hate her. Don't care. This time I am going to die, if it kills me. Stuck my head in the gas oven yesterday when Dorothy was out. No good. I had to leave off to be sick. I couldn't bring myself to be sick in the oven, though I needn't have worried. There was nothing in my stomach but slime.

Here she comes again, Anna, my little girl, saying, 'Daddy?'

Yes, darling? Why do you sound so guilty? What have you been up to now? You look like a badly wrapped butcher's parcel in your scarlet gym slip, and there is a smut on your little white face. Well? Out with it. Honesty's the best policy, my child. I'll beat you anyway, but I'll beat you harder if you lie.

'I did write to you, Daddy, but there was a postal strike.'

Indeed? I'll admit that sounds quite plausible, but . . . Write? Write? That doesn't make sense! *Jesus*, this is real!

I snatch the covers back from my head and stare up at her. Oh . . . This is Anna? She is very brown, very beautiful and sad. No, she can't be here. This is just a worse delusion than usual. Still . . .

'Bu?' I reach out to touch her, but . . . she will burst like a soap bubble if I touch her . . .

A scalding tear falls on my cold wrist. It is Anna's tear. Illusions do sometimes weep, but their tears do not scald me, their arms to not gather me, hold me, so that I feel warm, protected, safe again. Anna is real. Really real. Oh, thank you, God! Thank you! You are not such a bad old bugger after all.

Anna curls up beside me and sobs her hot tears into the bony hollow of my shoulder, and through my own tears I whisper, 'Bu, bu.' There, there, my darling, don't cry.

'There, there, Daddy.' She is rubbing my shoulder. 'There. All better. All better now.'

But where have you been? It is so long since I saw you, and you have changed, though your tears, and your small, sweet body creeping into my arms, give me comfort and strength as they have always done. We lie weeping together for a long time, and at last are quiet. I could sleep now in perfect contentment with my daughter safe in my arms.

But she sits up, laughs wetly and wipes her face on a corner of the sheet. 'Bu? Bu?' I lift my shoulders and eyebrows as high as they will go. Where have you been? She looks puzzled, wary. Then she smiles.

'America was awful,' she says ruefully.

America! Oh, my God, I had forgotten! It seems so very long ago, so long ago that you told me; and I had forgotten. Oh, Anna, I thought you had deserted me, and all the time . . .

Oh, my God! I take it all back. You *are* an old bugger!

I close my eyes and fall back against the pillow, amazed at myself, relieved beyond everything. Anna takes my hand and cradles it between her small brown paws.

'Did you forget where I was, Daddy?'

Yes, God help me. Am I really the imbecile Dorothy believes me to be?

'No,' Anna says sadly. Has she read my mind? If I look as embarrassed as I feel, I suppose it is easy enough to read. 'It's my fault,' she says. 'I should have telephoned. Why are you in bed, Daddy? Are you ill?'

Not exactly, no. I'm starving myself to death, as a matter of fact. I slice my finger across my throat, and although Anna's expression cannot be said to have changed, I know she understands. She stares down at the eiderdown and does some five-finger exercises on the quilted bit in the middle. When she looks up again her mouth is grim, her eyes hard. I am afraid. If she says I am being childish, as Dorothy does, I will go mad with grief. But her mouth softens. 'Would you still want to die if I were with you?'

For her sake I must say yes, but I can't. God forgive me, I can't.

'No! Bu, bu, bu!' I want only you, my darling! I no longer want speech, strength, friends and freedom. I want to be comforted, not by cleanliness and order, but by understanding. I want your love, for I cannot live without it.

Anna plays with my fingers, counting them solemnly as I once counted her toes when she was a baby on my knee.

'It's all right,' she says. 'I won't leave you again, Daddy. I've changed. I know – no, I don't know what I am. But I know what I am not. I know I'm not capable of leaving you in misery. I love you, and your misery is mine. Do you understand?'

She smiles and reaches out to touch my face, smoothing my tears back to my hairline. My hair is quite grey now, Anna. Had you noticed? You have given me my reprieve, but I feel strangely sad. You love me, and my misery is yours. I don't deserve such a gift. I have never felt so about you. Your misery has been my pleasure and my satisfaction, your tears my nourishment, your fury my joy. Do *you* understand? No, bless your heart, you do not; and your lack of comprehension is like the moon, the stars and all the pretty flowers to me.

Anna jumps off the bed and grins. 'Shall we have a picnic?' she says. 'Let's have cocoa and cheese sandwiches and cake! Shall we?'

Gorgeous little witch! I'll be sick, but yes, let's have a picnic and spit in Dorothy's eye!

Cocoa has never before moved me to tears, but there is a first time for everything, I suppose. Ah, the caress, the silken warmth, the sweetness on my tongue. Ah, the tender, soothing passage of warm ointments in my throat, the heavenly satisfaction of giving my gut something better to gripe against than itself. There is heat in my blood for the first time in a week. I am strong. I could leap the moon!

Anna is very jolly now. She sits cross-legged on the bed and I can see the lacy crotch of her sweet little drawers. It does not matter. We are friends, intimate and relaxed, like lovers between love, talking politics in bed. She tells me the tale of her travels and I am incredulous, bewildered at the sudden breadth of her experience and the depth of her understanding. She loathed Charlie, praise be to God, but has some compassion for him too, which she denies; though it is clear to me who loathe him so much more. The bastard offered to adopt her when Emma died. I refused — quite courteously — and he asked what right I had to deny him: Anna was *his* niece! Christ! Anna says, rather painfully, that he is very generous, but she thinks it is because he knows he is not loved. She says, 'I often wished you were more generous, but now I'm glad you weren't. It's impossible to appreciate endless generosity, you know.'

Yes, I know; but a little generosity would have done you no harm. I wonder how you have learned to be so forgiving? Not from me, that's certain.

'Daddy?'

'Bu?' Out with it. I see you are afraid of the question you want to ask, but what can I do to hurt you now? And what would I do if I could? You have acquired, rather late, a generous, loving father. Much too late.

'Daddy? You were . . . very strict, weren't you? You didn't, I mean, everyone else I knew had so much more . . . freedom; so much more — do you know what I mean?'

Yes, which is fortunate for you. I wonder if you finish your sentences when you speak to other people. You are like a Scrabble game with half the letters missing, though I am scarcely in a position to criticise. All my letters are missing.

'Was it because,' she goes on haltingly, 'you didn't . . . like me? Because I wasn't like . . . Mummy?' Poor child, she has wanted to ask that question all her life.

Would I have been any happier if I had made Anna happy? I doubt it, but it's not too late to give it a try.

'No,' I say, surprising us both with the firm timbre of my voice; although it is as far as I can go. The only other word which comes easily to mind is tea; which seems hardly adequate in the circumstances. I smile and pat Anna's hand, wishing I could explain, silently offering God my eyes, my legs, my left hand too for the words Anna wants to hear from me. I love you, Anna. I have always loved you. You are the wheel that turns the world, the only lily in the desert of my life. Read my mind, Anna. Read it, and try to understand. I denied you everything you wanted, not for your wrongs but so that you would seek consolation and find it in my arms. It was because you were so like Emily, not so unlike her. I was wrong. For one thing, although you still look like her, share her voice, her gestures, you are someone else. I have made you into someone else. Emma had a happy, free and easy childhood. She had a mother! A brother. A fond, indulgent father. Emma had friends. You had only me. It was what I wanted for you. Only me. I'm sorry, Anna. Read my mind. Understand me. I am sorry and I admit that I deserve everything I am getting – except you. You are too good, as your mother was too good, for me.

Anna seems happy now. She has relaxed. She smiles, but there is still something on her mind. She blushes again.

'Daddy? Uncle Charles – he's nothing like Mummy, is he?'

'*Bu?*'

I am so amazed I fall back and crack my skull against the headboard. My face is doing something peculiar. It isn't crying, but I'm not sure – oh, Jesus, I'm laughing! What an extraordinary sensation! And here comes Anna, laughing too, her darling brown arms outstretched to hug me. 'Oh, thank the Lord for that!'

Her laughter fills my feeble heart with strength, my mind with hope and my poor, betraying eyes again with tears.

Anna creeps closer to me, closer. We are both sitting cross-legged, our knees interlocked. She rests her head on my shoulder and her arms encircle me. For a long time we sit, rocking each other gently, like two sad chimps in an empty cage, yearning for the trees.

Chapter Twenty-Two

America was another stage in my crash-course to maturity, hardening my crab-shell and cooling my heart by many irrevocable degrees, so that I came home changed; disillusioned, but confident as never before.

Uncle Charles, whom I had never seen, had existed in my imagination much as my mother did, on a mysterious, unattainable plane. My mother lived in heaven, Uncle Charles in America. He was wealthy and grand, and, unlike my mother, he always remembered birthdays and Christmas with lovely gift-wrapped parcels, booklets of snapshots and onion-skin letters which rustled between my fingers. The letters were fluent and lively and told me that Uncle Charles was as talented and clever as my mother had been. He painted, played the violin, wrote poetry and was 'a wizard at carpentry, an example of which you will see in our cottage at Cape Cod'.

'Hmm,' was all my father said to this when, as was the rule, I read my letters to him. His lack of interest surprised me because, although he was an engineer, he was also a self-taught cabinet maker and working with wood was one of his greatest pleasures. 'Hmm,' he said to the violin-playing too, although next to my mother's memory his chief love in life was music; and, 'Hmm,' he said when Uncle Charles bought an English sports car, the very model my father coveted.

When I was twelve, Uncle Charles enclosed with the usual snapshots a short letter for my father, inviting us both to go to America for a vacation. 'Hmm!' my father said, and after showing me the letter he screwed it up and threw it in the kitchen boiler. I was devastated.

'Don't you like Uncle Charles?' I asked incredulously.

My father half closed his eyes and shrugged. 'Not much.'

'But why? He's Mummy's brother!'

'Hmm,' he said.

But I liked Uncle Charles enormously. He was always saying how much he loved me, how he longed to see me; and he approved of everything I did. He sent me a cheque for fifty dollars when I passed my O-levels, and told me I was as clever as my mother. I blushed when I read this bit out to my father, whose only comment about my O-levels, of which I passed eight, was, 'How any daughter of mine can fail physics is beyond me.' And he paid my fifty dollars into the bank account to which I would have no access until I was twenty-one.

Aunt Luce, Uncle Charles's wife, sometimes wrote to me too. She was less intelligent than Uncle Charles and she often spelled things wrong, but her letters oozed a delicious sentimentality. She had longed to have a daughter of her own and having a niece, an English niece, was the next best thing. She adored me. So did Paul, my cousin, who was a year my senior and devastatingly handsome. In my adolescence he had been the love of my life, and I had carried his photograph discreetly sellotaped to the inside of my school satchel until my father found it and walloped me. At eighteen, with the prospect of meeting him in the flesh at long last, I fell in love with Paul all over again, though the flirtation I allowed myself to imagine went no further than holding hands and murmuring sweet nothings.

But these things aside, my chief delight at the prospect of meeting my American relatives was the idea that through Uncle Charles I would meet my mother, and discover through him the secret, until now withheld, of her perfection. I did not consciously think as much, but I believed that through my uncle's example, his childhood reminiscences, his loving advice, I would meet my destiny and come home again with my mother 'in my eyes, my mouth, in my heart and in my understanding'.

It took only a minute, upon meeting him, to discover that Uncle Charles was a genetic accident, unlike my mother in every possible respect. I forgave him his American accent almost immediately (after all, it was twenty-six years since he had heard English spoken properly). But I did not forgive his opening words, which were not, as I had fondly anticipated, 'Anna! My darling! At last! At last!' but, 'Well, hiya, kid!' Accompanied by a resounding slap on the back.

Aunt Luce was, at least initially, more satisfying. She clutched me to her chest, sobbing, 'Honey; oh honey, honey, you're so beauriful, so beauriful, so beauriful!' quite loudly, bang in the middle of Kennedy Airport. I blushed and felt my Englishness, like a hard-baked pie crust, sealing me up to cook in my own juices.

Uncle Charles, apparently understanding my embarrassment, dragged my aunt away from me, but then he barked, 'Jesus! Stop makin' such a goddamn fool of yourself, will ya?' which made fools of us all and caused me to look back longingly in the direction of home. I imagined how my father would have greeted me if he had been Uncle Charles. A sparkling smile, a warm handshake, a kiss on the cheek, a courteous enquiry about my journey, a gentle comment about my tiredness. I had seen him do it dozens of times to other people, and I liked it much better. Homesickness began there, and did not end until, more than three weeks later, I erected again an international barrier between myself and my loving relatives.

Perhaps the worst thing about my trip was that it coincided with the first anniversary of my father's stroke, and once I had realised it I couldn't get it out of my mind. I knew that for him, with no hope of cure, with nothing to do, no friends, no future – and now, no daughter – it had been a year of hell beyond comprehension. I wrote a long, lively letter which I hoped Aunty Dorothy would read to him, but when I asked Uncle Charles for stamps, he laughed and said there was a postal strike. I felt sick with guilt. At night I lay awake in the awful heat, wishing I could go home to take my father in my arms and tell him I loved him still. My love was something he had taken for granted; but I could not excuse myself for taking it away from him now, when no one else loved or cared for him. I hated myself, loathed, abused, and then excused myself. I had done my best! The dark night of a Massachusetts heat wave has no forgiveness in it. I writhed in my bed, weighed down with humidity and guilt. No, no, I had done my very worst, made everything more sad and desperate than it need have been. I was beneath contempt.

Uncle Charles was not, however, and I gave him his full measure of it, and, for spite, the even greater measure of contempt which should have been mine. I had been in America for rather less than an hour before I discovered that Paul was spoiled and ignorant; that Aunt Luce was three parts gone to raving melancholia, and that Uncle Charles (who had driven her there and was working very hard on part four), was a bully, a braggart and a liar. He had far more money than sense, and he spent it as though it were sweat, another of his apparently limitless secretions. He spent it on me, and my protests at his generosity were genuine, almost desperate, for I wanted no burden of gratitude to contaminate my feelings toward him. He overthrew my protests, yelling, 'Hey, nothin's too good for you, honey! Nothin's too good for my own flesh and blood!'

My skin crept with horror and my blood ran cold to be reminded that I had genes in common with Uncle Charles; but seeing the futility of arguing, I thanked him and smiled frostily.

My frosty smiles – a new talent – reminded me of my father. When I realised that Uncle Charles worshipped the ground I walked upon, and that, therefore, I had infinite power over him, I was reminded of my father again. That power went to my head like champagne, or, no, more like gin, for there was little joy in it. I pitied Uncle Charles. I knew what he wanted. Through all the pride, the brag and the bluster I heard him cry, 'Love me!' – and could not have loved him to save my life. I found that I had inherited a strong sadistic streak (from my father) and even while recognising that my power would hold no sway over a better-matched opponent, I enjoyed trampling on my spineless, mannerless, adoring relative, even while I hated myself for doing it. Hated myself. I thought I hated Uncle Charles for destroying the illusions of a lifetime, but I was wrong: I hated myself.

The dreariness of being trapped with disillusionment for three and a half weeks was relieved by only one happy accident. The mosquitoes, which were eating everyone else alive, never once came near me.

'It's her English blood,' Uncle Charles told everyone loudly. 'Too rich for the little bastards!'

'Too cold.' Paul muttered under his breath.

To my horror, Paul had kissed me once at a drive-in movie. I said, 'Leave me alone, please. Between cousins it's incest.' I knew this was not true but he was stupid enough to believe it, and he treated me like a leper afterwards.

While I waited with barely concealed impatience for my homeward flight at Kennedy Airport, with Aunt Luce crying buckets into my shoulder and Uncle Charles bawling, 'Will you shut up? She's *my* bloody niece for Chrissake!' I felt something sting my ankle. I slapped my hand against it and was splattered with blood – my own, I suppose – from the biggest mosquito in the entire continent. By the time I left, politely and distantly saying, 'Thank you for having me,' my ankle had swollen to the size and shape of a prize marrow. I felt it was symbolic, an act of God; the act of a particularly vindictive God, who, if it had really been His intention to wreck my dreams, was now muttering smugly, 'That should put the tin lid on it.' It did. 'Thank you for having me,' I repeated bitterly, to Him.

But I was unwilling to lay almost a month of my life to waste, and on my journey home I re-wrote the tale of my travels (as I have since discovered all travellers do). My relatives became endearingly comic, fond clowns with smiles drawn in. The wearying sun and brutal humidity which had almost killed me became mere pin-pricks of suffering for a glamorous tan. My history research – ignored save to collect piles of leaflets from museum desks – became 'thrilling, fascinating', and New York City, the noise and dirt of which had appalled me, 'pulsed with life and excitement'.

By the time I reached my musty bed at the flat, having recited all this and more to an awe-stricken Libby – who had slogged her entire vacation behind the sausage and bacon counter at Lipton's – I only vaguely remembered that I had hated it. It was, after all, Experience.

My trip had seemed interminable whilst I was away, but when I had slept off the effects of my homeward journey the significance of time was lost. Why had I been so worried? A month was no time at all! My father had probably not even noticed I had gone. Nevertheless, the sophisticated traveller who set forth from the flat, enjoying the envious glances her 'glamorous tan' received from a rain-bleached England, became, long before journey's end, a shame-faced truant coming home to face the music.

Aunty Dorothy raised her eyebrows at me. 'Well, well, the traveller returns. Thank you for your letters.'

'There was a postal strike.'

'I believe you.'

I blushed and looked at my shoes. 'Where's Daddy?'

She glanced up at the ceiling and for a horrible moment I thought she meant he was in heaven.

'In bed.'

'Why? Is he ill?' My heart was pounding to choke me. Was this why I had been thinking so much about him? Had he been sending me thought-messages?

'No more than usual,' Aunty Dorothy said carelessly. 'He's trying to kill himself, that's all. Good luck to him, say I.'

I had an overpowering wish to tear Aunty Dorothy's throat out with my teeth, but I had learned something in America. I gave her my most frosty English smile. 'What keeps *you* alive?' I asked quietly. 'A motor?'

She swore at me, and I walked upstairs very calmly, but I was shaking with rage and terror. I stopped outside my father's room and prayed, 'Don't let him be dead. *Please.*'

He looked almost skeletal and his hair was quite grey, his face sunken and yellow. I wept, and then, pretending ignorance, asked why he was in bed. Paradoxically, the next hour was the happiest I had ever spent with him. He was overjoyed to see me, and when it became clear that he had forgotten where I was, that his despair had sprung from not seeing me for a month, my happiness was complete. He loved me. I could no longer deny it. He loved me! I was his only reason for living! We wept together, held one another, snuggling close until the tension of our separate longings dissolved and we were content. I knew that I could not leave him again, not for pity this time, but because in leaving him I was leaving part of myself. I knew that while he lived in misery, I must live in misery too. I knew that if he died in misery a part of me would die, and that I would spend the rest of my life carrying my guilt like a gangrenous, stinking limb, unable to bear the pain of it. That guilt, and the sensation of being separated from myself, had been unbearable for a mere month. I knew I could not survive a lifetime of it.

When my father fell asleep, I lay beside him, stroking his hair. Our lives would be hard, I knew, but easier than before. I had grown, had tasted freedom, tasted power. I had discovered something of my own strengths, and weaknesses. I didn't have to make the same mistakes again. Independence had done its work for me, but now it was over.

I fell asleep stroking my father's hair, and when I woke again he was stroking mine, his eyes soft and smiling.

'Daddy, I've thought it all out. I know what to do.'

'Bu?' He grinned, teasing me. 'Bu, bu. Bossy.'

'Someone has to be.' I sat up, laughing. 'And I'm getting quite good at it, you know.'

'Bu.' He nodded and sank back against his pillow, pretending sheepish submission. 'Bu?'

'You can't live with Aunty Dorothy, can you?'

'Bu! Bu!' He shook his head violently, pounded his fist on the bed, shook it at the door. Oh, he hated her.

'I can't live with her either. So we're moving out, you and I. We'll find a nice flat —'

'Bu?' He snatched at my hand. He was frightened. I'd done it the wrong way.

'Daddy,' I said firmly, 'I can't give up college. I won't. But I can't live with Aunty Dorothy any more than you can. It would be wrong, anyway. I'd end up as the whipping boy, and I've had —' I stopped and averted my eyes, giving myself no marks for tact.

My father nodded sadly. He knew precisely what I meant.

Slowly, carefully and as tactfully as I could manage, I presented the idea of moving into a flat, leaving Aunty Dorothy in the house. My father did not like it, but I knew there was no other way to save both of us.

'We could go to the opera,' I offered slyly at last. 'Invite Myra to tea. We could go to concerts, art galleries, the theatre . . .'

My father narrowed his eyes. He had never been susceptible to coaxing. I was scared. Then he slapped my arm, threw his head back and wheezed his silent, gasping laugh.

'Done?' I asked breathlessly.

'Bum!' he agreed, and shook my hand.

I conducted a very strained interview with my aunt. She called me a sanctimonious little bitch, a sentimental fool, a blind, besotted, suicidal lunatic.

'Do you think he gives a damn about you?' she demanded. 'Max Knighton has never cared for anyone but himself, and you can take it from me, Anna, he hasn't changed. You're selling yourself down the river for nothing at all!'

Everything she said had a ring of truth. My confidence in my father's love lurched and faltered. But it changed nothing except to dull the gloss of my happiness.

'You're probably right,' I agreed quietly. 'Except for the last bit. If

Daddy dies for want of anything I might do for him, I'll never forgive myself. I'm not selling myself for nothing. I'm buying a clear conscience, which is worth a great deal.'

Aunty Dorothy laughed. 'And how long do you suppose you'll keep it?' she enquired nastily. 'You bought a clear conscience once before, Anna, but it was too heavy a load. I don't see how your shoulders could have become so much broader in the space of six months!'

'They haven't,' I said. 'But my mind has. I know how much weight I can carry now, which is why we're moving out. I can't carry this house. I can't carry the travelling. I can't carry the time they take. Without them, Daddy will be light enough; lighter to carry with me than to leave behind with you.'

'For God's sake,' she said contemptuously. 'You'll never shake him off if you take him with you now! You could shake off a guilty conscience.'

'How would you know?' I was tired of her, tired of being polite in the face of her insults. 'You haven't got a conscience.'

She stared at me. For a moment I thought she would hit me. Then she laughed. 'God,' she said, almost pleasantly, 'you're such a bore, Anna.'

It was so unexpected that I found myself laughing too. 'Blood is thicker than water,' I said mischievously, and she laughed again.

'*Touché*. We're a pair of bores, heaven help us.'

It was rather bewildering. I had hated her all my life, but now I understood and liked her; not much, but enough. After all, she had nothing to gain now. She was only trying to save me from myself.

I expected to have difficulties finding a flat, but Myra and Libby, both understanding the urgency of the situation, helped, and we found a place in less than a week. The rent was astronomical, but the place was perfect: a ground-floor flat in a converted convent. There was a neatly fitted kitchen, vinyl-tiled floors, gas central heating. The main door opened to the street, but at the rear, where wide, arched windows opened to the ground, was a garden with willow trees and rhodedendrons.

I moved in almost immediately and slept on the floor. I had done an inventory at home, putting labels on all the things we would take with us. This was the hardest part of the whole move. I did not want to leave my aunt with nothing, but neither could we afford to buy everything new. Should she keep the frying pan, the cheese grater, the kettle? Eventually, seeing no alternative, I did my best to pretend she did not exist and took what we needed. My grant had not yet arrived, and until my father could move in with the furniture I lived very frugally on cornflakes and toast.

One evening when I arrived home from college, I saw a man falling down the stairs. He did it very quietly, and when he reached the bottom he sat up and rubbed his head, looking back the way he had come with a mildly offended air.

It looked like a scene from a Chaplin film and I laughed. Then, realising how unkind that was, I apologised and asked if he was all right.

'Yes,' he said. 'I'm going to a party, actually.'

I laughed again. I couldn't help it. I had the ridiculous idea that he had done it all just to make me laugh, which was impossible because I had never seen him before.

'Oh,' I said. 'You look as if you've just been to a party. Are you sure you want to go to another?'

'Can you suggest an alternative?'

'How about a cup of coffee?'

He smiled, and the smile came from inside him, through his eyes. 'That's very kind of you,' he murmured. 'Thank you.'

His name was Frank Guard and he lived upstairs. By the time I had made coffee I felt I had known him all my life, yet still there was the excitement of not knowing him, and the pleasure of finding out. He was slightly shorter than my father, with a good set of shoulders and nice slim hips. When I took his clothes off in my mind (something I had never done before and did now almost without realising it) his body was perfect: lithe and strong. His hair was slightly wavy, the sort of brown which I suspected had been very fair when he was a little boy. His eyes were a soft, soft blue with centuries of kindness in them. I could not stop smiling, laughing. Everything he said seemed sweet and funny.

'Oh, thank God,' he muttered.

'Thank God what?'

'Lovely teeth.'

He was a dentist. I laughed again and he kissed me. I did not pull away. I couldn't get close enough. He was the most beautiful man I had ever met.

We went to the party together and afterwards talked until dawn. We had cornflakes for breakfast. He laid down his spoon and smiled at me sleepily.

'Anna, I love you.'

'I love you too.'

It was odd. We both laughed.

'Will you marry me?'

'Will you marry my father?'

'Yes. I'll propose to him later.'

Chapter Twenty-Three

Life is quite different here and I feel lighter, freer, as though I had escaped an even greater oppression than I was aware of suffering. The flat is clean and new, and our things look well in it. The large plate-glass window fills the place with light, picks out the colours in the rugs, sets patterns dancing from my whisky decanter and reveals a lovely view of the cathedral, which rises, October-misted, above the trees.

Anna, too, is quite different. She moves more quickly, laughs more readily and talks to me without restraint, as if we had always been the best of friends. I cannot claim to like some of the things she says. Her tales of the flat – the one she shared with Libby – make my flesh creep. Everything is reported in the third person: Chris was drunk; Libby hitched-hiked to Manchester; Cathy slept with a different boy every night.

'Cathy,' Anna says with a smile, 'is very naughty.'

Hmm. But you can't tell me that my innocent darling remained an innocent darling with all that going on! Nevertheless, I cannot imagine Anna . . . Best not to. Imagination can be a swine to a man with my handicaps.

'You mustn't be shocked,' Anna says kindly. 'Things are different, nowadays. People aren't as sheltered as they were when you were young.'

She makes me smile. I've never heard of anyone who led a more sheltered life than Anna's. And as for me! Sheltered! I could tell her a few tales! I wouldn't though.

I don't think Anna would believe that I was bedding her headmistress for the best part of five years, although it gave me a few private chuckles at the time.

'Oh, she's lovely, Daddy! She has the loveliest red hair, and a lovely gentle voice, and she never shouts, even when she's cross with the big girls!'

Ah, but she screams when she comes, my darling. And did you know that she has lovely red hair growing in a sweet little fuzz from her nipple? Right breast. Nice breasts. Everything about Lou Hamshire was nice, except the things she did in bed. And they were delightful.

You see, Anna, she would keep writing to me, asking what was the point of paying out good money for your education if I would not allow you to take part 'in the wider life at St Lydia's'? A good education, she said, was not merely a matter of maths and geography learned at a desk. There were Saturday morning hockey matches, after-school choir practices, trips to the theatre with Miss Limpet-Fotheringham-Smythe (lisle stockings, stockinette knickers and pearls), and, as a final outrage, a four-day excursion to Cherbourg with Ma'm'selle (co-ordinated woollens and buck teeth). Miss Hamshire changed her tack at this point. If I was having 'difficulties' she said (for she knew the fees were quite a strain for some parents), she would be charmed and grateful if I would allow her to pay your fare from the school fund. Hell's bells! And I had sent you to a private school to avoid social workers!

I had dealt with the deputy headmistress on enrolment day, and had no idea Lou was so attractive. Not young, of course: I could give her very few years. But she was extraordinarily well preserved, and one knew at first sight that she had never worn stockinette in her life. She was quite a bonus, quite a challenge. Fortunately, I was wearing a new suit (that oatmeal tweed one you like so much) and I looked like the monkey's uncle – silk tie, gold cuff links, beautifully polished brogues. It scotched her ideas of my difficulties before we had finished shaking hands.

'Oh dear,' she said, and grinned delightfully. 'I've made a dreadful mistake, haven't I?'

'No. No, indeed.' I grinned too and plucked an imaginary hair from my lapel. 'I was wondering if the school fund would pay my tailor, as a matter of fact.'

So we began with laughter, which was very good.

We sat in little chintz armchairs by a window which overlooked the tennis courts. They were not the only chairs in the room, nor by any means the most comfortable for a man of my size. I thought at first Miss Hamshire had suffered a lapse of courtesy, but then I noticed the girls who were playing tennis; big, strapping creatures with short skirts and frilly drawers. Miss Hamshire was no fool. I didn't know whether she was testing my eyesight, my moral fibre or my intelligence, but I turned my chair slightly, declaring myself a man of unimpeachable character with nothing more than the problems of fatherhood on his mind.

'Anna,' Miss Hamshire said gravely.

'Yes,' I agreed. 'I should have told you before, of course, but one likes to keep one's "difficulties" . . .' Another smile; they're always useful. 'One likes to keep certain things private when one can. I appreciate, however, that privacy can be a mistake if it creates misunderstandings, so I'll do what I can to explain.'

Miss Hamshire had been properly brought up, and the mention of broached privacy disadvantaged her neatly.

'Anna is a rather unfortunate little girl,' I began.

(Have you ever noticed, Anna, how often I referred to you as 'a little girl'? You were never a mere girl, never a child, rarely my daughter; and this was no accident on my part. It was a trick. I have a hard face, with a history of bitterness in my eyes. I cannot always disguise it, did not often need to, except where you were concerned. That was why I called you 'Anna, my little girl', for the impenetrable smoke-screen of tenderness it created. Discretion is the dirtiest part of lust. It is like sweeping dust under the rug. Only the most malicious of women – like Dorothy – suspect it is there.)

'Anna is a rather unfortunate little girl,' I informed Miss Hamshire, and she frowned sympathetically.

'Her mother, of course,' she said.

'Yes. My wife died – seven years ago. Anna was four. She became very withdrawn, but I was in . . .' I looked away. It was a genuine breakdown. I could never say 'my wife died' without seeing her dying, hearing the nurse whisper, 'She's gone.'

'I was in no fit state to care,' I went on softly. 'My mother took care of Anna and they became very close. Rather too close, I'm afraid.'

Miss Hamshire looked puzzled, but I knew she had not yet twigged my game.

'My mother died when Anna was five. It was, to put it mildly, rather devastating for us both, but Anna was inconsolable. She had the idea that everyone she loved . . .'

'Poor Anna.'

'Oh, it gets worse. If you can bear it.' I smiled. Self-pity has a limited attraction, and is even less attractive in men than in women. 'After my mother's death, my sister took care of Anna. I was deeply grateful. She was a clever woman and could have had a career of her own. But men are rather selfish creatures, as I'm sure you know.'

That was a good move. Miss Hamshire smiled. She knew.

'And once she had taken the bit I simply gave her her head. I was prepared for the responsibility of bringing Anna up without aid, but since it was not necessary . . .' I shrugged. I also looked deeply ashamed. Miss Hamshire was riveted.

I looked her straight in the eye. Nice eyes. Soft and grey with well-tended laughter-lines at their corners.

'It was a long time,' I said slowly, 'before I noticed that Anna had begun to stammer – you've noticed she stammers? – and it was even longer before I understood . . . why.'

I looked at my hands. I twirled my wedding ring. I did not look up. 'My sister was, she was treating Anna . . . somewhat roughly.'

'I see.'

I hoped Lou did not see what I saw. I hoped she saw a big, butch Dorothy wearing leathers and wielding a bull-whip and Anna – minus the lavatory brush – stammering broken pleas for m-m-mercy.

'Anna is very young, Miss Hamshire,' I said, risking a note of severity. 'She is much younger than her years. She has been bereaved, betrayed; and while such experiences can devastate people of greater maturity, for such a little child they inflict wounds which, at best, leave lasting scars. I do not hold myself blameless in the infliction of her wounds, but I will not be held to blame for . . .'

I sighed, smiled and looked humble. 'Forgive me. As you can see, I feel rather strongly about it all. I am doing my best to heal Anna's wounds, Miss Hamshire. She needs security. How can I supply it?'

Oh, clever Max, and clever Miss Hamshire! She smiled archly. 'I'd be teaching my grandmother to suck eggs, I suspect,' she said. 'You tell me.'

'A quiet life with no surprises. A steady routine, regular hours, plenty of sleep.'

Miss Hamshire's smile softened, warmed. 'And no trips to Cherbourg?'

'Quite so.' Our eyes met in mutual sympathy. 'You agree?'

'I agree. Thank you for explaining it all so fully, Mr Knighton. I know it was not easy for you.'

Her smile was rather strained when she shook my hand. 'We'll take great care of her.'

'I'm sure you will. Thank you.'

She was smaller than I had first thought, but she somehow managed not to look up to me. Had I slipped up somehow? Had I fooled her, or was she merely allowing me to think she was fooled? Had Anna said anything indiscreet? I was not entirely certain I had won.

I worried about it for weeks before telephoning Miss Hamshire to ask her to dine with me. I anticipated a tactful refusal and was rather surprised when she agreed. Our dinner, in a quiet hotel miles from anywhere, went very well. We scarcely mentioned you, Anna, but I was still not certain I had won. It was she who suggested, after a further dinner engagement, that I take her to bed. I thought she was testing me. I refused, teasing her out of it, laughing at myself and my confessed desire. She seemed rather hurt.

'I suppose you aren't accustomed to being seduced?' she said.

'No. But I don't find it at all painful. Are you serious, Lou? Or are you merely coercing me into increasing the strength of your hockey team?'

She laughed. 'I'm serious, damn you.'

I raised my wine glass, solemnly toasting her good taste. 'In that case,' I said, 'I consider myself seduced.'

She was a much better lover than I had anticipated. She didn't natter, as some women do during the preamble, on inconsequential subjects, and she had a deliciously mucky laugh which incited me to give her more satisfaction than I had originally planned. Then, at the most amazing moment – midway between a gasp and a groan – she said, 'You don't think you're taking this security idea too far, do you?'

'*What?*'

'Anna.'

It was lousy timing. I almost died on her, but I was an expert at realising my opportunities and I immediately suspected that Lou had used the ploy not to catch me out but to prolong her 'agony'. I knew how to prolong it! I sat on the edge of the bed and reached for my clothes.

'Max!'

'I never mix business and pleasure.'

'Bugger business,' she said, and wrapped both legs around my waist. I had won.

Rather against my better judgment, I became extremely fond of Lou. I told her I would never marry again, and she accepted this cheerfully enough. We talked a great deal: politics, music, art – never religion.

Religion is one of my weak points. Too emotional. An intermittent love affair is no place for emotion. We ate pasta in bed, and then I dressed, kissed her and came home to you and your baby-sitter.

I was not always at the Watersmeet, Anna. I am not quite the gentleman I pretend to be. Are you shocked?

'Do you want spinach or carrots with the liver, Daddy?'

Pasta, please. Tagliatelli with mushroom sauce.

'What are you grinning at?'

Wouldn't you like to know!

Anna smiles warily and makes for the kitchen. 'Libby's coming round after dinner,' she says distantly.

Poor Anna. She can understand my griefs. They make her feel useful. An unexplained gleam in my eye foxes her utterly.

Eventually, and I think rather sadly, Lou ditched me for a banker who seemed more likely to marry her. I missed her much more than I liked to admit. There were others, of course, but none who could talk as Lou had talked, or laugh as Lou had laughed; and none so good between the sheets. But she did not marry the banker. Something happened. I can't remember, but wherever the memory is, there is grief in it.

Anna's cooking continues to improve, and, paradoxically, we eat better meals since we have become so poor. Anna worries about money, and consequently takes more trouble with the shopping. She can make a tiny lamb chop stretch to a feast, and makes solid nursery puddings in the vain hope of adding some flesh to my ribs. The worst thing about poverty is instant coffee. It tastes awful, but on this occasion Libby's arrival sweetens its bitterness and brings another gleam to my eye. Libby's a stunner. She is tall and rather bony like myself, and although she speaks seriously and intelligently, seeming at least five years Anna's senior, she laughs a good deal too. She sits on my knee (being careful not to establish her weight on it) and says, 'What shall we do for a giggle?' Anna could not hide her dismay the first time this happened. I think she expected me to throw Libby off with a scream of outrage. When, instead, I whispered a lascivious 'Bu, bu, bu,' into Libby's ear, Anna's eyes widened with disbelief.

'You're a disgrace,' she informed me pleasantly.

'Bu?' Who? Me?

'Yes, you,' she said.

It was a very happy moment.

'For a giggle', Libby and I are planning a Guy Fawkes's party for Anna. It was Libby's idea, of course. I have none of the words which might have suggested it, but she could not mistake my enthusiasm for the project. I gave her all the money I had and pressed my finger to her lips to pledge her to secrecy. I have given her more money since, saying, 'Bi-berps,' which is sufficiently like fireworks to get the message across. Anna, hearing me say it once, asked what was going on.

'He's got indigestion,' Libby said solemnly.

Anna was rather offended. She reads my mind very effectively now, but I get the idea that she does not like other people doing it. Not that they can. Anna can interpret the meanings of fifty different versions of 'bu', but 'bi-berps' is beyond her telepathic power.

Anna adores fireworks. Once, when the County Show coincided with her birthday, I allowed her to stay up late for the fireworks display. She was still very small and I stood her on a rail and propped her there with my arm. I remember the heat of her summer skin, her sticky hands clutching my neck, and the sweet, sleepy scent of her body. When the first flight of rockets went up she began to tremble.

'Frightened?'

'No! Oh, no, no! Oh, Daddy, it's beautiful!'

I laughed; but her passion was curiously awe-inspiring. She had jammed both hands in her mouth and her eyes were huge; glowing darkly, like necromancers' crystals foretelling the doom of the world. The other children – we were with the Townsends and their brood – gasped and yelled and jumped up and down, but Anna was quite still save for her quivering nerves, and quite, quite silent, absorbing every sparkling explosion as if it were to be her last joy on earth. I wondered what the hell I was doing to her. I hated myself. But then, as was always the way when I dared to risk the torment of self-examination, I hated Anna.

Long before the display was over I carried her back to the car. She fought me, stretched out her hands to sky and its canopied jewels.

'Oh! Oh, no, Daddy, please!'

I slapped her. 'If you're going to get in such a state,' I said coldly, 'you won't see the fireworks again.'

To the best of my knowledge, she never did see the fireworks again, except perhaps illicitly from her bedroom window on November the Fifth. But this year we are having Catherine wheels, rockets, sparklers and Roman candles – the whole bang-shoot. I can't wait to see her face! Will I giggle, as Libby expects, or will I weep and ask God to let me begin again? Another chance, another chance. I'll be good to her this time, God, I swear.

Libby tweaks my ear, 'Why so glum?'

I smile, to please her. Glum? I don't know what you mean. I'm not glum, my dear, I'm just . . . sorry. You think I'm quite a darling, don't you? But I ain't. I'm a bastard, Libby. Clean through. I wish you could hear me. They say confession is good for the soul, and my soul . . . Christ, my soul. But my soul is on the mend since we moved here. Life has become – quite interesting.

Myra pops in once or twice a week. She and Anna have become friends and they talk about Life in serious, womanly tones. It's mostly rubbish, but quite fascinating for me. They often forget I'm here. I feel like a fly on the wall of a harem. I know things about menstruation, perspiration, cleansing milk and hair conditioners which have quite escaped me until now. Myra is no longer my speech therapist. She has given up. It was hard for her to tell me so, but I watched her distress with quiet amusement. I gave up a long time ago, and it came as no surprise to learn that my case is hopeless. I like her better in her capacity as Anna's friend, anyway. I often resented her professional power over me, and it is easier to think of her – with Libby and the others – as one of the children.

I have met most of Anna's friends. I was shy at first, ashamed of myself, but they were very easy to like and one of them – his name is Dave – has encouraged me to take up bird-watching. 'Good place for it here,' he said. 'If you put out food for them I reckon you'll see a dozen different species a day.'

He spoke as though I were perfectly capable of answering him, and more out of gratitude than interest, I fed the birds. Now I am a keen ornithologist and have added bird to my immediately available vocabulary. In spite of all Myra's work, my spontaneous words are still limited to tea, money, no and bugger. I use them for everything, but now that I have bird too, I shall try to dispense with bugger. I've never been happy with it.

Frank. I try to forget Frank, but I can't. He works at the dental hospital down the road. Anna asked him to fix up our new vacuum cleaner. She said there was a 'chap' in the flat upstairs who would do it, and he came down with his screwdriver. I liked him immediately. Fine eyes. Fine hands. A very gentle man, and a gentleman to boot.

'Frank is a dentist,' Anna said brightly. But her eyes were flittering all over the place. She could not look at me. She could not look at him.

Frank was a little startled at having his professional references presented to me in such a way, and he looked at her sideways, his eyes warm with amusement. His eyes. Her eyes. They told it all and I could not bear it; but before I could faint, Frank aimed his screwdriver at my mouth and smiled. 'So now you know,' he said, knowing that I knew what I knew. 'Open wide, sir!'

He made me laugh. There was nothing I could do. They are in love, and if I had been forced to choose I know I would have chosen him for my daughter. But I try not to think of it.

Frank has a motor car. It is the sort of vehicle I would not normally deign to spit upon, but things are not normal any more, and I can't spit anyway. We go out in this disreputable heap of tin every weekend. Anna sits in the back with her fingers crossed while Frank describes all the bangs and rattles in loving detail for my fascinated, and utterly appalled, ears.

'That's the exhaust,' he says; 'I think the string's worn out.'

'*Bu?*'

He laughs. 'Is there another way to hold an exhaust pipe on? I've tried chewing gum, but it dries out and drops off.'

I'm never sure he's serious. He seems to care about serious things. He thinks deeply, speaks – when he speaks to Anna – with a gentle earnestness, a wisdom and kindliness which are extraordinary in a man so young. He is twenty-eight. Anna says he suffered from asthma as a child, which might account for it. Children who are sick and lonely often become wise beyond their years, and they learn something of humility; the saving something which escapes the rest of us until too late. Yes, that is Frank's secret. He takes everything seriously – except himself. For Anna's sake I am glad he is wise. For my sake? Well, he makes me laugh. Even more importantly, he cleans my teeth! Frank is a jewel. I can laugh and run my tongue over my teeth without feeling horrified.

Anna is still a rotten housekeeper but she is more organised here than at home, and happiness gives her energy. I do a lot to help. I push the vacuum cleaner, do the dusting. I can't fold Anna's clothes, and once in a while we have a reprise of the old days, with me dragging her to her room and wagging my finger at the mess. She still has the grace to blush.

'Sorry,' she mutters, 'I'm incorrigible, aren't I?' And then she grins. Little beast.

But the truth is that I no longer care about her faults. Her virtues have taught me to give and take. It's a great relief.

Chapter Twenty-Four

My father suffered his second stroke on the eve of his fifty-second birthday. It was nothing like the first and the doctor called it 'an accident' – a minor haemorrhage. I didn't know it had happened. He seemed quite well and happy, although there wasn't a great deal to be happy about. I was in the middle of my Finals, worn thin with worry over money; and I was glad the weather was fine because I had holes in my shoes and not even the price of a stick-on sole in my purse. I had never regretted taking the flat, but my grant did nothing beyond paying the rent in advance and the gas bills in arrears. After that we were on the bread-line, at the back of the queue.

My father had enough to eat, but I suppose I did not. And while he had clothes enough to last a lifetime, I did not. He came first in everything, not because I was so unselfish, but because he was so helpless. It was like having a child. The child eats while the mother goes hungry. I didn't starve, exactly, but I ate what I could while Father ate what he needed.

And on the eve of his fifty-second birthday he didn't swallow it. I failed to notice it at first. I was worrying about my exams, wondering if I had enough energy to study all night. When I looked up I saw that my father's cheeks were puffed out like a hamster's, and when he opened his mouth to put in another forkful, a mash of spinach and gravy oozed out and dribbled down his chin. He seemed not to notice, which was odd, because he hated being messy. I watched him. Another forkful went in, another mess dribbled out. His mouth was full of food and he did not know.

I explained it, trying not to embarrass him. He seemed not at all embarrassed, simply interested, almost amused. I told him to swallow. He couldn't. I gave him a bowl to spit into. He couldn't spit. At last, blushing for him rather than for myself, I emptied his mouth with my fingers and nearly fainted to discover how much he had stowed away. His plate was almost empty, but he had swallowed nothing at all.

I was frightened. I made him try again and stroked his throat to make him swallow, but after an hour of trying, of mashing the food to a pulp and doing everything short of ramming it down his throat with my fist, he had swallowed scarcely enough to keep a sparrow alive. I was almost in tears, but he seemed quite fascinated, his eyes wide and bright with interest.

The doctor said it would wear off, but the next day he decided that a few days in hospital would sort it out. I was very relieved until I realised that he did not mean to send my father back to Myra's hospital, but to another place on the far side of town which he said was geared to the chronically sick. When we arrived there it took me less than a second to realise that it was a geriatric hospital, with walls the colour of shit and a stink to match, with one nurse to thirty beds and inmates who howled and sobbed in the throes of *senile dementia*.

I seemed to be freezing from the inside out, but my father was still blithely unconcerned. He was smiling as we walked down the ward. Then a man screamed and suddenly my father was terrified. He scrabbled for my hand, his face turning an ashen grey as if he had only then realised what was happening.

'Come along, dear,' the nurse said, and pulled me away. Behind the curtains, while she helped him undress, I heard my father sobbing: a horrible, choking sound. I stood there, horrified, knowing that I must leave him and that I was leaving him in hell.

I dragged myself away. It's a worn way of putting it, but there is no other expression to fit such a sensation. I stood outside that stinking ward for ages, feeling that I was attached to my father's heart by elastic. The elastic was at full stretch, too strong to be snapped, and when I attempted to move, my feet went nowhere. I was senseless of everything except my father's terror. Gradually I became aware of myself. I was trembling. My elbows were pressed against my ribs, my hands splayed and rigid, my lower lip pulled down to expose my teeth. I attempted to relax. I thought, 'Exams. Work. Three years. *Move!*' But I couldn't move. I could hear my father's sobs, not in reality, but echoing in my head as though each sound had etched its mark there for ever. The sounds were not real, not human, but the cries of a soul in torment, denied the last right of all, to scream, 'Let me out!' And I couldn't. I couldn't let him out. I had no choice at all. If I took him home, he would starve to death.

Having no choice was the horror, but it was the truth, and so at last the comfort, if one could call it that. I held my breath until it hurt, and then, exhausted, relaxed enough to walk away. It was an old trick, one I had learned as a child, but then the difficulty had been not to walk away from my father but to approach him.

'Anna, come here.' He rarely shouted, but he had a way of snapping commands in a voice which invariably froze me to the spot. The elastic attached me to other things then. I dragged myself towards, not away from him, for I never knew what would happen when I arrived. Sometimes he would simply issue another command, 'Put your coat on,' or 'Wash your hands.' And sometimes he would slap me and shake me for crimes I scarcely recognised as my own.

But I did not hate him. I went on loving him, aching to know that he loved me. Sometimes he did. Sometimes I was sure he did. When I had nightmares he would come to my room, stumbling with sleep, bare-footed, bare-chested, grumbling drowsily, 'S'awright, darling. Only a dream.' And sometimes he would collapse on the bed at my side, throwing his arms protectively over me, 'On'y a silly ole dream,' before falling fast asleep without ever having properly wakened. He loved me then. I was sure he loved me then. And when I hurt myself, when I fell down and scraped my knees, he would pick me up to rub or kiss it better. 'Brave girl. Don't cry. All better now.' He loved me then.

But he loved me most when we had quarrelled and I hated him, oh, hated, hated him – and then was terrified that he hated me. 'I'm sorry, Daddy! Please, please forgive me!' And he would take me in his arms, rubbing the ache from my shoulders, kissing the tears from my face. He loved me then, in the quiet lull after the storm. He stroked me, soothed me, comforted me. He called me Daddy's little girl, Daddy's baby. He called me his darling, and he loved me, I know! But he never said it. In all my life, my whole life, he never gave me what I wanted more than all the kisses in the world. He never said, 'I love you.' And I never, really, believed he did; for in the next day, the next hour, the next minute he might say, 'Anna come here,' and flay me alive with his voice.

I thought at the time that I was in the grip of some kind of divine justice, with motives which were as yet beyond my comprehension; and I was planning to marry Frank before it fully occurred to me that my father had been gratuitously cruel. It occurred, but I still could not believe it, because I could always find reasons for his treatment of me – perhaps misguided ones, but still part of the divine pattern.

I dared not think that it was he who was now held in the grip of a divine justice, because that rendered God more cruel than my father had ever been, and I needed to know that God was good. I had left my father helpless, sobbing, starving in hell, and if God was not good . . . If God was not good he would never be let out.

'God, please. Oh, God, *please!*'

I rang Frank and tried to tell him what had happened.

'I'll come down,' he said, and hung up before I could say no. His unselfishness amazed me. He had left the dental hospital a few months earlier to buy himself into a practice in a small cathedral town fifty miles away. He had said goodbye to ten years' savings overnight, and now was poorer than we were, living on a diet of boarding-house breakfast and shelled peanuts. He still managed to keep his battered old car going with what he called 'chewing gum and bits of string', though he was, in fact, a perfectly capable mechanic, and looked just as happy in a greasy boilersuit as in his starched white coat. He never missed visiting us at weekends. Sometimes he arrived with oil on his face and a rueful smile – three hours late. And sometimes he arrived with a bunch of dog-daisies he had stopped to gather from a hedge, whispering, 'Pretend they're red roses.'

'How many?'

'Two dozen.'

'Two dozen? For me?'

We pretended a great many things. Most of the very best things were pretend, except the best thing of all: I loved him, and I was going to marry him. One day. When we could afford it. When things worked out.

I loved Frank. But something was wrong. I knew he was the right person for me to marry, and yet – not quite right. The thought of losing him was agony; the thought of living with him for the rest of my life, frightening. I did not understand him. He was a private, deep man. He said he loved me, and yet seemed quite self-contained – without any needs which I – rather than any other woman – could supply. He was utterly dependable, totally trustworthy. He was safe. When I thought about life without Frank it was like coming to the edge of the world and seeing nothing but darkness before me. But when I thought of Frank's life without me, it went on just as before, as though I had never existed. Sometimes I wondered if I had been deceived and that his 'private depths' were mere shallows.

But he was coming to comfort me. He was coming to drive away the echoes of my father's sobs. I did not need to understand him, if only he were there to understand me. On the way home from the hospital I bought a pork rasher at the market, some vegetables and a banana, and when Frank arrived I had scraped together a fairly substantial meal.

When we had finished the banana (half each) and custard, he smiled blissfully and said, 'You're gorgeous. I was famished.'

'You only love me for what you can get.'

I was joking and immediately regretted it. One of the very few advantages in his moving away was that we could no longer sleep together. A middle-aged couple had taken his flat upstairs and at weekends, although Frank slept in my bed, I slept on the sofa. I could not bring myself to sleep with him while my father was in the flat.

Sex was very important to Frank. I had had enough experience of men, before I met him, to realise that it would be important, and I made it a priority to tell him that I was still a virgin. He laughed.

'Oh, dear. Is it terminal?'

'I'm not sure. I know it isn't infectious. And I believe there's a cure.'

'But you think the medicine might be worse than the disease?'

'Something like that, yes.'

He changed the subject. Some time passed before he mentioned it again, and then it was a casual remark slotted between, 'Pass the spanner,' and, 'Anything to eat?' Eventually though, he taught me all about it, told me the things which should please me and the things which pleased him. I accepted everything he told me, tried to cooperate – and hated it. He tried so hard to make me like it, and he was so gentle, so thoughtful; it made me want to cry for him when nothing happened. I shivered and trembled, hating his eyes on my body, feeling irritated by his stroking hands. We both had very bony hips, and the pain of our bones grinding together was excruciating. He did not feel it. His passion frightened me. He was usually so quiet and controlled, and the person who gasped and groaned, screwed up his eyes, bared his teeth, was a complete stranger to me.

Many of my relatives – including my mother – had died either of strokes or heart attacks so I was advised against the Pill and had little faith in other forms of contraception. Frank was reassuringly efficient about it and I had done everything the clinic had advised, but I was certain something would go wrong. The feelings inside me conjured up images of unwanted babies. I kept imagining my father's face when I told him, heard him say, 'Pah!' and turn away, hating me for the rest of his life.

But now his life seemed close to its end. Frank sat in an armchair and I sat on the floor between his knees. I told him again about the hospital. I described again my father's terror, heard again the echo of his dreadful sobs. Frank listened in silence, hugging me, occasionally kissing my hair. When I asked if he thought my father would die, he said, 'I don't know, Anna' – which somehow made me more certain that he would. I hoped he would. I could not bear to see him suffering so. I knew death was the only dignity left to him, and if I could have bought his death that night, I would have sold my soul to raise the price.

I think he had already died in my mind, because having unburdened my horror and had Frank, through his warmth and gentleness, take it from me, I did not think of my father again. I felt so grateful to have Frank there, and it was he, for the first time in years, who filled my thoughts. I would be a good wife. I would never let him regret marrying me. I would make him laugh when he was sad. I would strengthen him when he was weary. I would be at the centre of his world. I warmed to him that night. I felt my own desire – only fleetingly, but it was there to be nurtured by love. And when the grinding of our bones killed it, I knew its death was a temporary thing, soon to know resurrection.

'Christmas?' Frank mumbled sleepily.

'Hmmm?'

'Weddin'. You, me. Uh?'

'No money, Frank.'

'Hell with it. Love conks all.'

I laughed, and we fell asleep.

My father did not die – except a little bit more. I visited him every day for three months, and watched while he died a little bit more each day. They drip-fed him for a while, taught him to drink through a straw and gradually to eat again. For weeks he wept when he saw me, wept when I left, and then he accepted that I could not take him home and his face became quite passive, sadder than I had ever known it.

He got up and shuffled to the dreary hall they called the day room, to sit there, unmoving, for hours. For the first time in his life he began to look unkempt – through no fault of his own. He could eat, but his mouth had lost sensation and he frequently dribbled and spilled his food. His skin acquired a greasy shine and he wore open-necked shirts against the heat which stirred the sluggish circulation of his senile companions. He was pitifully thin, and the scraggy skin of his neck ended in a deep hollow between his collar bones, where sometimes would lurk a pool of sweat or some breadcrumbs. He smelled of tinned soup.

The hospital staff were kind, but massively overworked, and I knew that Frank and I were the only people who ever talked to him. We waited a long time before we told him our wedding plans. I told him about my Finals first. I had won that battle, at least.

'Not a First,' I told him ruefully. 'But it's the next best thing. Are you proud of me, Daddy?'

He moved his head very slightly. I could not tell what it meant. I waited until I left the hospital before I cried.

When we told him that we would get married at Christmas he looked briefly into Frank's eyes and then rested his cheek tenderly in his hand, gazing into a dull and lonely distance. His hand was curved like a crescent moon and he rested his face on it not for support but for comfort. It was as though, being robbed of all solace, he strove hopelessly to comfort himself.

Frank swore obscenely under his breath and marched out. He was not given to using bad language. 'Bloody hell' was as far as he usually went, and then only when one of the Riley's more important bits fell off. Was he hurt because my father had not been overjoyed at our news? I was.

'Aren't you pleased, Daddy?'

He looked up again, staring at me as if wondering who I was. Then he sighed softly, as though all violence, all strength, all power were taken from him and, save for the act of dying, he was indeed quite dead.

When Frank came back he was smiling. He crouched at Daddy's feet and held both his hands, shaking them briefly to command attention.

'We're getting you out of here, Max,' he said. 'Do you hear me?'

My father frowned, and then he turned his head and stared at me.

I did not know what Frank had done, but he never lied or made hopeful inventions, and if I could trust him with the rest of my life I must trust him with my father's life too.

'Yes,' I said firmly. 'We're getting you out, Daddy.'

He touched my face with his fingertips and smiled; but it was as if he had forgotten how to smile, believed he could not do it any more. His mouth opened wide and his drawn, almost fleshless cheeks formed into two pale little crab apples, which emphasised the dark hollows of his eyes and made the eyes themselves as bright as naked souls. His suffering tore me in half, and it was all I could do not to howl like a dog in the dark for our release from chains we could not bear.

Chapter Twenty-Five

My son-in-law is the first good man I have ever known. Where did Anna find him? She says, 'At the foot of the stairs.' And sometimes I wonder how he came to fall, and from where. I have seen good men with God in their eyes and snakes in their tongues, seen good men with God in their acts and hell in their motives, seen good men who would eat your soul; but I see no harm in my son-in-law. He is good. He has no vanity, no envy, no pride, no violence, and yet all of these, trapped not in his heart to hurt him, but in the palm of his hand, held like fine tools, to make and to mend. He raised his fist to me once. I had lost my temper (still do, sometimes; can't help it) and had taken Anna by the throat. Frank raised his fist and I was terrified. My heart drained of rage. I was ashamed, grieved. I thought I had lost everything.

Anna sobbed, 'No, no! He can't help it! He didn't mean it!' And Frank held us both in his arms.

'I know,' he said gently. 'I didn't mean it either, but I can't let you hurt one another, can I?' He led me out to the garden, telling Anna to dry her tears, make some coffee, cheer up and forget it.

'Now,' he said. And I knew what was coming — lay hands on her again, old man, and you're for the geriatric home. 'Now,' he said, 'what are we going to do about this sodding car? Give me a hand to bleed the brakes, will you?'

To make and to mend. We would all enter heaven's gate if to make and to mend were our only purpose, and I see in Frank that the words are his goodness, the only goodness a man can have. He has all my skill and more with inanimate fabrics — metal, wood, stone; and his hands, though smaller than mine, are the same: broad backed, long fingered, with knuckles like wood-knots. They are strong, sensitive hands which can play a screwdriver like a clarinet, ring a sledge hammer like the knell of doom.

And he makes us laugh. He makes me laugh at things I had never known were funny, forcing me to see life from another angle, to abandon all that has gone before — and accept things as they are.

We moved from the flat soon after the wedding and came here, to a cottage which seems to be nowhere and yet is within walking distance of the town where Frank works. We chose the cottage together. It was empty, save for a cardboard box and a pile of old newspapers, and there were six different layers of wallpaper on the sitting-room walls, their designs a history one could peel off by generations. We sat on the windowsills and I stared out into the garden, a jungle of seedling elders, stinging nettles and ghosted willow-herb. I was saying to myself, 'Oh, no, not here'; but without violence. The cottage was dank and primitive with a chemical lavatory somewhere among the nettles; but I knew it was not as bad as the hosptial. I knew I could live here, if I must. After the hospital I could live anywhere: in a hole in the ground, up a tree, anywhere. Just let Anna be there too. Anna – and Frank, my son-in-law, my salvation.

It was he who let me out. Anna had tried, but she was too young. I was caught in a machine too big for her to handle, a treadmill she lacked the power to stop. Frank just walked into someone's office and said, 'I am taking him home,' and they said, 'Yes, sir. Certainly, sir.'

He let me out. I thought I was there for ever. I scarcely remember it now except in nightmares, but I never forget the nightmares. The grief of it. The fear.

I lost track of time. For weeks I lived in terror of the rats on my bed. Most of the time they sat quite still, bald, malevolent things. They stared their malice at me while I sat rigid with terror, staring at them. Sometimes they jumped! And stretched their legs, yawning the boredom of their evil vigil. Sometimes they crept – when I wept – over my face, eating my tears. After a long, long while, I noticed that only one of the rats crawled over my face. Later I discovered that the rats were my hands.

For a long time I lay in a temple with ochre walls, hearing the screams of sacrificial beasts, watching the priests at their devotions. I heard someone cry, 'Sinner!' and another scream, and suddenly I knew that they were sacrificing men at the altar and that I was next.

Later, when the delusions ceased, I heard the cry again. It was a fat woman in a green overall, shouting, 'Dinner!'

But reality was worse than delusion. Reality was a man who sat in a chair beside my bed, staring at the wall, eternally droning the same agonised phrase: 'I want to go home.' He tore the words from my own heart, scooping them out with a blade of steel, making me bleed.

Reality was inhaling soup and warm tea in my attempts to swallow them; panicking, choking, hearing the nurse say, 'Woops!' as though my agony were of no importance.

Anna was reality. She came every day. At first she said, 'Soon,' and then, 'In a little while,' and then – nothing. I knew she would never let me out. And I had been there before – in hell – knowing I would never be let out. I knew how to deal with it.

When she comes, feel no joy. When she speaks, pay no heed. When she smiles, look away. When she weeps have no heart. When she leaves, feel no grief – and survive. To die.

I did not die. Frank let me out and Anna wept for two days. God bless her, she was too happy to stop crying. Too happy, and too grieved by her own helplessness to help me. They would not listen to her. She was too polite, too shy, too obedient to understand that she could break the cogs of that frightful machine. She was too polite, too obedient; all the things I had taught her. She was nailing me into my coffin with my own hammer.

The wedding was quiet and rather sad. We had no money for frills. Anna baked the wedding cake and Frank provided a dozen bottles of champagne – brewed from pears, I suspect. The guest list was painfully brief. Frank's parents, his brothers and sister-in-law, Libby, Chris, Myra, Jenny Cole – a staff-nurse now, at Guy's – and Dorothy!

'How are you, old boy?'

Well, let's put it like this: not dead yet, thanks.

I have forgiven her. No, I have not forgiven her. But she sent Anna my mother's wedding gown, aloofly claiming to have 'no immediate use for it'.

It's a good thing there were so few guests. Already there are ten people in the world wondering why the bride and her proud father wept buckets throughout the ceremony. Eleven. I am wondering why Anna wept. Twelve: for surely Frank must wonder, and be afraid.

After the wedding we began house-hunting. Anna wanted 'a cot beside a hill' with a bee-hive's hum to soothe her ear, and Frank, who hated the idea and would have greatly preferred something sensible with a damp course, eventually came home to announce, 'We've got a cot, and it's got a hill, but beehives is extra, madam.' He seemed rather distraught. We soon knew why.

'Where's the lavatory?' Anna whispered.

'Lavatories is also extra,' Frank said.

Anna crept away to explore, her hands rigid with shock. Frank stood in silence, his gaze piercing the structure of the place like a pen-knife into rotting timber.

From the scullery I heard Anna say, 'Well, at least there's a tap.' And then, 'Oh, God,' following a nasty rattling sound, 'it's bust.'

Frank's eyes did not abandon their narrow scrutiny of the room, but he said sharply, startling me because his voice was usually so soft, 'Don't say, "bust" Anna; it's vulgar.' She appeared in the doorway, the tap in her hand, her eyes big and scared, a flush of embarrassment on her face. Frank grinned. 'Say tits,' he finished, and kicked the fireplace to see if it would fall down.

I laughed so much I almost fell out of the window.

Anna thumped her husband affectionately and then sat on my knee, curling her arm around my shoulder. 'Do you like it, Daddy?' she said hopefully. 'Isn't it lovely?'

Yes, it was.

She went to the car to fetch our picnic. Frank squared his shoulders. 'It'll have to do, Max.'

'Bu.' Yes, I know.

'I can do the plumbing before we move in, but after that I'll need help. Are you game?'

I shrugged hopelessly. Game? What had that to do with anything? I was useless.

Frank lifted an imaginary hammer in his left hand and mimed knocking down walls. He took an imaginary paintbrush and mimed painting doors. Then he mimed flopping down in exhaustion. He glared at Anna who was laughing in the doorway, and in my own hollow voice he said, 'Tea!'

After that, I was game for anything.

Frank did rather more than the plumbing before we moved in. He turned the smallest bedroom into a bathroom, tore out and replaced the rotten windows, swept the chimneys and kept fires burning in every hearth for weeks on end. On the day Anna and I moved in with the furniture, Frank looked as if he had been dipped in cement and left to harden, but the cottage, though bare, felt as warm and as safe as the womb.

He built a work bench for me with a couple of vices to compensate for my useless arm. He smiled and said, 'I provide the vices, you provide the virtue,' and left me to it. He had no money and the new doors were old ones he had salvaged from another derelict cottage. They were panelled deal, filthy, and inches thick in paint. I cleaned, sanded and varnished one every week. I grew tired and lost my temper countless times. I threw things at Anna. But every time I finished a door, Frank thanked me and hung it in its appointed place. He never said, 'Well done,' because he knew they were not perfect and he knew I knew it. His failure to patronise me was not, I am sure, a conscious decision on his part. It simply did not occur to him to lie. But I got better at it. I gained confidence and felt pride, like rage, burning inside me. The last two doors were perfect. Frank opened his eyes very wide and a smile touched his mouth. 'Ah,' he said; and that was perfect too.

I was never jealous of him. He played no lovey-dovey games with Anna, although when I thought of their relationship I realised that it was all an elaborate game. They played at quarrelling, called each other names, clenched their fists, stamped their feet – and then fell about laughing just as I had begun to fear that a divorce was imminent. They played at intellectualism, discussing morality, politics, art and literature. They psycho-analysed each other. They cured the ills of the world whilst papering the kitchen ceiling. The outcome of their explorations was always a lapse into laughter and self-ridicule which seemed to annul everything they had said while at the same time rendering it more significant. The simple truth, I suppose, is that they were having fun, just as Emily and I had had fun, but Anna and Frank did it better. They were more evenly matched.

Frank did not serve his wife as I had served Emily. Anna helped with the renovation work, and while he made sure she did nothing beyond her strength, when she found problems and said, 'I can't,' Frank said, 'You can.' And explained how, without attempting to relieve her of the task. I had never thought of Anna as a worker, but with Frank nudging her and pride nipping at her heels – and me looking on in doubtful amazement – she worked like a mule, and frequently looked like one, especially at midnight when Frank had crawled to bed, exhausted, and she, equally exhausted, muttered, 'I'll just finish this bit.'

Each evening after dinner, when they had shared the washing up, we would all line up on the sofa, warm and satisfied, ogling the television. Anna rested her head on my shoulder, her feet on Frank's knee. Then, like a young bird hopping in at the sill, came the thought that was a stranger to me: I am happy. And God had no part in my life.

Happy? Without speech? Without women? Without dancing and friends, without power and strength? Without Emily? Yes. My life was peaceful and sweet. I was never bored, never lonely. The pride I had was the small, neat pride of one who has known the ultimate humiliation and no longer notices minor shames. I knew it would not last. I knew I was still on the prison ship and that my destination had not changed. But the ship was becalmed for a while and my ankles had grown numb against the irons. Yes, it is possible to be happy even knowing one's destination, even in dread of it, even though one is helpless to avert the horror. If I had known this before . . . If I had known this before I could have been happy all my life. I could have made Anna happy. I have spent my whole life crying for the moon.

It's too late now. I am wasted, I am dying. All hope is gone. And I am happy, damn it!

If I had known this at any time during those starving, freezing, murderous days in Germany, I suppose I would have been dying instead of merely fearing death. Perhaps I would have died happy, and I would have died good, without Anna on my conscience. But to have died without knowing Anna? No, I cannot regret so much, God, not even to save my soul. The most base misfortune has its small measure of joy. I learned that a long time ago and stupidly forgot it. Stupidly forgot. Is that what life is? A chance to learn with the choice of forgetting. A chance of heaven with the choice of hell.

We were off the coast of Norway when we were torpedoed. Later, I could grit my teeth and hold other men together while they screamed, but at that moment I was so scared I almost cried out, 'Jesus! Mother! Save me!'

I was asleep and then awake, fully dressed save for my boots. We were on the Baltic run, *en route* to Russia, and it was cold. Someone yelled at me to get out, but I couldn't get my boots on. My feet were swollen. I had two pairs of socks, thin ones and thick, felted sea-socks, and I could not get my boots on. Instead of screaming for my mother I yelled, 'I can't get my fucking boots on!'

The ship was going down by the head. When I eventually reached the side, I had both boots on but had not managed to force my heel down in the left one. I jumped for the boat – and the left boot fell in the sea. Later, looking despairingly at the remaining boot and trying vainly to think of a use for it, I slung it over the side to drown with its fellow. It was strange to be taken prisoner in my socks. It was wonderful, but I did not know it then.

They marched us to the train. Sixty miles across the snow. It took four days. My feet were cold. I almost wept for my boots, for their warm fur linings. But my socks built up a protective layer of ice underfoot, and when my feet swelled my socks stretched and went on stretching. Mine were not the only feet to swell, but leather boots do not stretch very much and their owners were too bloody British to complain of the agony they suffered until too late. By the time our journey ended, two weeks later, three men had gangrene. One lost all his toes. One lost a leg. The other one died. Most of the men were crippled for months afterwards. I didn't get so much as a blister.

I told no one about it. Not anything. Ever. To maintain a semblance of courage we called the Gerries 'goons' and laughed at them; went on laughing when we came home and our loved ones cried, 'What have they done to you?'

They all said it. Mothers, fathers, aunts; the grocer, the rector, the paper-boy. 'What have they done to you?' I began to imagine that Churchill had set up a Welcome Home Ministry with a slogan of its own, like 'Dig For Victory!' or 'Careless Talk Costs Lives!'

'Oh, Max! What have they done to you?' Even Emily said it.

I smiled carefully. I did everything very carefully in those early days at home, afraid of anything which felt too good lest it break my dream and I wake again, in Germany.

I shrugged. 'Nothing, really.'

'But you're so thin!'

'Worry, I suppose. That, and boredom. You're thin too, Emma.'

She blushed and turned away, wringing her hands, noticing it, clasping them behind her back, shoving them into her pockets.

I loved her too much. The dream was becoming too wild, beyond my control. 'I've missed you, Emma.'

She bit her lip upon tears. 'Oh! Er, me too. I mean, I've missed . . . oh, Max.'

She bowed her head and jammed her hands again into the pockets of a lumpy grey herring-bone suit. The wide lapels, padded shoulders and enormous buttons did not greatly become her. She looked like a new-hatched chick in a potato sack, and seeing her frailty, I forgot my own. I forgot that I was dreaming, forgot that I had lost hope, lost faith, lost God.

'Emma, I've never loved anyone else!'

'I know, Max.'

'I thought . . . I thought you'd be married by now.'

We had been engaged twice and she'd broken it off twice. Once for her independence and once for a London barrister. I was certain she would marry him before I could come home, and there was always the fear of never coming home, of not knowing how long it would last, who would win. And if they won? We did not think of that. The question would be asked – 'If they win?' – and one's heart would leap and shrink, freezing inside.

The answer was always, 'Don't think of that!' Is Emma married by now? Don't think. Feel no joy, no grief. Have no hope, no heart. Survive.

'No,' Emma said softly, 'I'm not married.'

I ached to touch her. I was afraid to touch her. I had become accustomed to being thin, stopped noticing it except in terror for my health; but now I felt certain the touch of my bones would revolt her. Her thinness was more healthy; wiry and energetic. She had worked her flesh away. Mine had fallen off.

We stood in silence, stiff as bare trees in a frozen forest. We felt the ice crackling in our joints, the air congealing between us. There were only two words in my mind. I could think of no others. I kept swallowing them, choking on them. Speak! Can't. Speak! Oh, I can't. *Speak!*

'Marry me!'

I could have sworn, as the words left my mouth, that I had screamed them, but I heard only a whisper. I did not look at her. I knew that if she had not heard I would not be able to ask again.

'Yes.'

It, too, was a whisper. It, too, was a scream. Its reverberations hung on the still, frozen air and crept through my ice-bound branches, gradually thawing, gradually warming my sap. Yes, yes, yes.

I moved at last. I turned my head. We looked at one another, slowly smiling. Both of us wept.

'Oh, yes, Max! I don't know why I've –'

She was in my arms. I would not let her go. I marched her down to the rectory before she could change her mind and we were married a month later, she in pre-war silk and I in post-war serge. I had put on weight by then, and it was wonderful to be strong enough to lift her up, to hold her high and shout, 'You're mine!'

She froze. 'No,' she said. 'No, Max. I am mine, not yours. Oh, I knew –'

'Don't! Don't say it, Emma!'

She did not say it. She did not say that she had been wrong to marry me, but afterwards, when we were calm, we talked about the differences which had kept us fencing for fourteen years. Fourteen years!

She said I was too powerful for her, too jealous and hard. Hard? Yes, but I was putty in her hands. She said she valued her independence more than life, and yet, when she was with me, she felt enslaved – as much by her own love for me as by my jealous, selfish power. Selfish? Yes, but I would have given her my head on a plate, studded with pearls. She felt it was wrong to betray principles to passion. 'Principles endure,' she said sadly. 'But passions . . .'

I wouldn't let her finish. I knew it was true for her, though it would never be for me. Other women were faces, bodies, voices; but Emma was her soul, more dear to me than my own. How could I explain so much? How could I reassure her?

'To say, "You are mine,"' I said, 'is no more a claim of possession than to say, "This is my right hand," which is not a possession but a part of me; one of the most precious, and the least selfish. It gives, Emma. It loves. It is shared, and others may hold it without taking it from me. You are my hand, Emma. You are my right hand.'

'Hands can hurt,' Emma said.

'But they do not hurt themselves. I could smash my hand with a hammer, but why should I? To punish it, restrain it, force it to my will?'

'Yes, I see.' She held my hand, turning it over, running her small fingers over it, so gently. 'Oh, Max, I can't believe you love me so much!'

'What do you want? Independence? Your career? Friends of your own? Have them, Emma. Take them, keep them, but love *me*! Tell me what you want, and if it's mine to give, it's yours.'

She blushed. 'I'm afraid it's rather ordinary, Max. But I'm afraid – feeling as you do – it's the last thing on earth you'd want to give me. I want you to share me.'

I turned cold, and closed my eyes. 'With whom?' I was thinking of the barrister.

'With our baby, Max. I want a child.'

I suppose my mind was still not clear of horror. I was still thinking of the barrister. 'Whose baby?'

'Yours, you fool!' She was laughing.

'Mine? You want my baby? *My* baby? Oh, Emily, you can have ten!'

I kissed her, lifted her in my arms, whirled her around until we were both helpless with laughter.

'You are mine,' I whispered at last.

'Yes.'

'You are my right hand.'

'Yes.'

Only God would think of cutting off my right hand twice. He's an imaginative bastard. One has to grant Him that.

Yet still, somehow, I survive. For what? Perhaps I still have some purpose, some use. Perhaps there is still something I must do. Surely He is not still waiting for my repentance? I will not repent. He took Emma, my right hand. He took my soul. And I will burn in all eternity, gladly, to prove it.

Until then I can be happy in my small way: loving Anna, loving Frank. I am standing on the deck of the prison ship, watching the dolphins at play. But already the wind is changing. The cottage feels solid now, is clean and comfortable, and there are roses in a jug on the table. But Anna wants new carpets, new clothes, a car of her own, and there is no money. Anna is looking for a job, and every time she picks up the newspaper fear stabs me again. She is taking another step forward and I know I must take another step back.

Chapter Twenty-Six

Our first year of marriage disappointed all my expectations of romance, security and happy endings. We were up to our eyes in debt, up to our ears in work. I spent our brief honeymoon behaving as much like a sex maniac as possible, though in spirit I was still clinging to the edge of the bed, wondering why God had invented it. There must, I thought, be easier ways of propagating the species.

Had I been asked to explain, on our honeymoon, the things I hated about sex, I probably could not have done so with any hope of being understood; but when we came home again I could have summed it up in two words: my father. How could I make love to Frank while my father was sleeping – or perhaps listening – in the next room? Just the thought of it – and I imagined his outrage in blood-chilling detail – made me cringe. It was useless to tell myself that my father would expect me to do such things. I was married. I had become respectable. 'It' was now a permissable act. But try as I might, I could not make myself believe this, and every time Frank touched me it was as if the bedroom wall had disappeared, allowing my father to watch our every move. My sex-maniac pretensions forgotten, I lay like a board, gritting my teeth and moaning with embarrassment every time the bedsprings creaked. My moans might have given Frank some encouragement had my rigid muscles not given the game away, and once, in an unprecedented display of temper, he sank his teeth in my ear and growled, 'Will you relax, for God's sake? It's like trying to screw a brick wall!'

My astonishment relaxed me immediately, but on another, even worse, occasion, I groaned, 'Oh, hush!' and attempted to smother his climactic yell with the spare pillow.

Frank mastered his fury with typical restraint, but afterwards it was as if the bed had been fenced down the middle. I was so appalled at myself I could scarcely breathe. There was an awful silence. Frank uttering the occasional sigh at his edge of the bed while I swallowed tears at mine. I knew I deserved no forgiveness, and I lay in silence until I could bear the disgrace no longer.

'I'm sorry! Oh, Frank, I'm so sorry!'

He did not move except to fill his lungs for another sigh, but after a few moments he reached out and held my hand.

'Oh, Frank, I'm sorry, sorry, sorry!'

He laughed wearily and pulled me into his arms. 'Don't be so tragic, Anna. It's only sex.'

'Isn't that why we got married?'

'No, we got married for love, you idiot. Don't worry. There's too much strain at the moment. It'll be all right.'

I believed him, and loved him more, at that moment, than ever before. I should have become accustomed to it, but to be absolved without doing penance, to be forgiven without first being punished still seemed miraculous to me. And strange. Sometimes – always rejecting the thought as being too ridiculous for words – I felt it was wrong. It brought a funny, competitive element into our relationship: if he could be so good to me, I wanted to be doubly good to him. But he always won. His generosity seemed endless, and his love for my father brought tears of gratitude to my eyes.

Frank loved him far more purposefully than I had ever done. He had not known my father as an able-bodied man and was saved the prejudicing contrast of 'before and after' which led me to think of Daddy as a helpless invalid. I saw my father as a man without a right hand. Frank saw him as a man with a left hand; a hand he could be expected to use. I thought at first that Frank was humouring him, letting him feel useful even though he was useless, and I dreaded the consequences of the deceit. But it was no deceit. When the cottage, only a year after we moved into it, had been fully restored, we could attribute at least a third of its comfort to my father's unaided work.

He had lost a great deal of natural skill, but his love of perfection had survived the stroke intact, and although he worked slowly, and frequently lost his temper, he would not relinquish a task until he was satisfied with it. Frank never offered to help him. Sometimes, when my father threw his tools down in despair, I would beg, 'Can't you help him, Frank?'

'Nope. If he wants help he knows where to find me.'

'You're mean! You know he's too proud –'

'If he's too proud to ask for help, he's too proud to accept it. Leave him alone. Let him work it out his own way.'

I eventually learned to cope with the idea of my father doing straightforward jobs, like sanding doors and painting skirting boards, but when Frank asked him to repair a broken Windsor chair I was terrified. So was my father. Frank had reclaimed the chair from the back of a dust cart.

'It's very old,' he said, rather unnecessarily.

'Bu!' my father agreed, but his eyes were popping, and his lower jaw had collided with his ankles.

The chair seat had a split down the middle and three of the rungs had broken in half. One of the legs was missing entirely.

'What d'you think?' Frank demanded optimistically. My father shook his head, fluttering his fingers at the chair as though to touch it would be to endanger his health.

Frank shrugged. 'Oh, all right. If you don't think you can.' He fingered the chair-back lovingly. 'I just thought, a few screws.'

'*Bu?*' Even I, who knew nothing about woodwork, clearly heard my father shriek, 'Screws? Are you a heathen?'

Dowels were the thing, apparently, and although Frank was well aware of the fact, he maintained a show of ignorance until my father's righteous indignation had propelled him to his work bench.

The repair took three months to complete, and although my father lost his temper countless times, he took it out on me, or on his tools, or in wild, kicking rages which bruised his toes but otherwise did no harm. When he had repaired the jagged split in the chair seat I found him stroking it lovingly, with tears pouring down his face.

'Bu, bu, bu,' he crooned, pointing to the repair so that I could inspect it and approve, though it was, in fact, invisible. Where there had been a splintered crack was now – nothing, save at the edge of the chair three perfect circles to show where the dowels had been inserted.

I could scarcely believe he had done it; with one hand, two vices and more courage and skill than I could comprehend. I wept over it with him; and when Frank came home he said, 'Oh,' in a choked voice, and walked out. I think he wept too, somewhere else, where we couldn't see.

The chair did not have any nails or screws, and when my father came to reassemble it – each piece already smoothed and polished to a satiny finish – it was 'merely' a case of fitting round pegs into the round holes provided. But the pegs and the holes – ironically reflecting my love-life – were not inclined to get together. When my father pushed one of the joints together, another joint sprang apart. He lost his temper and threw a hammer at me. I caught it without turning a hair (his temper, like his tears, was something I had grown accustomed to) and made him have a tea break. When he was calm again I made the mistake of suggesting that he wait until Frank came home.

'No!' he roared, and rushed back to the workshop to claim the chair as his own.

When Frank came in I told him what was happening and confessed my tactless stupidity.

'Tell him dinner's ready.'

'But it isn't! I haven't even –'

'Lie,' he said.

When I went to the workshop the chair was no further forward, just a seat with three legs, the fourth still refusing to go home. My father was breathing through his teeth. He looked like a wolf worrying at a dead cow. It was too big for him, too awkward, but his memory of hunger was too recent to allow him to believe that he had had enough.

'Time for a break,' I said, cheerfully prophetic. 'Dinner's –'

My father picked up the chair seat, swung it around his head, yelled 'Aaaaaarrgh!' and hurled it at me. The chair hit the wall at the exact spot my head had been a second earlier. The three fixed legs twanged off in all directions and the seat, split neatly in half, landed in my lap. When Frank ran in a moment later, my father and I were both sitting on the floor, rocking one another and crying our eyes out.

For hours no one spoke. Frank led my father to a chair and me to the kitchen. I cooked dinner. No one ate it. My father looked exactly as he had looked in the hospital: grey-faced, his head resting helplessly in the palm of his hand. I thought it quite likely that he would die in the night. Frank sat at the table doing his accounts, but occasionally he looked up and stared at my father for minutes at a time. Eventually, my father looked up too, and their eyes met. Frank raised his eyebrows and performed a curious, barely perceptible grimace which involved pinching his nostrils together and curling his lip. It was, for all its economy, an expression of freezing scorn. I went mad. I hit him.

'How dare you!' I yelled. 'How *dare* you! He couldn't help it! He's only got one hand, you callous, sanctimonious –'

'Bu!' my father said. He stood up and patted my arm, looking at me very sternly. 'Bu, bu!' That's quite enough of that, thank you.

He directed an even sterner look at Frank. 'Bu!' And I'll thank you to mind your own damn business!

Then he went back to the workshop and repaired the chair all over again.

When it was finished, and quite as beautiful as before, he calmly summoned Frank, who calmly fitted all the pieces together. They looked at one another in silence, both suppressing smiles, pretending to be fierce and proud and independent; but although there was at least three feet of space between them I felt that they held one another close, and loved one another as they had never loved me. I was not jealous. It was very beautiful. (Perhaps I was, just a little, jealous.)

The car and the cottage consumed money a good deal faster than Frank could earn it but, although he worried, he never once complained. In the few hours when he was not working – he rarely went to bed before one and was always up at seven – he would slump in a chair with his eyes closed, and I was happy to let him rest. It made me feel good, and somehow useful. But he was never asleep. Eventually he would open his eyes and say, 'I've been thinking,' and come up with a plan for converting the attic, building a fish pool or making a fortune from reconditioned false teeth. He spent quite a lot of time 'making a fortune', but it was always something ridiculous. After a while I realised that he was not interested in making a fortune but was simply diffusing, through creative humour, his anxiety about the mortgage, the bank loan and the price of Riley spare parts.

But our evenings and weekends would have been much happier had not so many of them ended in bedtime misery. Frank managed, for a long time, to trap his disappointment between the sheets, behaving each morning as though nothing awful had happened the night before. He brought me tea in bed, cracked jokes to make me smile, tickled my feet to make me laugh. But Frank's patience was not infinite, and our misery, by slow degrees, overspilled, following us into the day. We did not quarrel, but we avoided meeting one another in doorways, where before we had touched; and the fond teasing which had played such an important part in our relationship, became strained, and then faded to distant courtesy.

Sometimes I saw knives in Frank's eyes which never quite clashed with the knives in mine. I ached to confront him, to tell him my feelings, including my belief that I did not deserve all the blame. But how could I tell Frank he was doing it wrong? After all his goodness to me it would be the final insult. Besides, I didn't know what he was doing wrong. All I knew (because he had told me so) was that sex was an act of sharing, which both partners should enjoy. He enjoyed it. His enjoyment was soured by my inability to reciprocate, but he enjoyed it, nevertheless. He had, therefore, something which he was not sharing with me. Or was he sharing it? Was I simply refusing to accept it? No, because afterwards, when he fell asleep, I wondered what he had felt and was jealous that I had not felt it too.

I was determined to find a solution, and after hours of deep thought and frantic rehearsal I would find the exact words and the precise tone of voice to explain it all without hurting either of us. I performed most of my rehearsals in the garden, thanking God that we had no neighbours to overhear me, and sometimes thanking God that dandelions can't blush. 'Hey, Frank, I think I know what's wrong with me. Why don't we try . . . ?' But it was all useless. As soon as Frank came home my tongue relapsed into its old, childhood fault, tying itself in knots and finally uttering something quite different. 'Hey, Frank . . . I've mowed the lawn.' (I always mowed the lawn, so this probably made him think me mad, as well as frigid.) After a while I gave up trying, knowing that it would be impossible for me to broach the subject with Frank in cold blood. I wanted a fight. I wanted rage; the only release I had ever found for my inhibitions.

But even our quarrels died at their source – my father. He was acutely sensitive to atmosphere, and when Frank and I, poised at the brink of a full-scale row, became snappy with each other, he would watch us with undisguised fear in his eyes. One glance at him then, and the towering column of my rage reduced itself to a sour, burning puddle in my gut. Frank had often accused me of being too imaginative, of borrowing trouble, and when my father's fear thwarted my rage, I knew that this was true. If I had not imagined his feelings, borrowed his pain, I might have found the strength to ease my own. And Frank's. But I understood my father's terror. It was the same as my own, differing only in its details. If we should lose Frank . . .

If we should lose Frank, our lives would become a wilderness. We could not bear the loss. But I had the power – somewhere – to hold him. My father could only watch, and helplessly pray that I find it.

As Christmas – and our first wedding anniversary – approached, Frank's mood suddenly lifted. It was as if he had taken a deep breath, viewed the situation objectively and decided to give it another try. We celebrated our anniversary very happily, very cheaply and very early, with due respect for our bank balance and for my father, who panicked (and usually lost his temper) if we stayed out late. At times like these, I was still scared of him. His temper, when he lost it with inanimate objects and aimed it at me, frightened me scarcely at all. But coming home late involved too many memories, too much guilt, and I had been known, more than once, to cower outside the porch, desperately begging Frank, 'Will you go in first, please?'

On New Year's Eve we were invited to a party at Frank's partner's house, and although Frank had lost his taste for parties, he agreed to take me. We prepared my father for an extremely late homecoming and offered to ask someone to sit with him until we returned. He declined. Since his second stroke he had become increasingly shy and self-conscious, and even when the milkman came in to be paid he would avert his eyes, his face tortured with embarrassment.

'We'll be *very* late,' Frank reminded him again.

'Bu,' my father nodded, but his eyes were huge with anxiety.

'Are you certain you don't want company?'

'Bu.' Another nod.

'You won't be nervous? Are you sure? It'll be at least two o'clock before we get home.'

My father fluttered his fingers, rubbing them together indecisively, but he made no attempt to say anything. He nodded again and turned away. He was obviously very scared, and I turned to Frank, the words 'Let's not bother,' on the tip of my tongue. He frowned, shutting me up with a discreet shake of his head. He never said as much, but I guessed he sometimes suspected my father of manipulating us. I was quite certain he manipulated us, but I pitied him too much to resent it, even when, after looking forward to the party for weeks, I began to wish we weren't going.

We didn't go. It snowed all day, and we knew, by teatime, that we could not get there. Frank spent most of the day keeping the drive clear, but when he came in to announce that the lane had become impassable, I felt a perverse pang of disappointment which almost brought tears to my eyes.

'But I bought a new dress!'

Frank laughed and hugged me, rubbing his frozen nose against my cheek.

'Never mind.' he said. 'Let's have a party at home, just the three of us.' He smiled, whispering seductively, 'And later, just the two of us. Max, get your glad-rags on. We're having a party!'

My father's anxious face underwent an immediate transformation, and he grinned, flapping his hand approvingly at the snow as if to say, 'See! God's on my side!' He was thrilled to bits. So, when I thought of it, was I. Even if we had gone out I knew I would have spent the entire night on pins, worrying about my father and wanting to go home. God was on my side, too. Sometimes.

We dressed up and I cooked a gorgeous meal. We had candles on the table, soft background music. My father played host, bowing and smiling as he poured the wine, and his excitement delighted me. I had his whole attention, was the sole object of his charm, his smile, the gentle flirtations I had coveted for so long. I knew it had no meaning. I knew that he was using me to create an illusion: of other evenings, other women, of the man he once was. He was acting out the old, seductive role for his satisfaction, not mine; but I found myself able to accept his attentions in the same spirit, selfishly extracting my own pleasure from the performance, wryly admitting that half a loaf is better than no bread – and that late is better than never –.

After dinner, Frank played some Strauss waltzes on my father's old gramophone and we danced, giggling self-consciously and stepping on each other's feet. My father was squiffy. He tapped Frank's shoulder. '*Bu?*' My dance, I believe.

'Crikey,' Frank said. 'Two sherries and she's anybody's!' And he sat down, pretending to be offended.

I thought my father would dance as Frank had danced, with more apologies and giggles than skill, but as soon as he took me in his arms I took flight. It was as if he had never been ill. It was as if no time had passed since I was seventeen and he had come home laughing, saying, 'I've danced all night!' He wedged his right arm in the small of my back and guided me with his left, and it was as if he had been re-born, healed, restored. All his old power was there, the hard sexuality of a man in his prime. I loved it, loved it. I loved him. Oh, I loved him! I could have danced with him for ever; but after a few minutes his right arm began to move independently up my back, dragging my dress with it, and the mood was broken entirely when I realised that my knickers were showing.

When we went up to bed, Frank watched thoughtfully while I cleaned off my make-up, and I felt a rare flutter of anticipation as I guessed at his thoughts. But my guess was wide of the mark, and when he spoke there was no invitation in his voice.

'You'll never do it,' he said flippantly.

'Do what?'

'Wipe that look off your face. Did you have a nice evening? Daddy was in fine fettle, wasn't he?'

He had never before referred to my father like this, and his voice had a sarcastic edge to it; but I was still too excited to care.

I turned to him, 'that look' still glowingly evident on my face.

'Oh, thank goodness it snowed! He was so happy, Frank, and I enjoyed it much more than if we'd gone to Mike and Caroline's. Didn't you?'

'It was all right.' He shivered and jumped into bed, pulling the covers up to his ears.

I looked at him in surprise, realising for the first time that he had been very quiet since our dance, playing his part much as Aunty Dorothy had played draughts: with a vaguely martyred air.

'Oh, come on,' I chided gently. 'He doesn't have much fun, Frank.'

'Mm.' He closed his eyes and drew up his knees, thumping his pillow irritably.

'Did you really hate it?'

'Nng. Don't leave the bathroom light on all night, Anna. I'm the one who pays the bills, if you recall.'

I was shocked. What was wrong with him? It was completely out of character for him to resent other people's happiness, even if he did not share it; and what had happened to his 'party' for just the two of us? Why wasn't he charming my nightie off?

'What's wrong?' I whispered.

'Nothing. I'm tired.'

He was furious. I knew him well enough to realise that. But I hadn't a clue why, and I found myself wishing he would turn over, smile at me and say, 'Come to bed, gorgeous.' It was the result I had expected of the evening. I almost wanted it. I did want it.

'Shall we make love, Frank?'

'Nng.'

'I'd . . . like to.'

He did not reply; so I crept away to brush my teeth and to attend to the bathroom light. When I returned to the bedroom, Frank was asleep. I stared at him in bewilderment, telling myself that he had caught a cold in the snow, or exhausted himself clearing the drive. I got into bed, deliberately jouncing it, deliberately brushing his shoulder as I lay down. He did not wake, and as I recognised my disappointment I smiled. Whatever had upset him, he had wreaked a neatly ironic revenge.

I lay awake for a long time, remembering our little party with a pleasure which even Frank's kill-joy tactics had not spoiled. I remembered too that evening long ago; my father's face, his warm, warm kisses.

'Oh, Anna! I thought I would never be happy again!'

What had happened that night? He had danced . . . with whom? Who had made him so happy? There would never be an answer now. My father had kept all his secrets and would take them to his grave. I had seen him strong. I had seen him weak. I had seen him dressed to the teeth and I had seen him naked. I had seen him laugh, seen him weeping – and he was still a stranger whose secrets were his own.

But I was changing. Having suppressed for years the more acquisitive side of my nature, I now began feverishly to want things. I was envious of Frank's partner and his wife, who seemed to have everything: a five-bedroomed detached with fully fitted luxury, two cars (neither of which fell apart if you breathed on them), two foreign holidays a year and one in England, which they didn't count: 'We only go for Mike's sailing.'

When I told Frank that I wanted a car of my own, a stair carpet, new curtains and a decent garden gate that wasn't held together with string, he mended the garden gate and ignored everything else. He did not care that we were poor, and his lack of concern infuriated me. His ability to accept the good with the bad, 'and treat those two imposters just the same', became, for me, a sympton of weakness, not of strength. I had spent my life watching my father force the circumstances to meet his terms, and it was frustrating to look on while Frank allowed the circumstances to dictate.

'Don't you care that we haven't any money?'

'Yes, it would be less worrying if we had some reserves.'

'But don't you want a new car? Don't you want the house to look nice?'

'What difference would it make if I did? I haven't the money to buy them, so it's like crying for the moon, isn't it? Anyway, they aren't especially important.'

'Why?'

'Why are dog-daisies nicer than red roses?'

'We can't live for ever on romantic pretences, Frank. There's no romance in pretending we have a stair carpet.'

He smiled and took me in his arms. 'You want a carpet so much?' he whispered. His breath tickled my ear and made my body remember one of its brief experiences of desire. I laughed.

'Yes,' I said firmly. 'So it's no use you trying to canoodle your way out of it.'

There was a prolonged silence. I suspected he was battling with our overdraft, and as his smile faded I guessed the overdraft had won.

'All right,' Frank said softly. 'You can have a carpet.'

Even for Frank, this seemed an unusually rapid capitulation, and I stepped backwards, amazed and disbelieving. His generosity had never ceased to astonish me, but this was the first time he had attempted to make a silk purse out of a sow's ear.

'Really?' I gasped. 'How?'

'You can get a job, and pay for it yourself.'

Chapter Twenty-Seven

Another stroke. I think. I think, I think I've had another stroke. Don't knowing, know. Not feeling any no pain. Everything every upsadaisy. Pain? No feeling. No feeling! Seeing. Green. Bright green and sparklers. Sparklers, darling. Hold it – so.

Little babies on the table. Small, pink babies cry. There, there. Don't cry. Oh, I'm laughing.

'Jewel a cup and coughing, had he?'

What? What? How funny!

Anna's lusting, rusting, dusting. House all pretty, soft and clean. My skirt is sheen. My shirt is clean. My shine is shoesy, shoesy, shiny shoes.

'Bu?'

'D'you want a cup of coffee?'

Culpa coughing? *Mea culpa* coffin. Want a coffin? Oh, *coffee*! Cuppa coffee! 'Bu!'

Clever Anna. She's biting a crook, lighting a brook, Anna is writing a book! Clever Emma. Anna.

Spider-spotting through the window. Pretty spider. Silver threaded curtains weaving spotted spider does. Window! Oh, bitter, bitter bits, bitter bits of glass and the biter bitten. Window. Widow. Widow-spider. I'm a widow!

Oh, don't cry! The window's cracked.

Don't cry. Daddy hold you. Hold the hand outside the window. No.

Another stroke? Can't be. Everything is funny and there is beauty in the dark green light. The sky is green. The trees green too, and all the flowers. Max! Another stroke?

No, you are still there, darling. Hold on. *There is still something to do!*

Who is speaking? Frank? Frank is a good man. Hold the hand outside the window. No!

Frank is a dentist. Frank is a good dentist. Frank is good. Anna found him on the stairs. He descended into hell. All fall down.

I am falling! I am falling! *No!* There is still something to do!

What must I do, Daddy?

Make it better.

How can I do it?

Hold on.

Hold the hand outside the window. No! Hold the spider, hold the widow's hand. No; they tell me I still have something to do.

Delaney was an Irishman. It is not generally known that the Germans hated the Irish.

Hold on! I am holding on. I will not hold the widow's hand with the spider's legs. I am holding on. I am telling you about Delaney. They took him away and beat him. Broke his arm.

They made us sit in the compound in the cold, cold, cold. Oh, cold! Cold is grief beyond grief, pain beyond pain, longing, oh, longing!

(Listen. I never let Anna be cold, no. I wrapped her in fleece and vicuna, and soft little slippers her feet.)

When his arm mended they broke it again.

They kicked over his coffee, let it bleed between the planks. Ersatz coffee, but it was hot, and he cried in my arms. He did not cry for his broken arm; he cried for his coffee.

Cold, oh, cold! But the Irish are an emotional lot.

Cold! We took the hut apart, little bit, little bit, and burned the little, little bits in the stove to keep us from the cold. Ah, but the hut was our ship and our defence against the cold, cold sea. Such are the choices of freezing men.

Hold on, Max. You will be calm. Now. Quite calm. There is still something to do.

What must I do? I'm tired, Daddy! I'm so tired . . .

Lie in my arms, my darling. Here, here in my arms. All better now. There, Daddy make it better.

But how can I do it now?

Hold on.

Lamley was a drunk with nothing to drink. Drank boot polish. Drank paint. Brasso. Drink anything, would Lamley. Screaming insects in the cold. Spotted spiders crawled upon his face.

Hold the hand, Max. Hold the hand outside the window. Hold the widow's hand.

Widow? Am I dead?

No!

You will be calm, Max. You will be calm.

Yes, yes. I am calm and all of me is happy, except – the bit that is frightened!

Of what?

The cold.

No, no.

Hunger.

No.

The babies on the table. They frighten me because they are not there. Look, they are petals, Max, just petals. Scoop them up and see. Oh! The babies are falling, falling, all fall down!

No, they are petals. Petals can't cry, Max. They can't be hurt.

Don't cry! Daddy, Daddy, Daddy hold you!

Pick up the petals one by one. Feel? Just petals. See?

Yes. Yes.

Now I am happy. All of me is happy, except – I am still frightened. Of what?

Of loneliness. Of death.

Death is nothing, Max, is it?

Is that why you are talking to me? You've been dead – a long time. I do not know how long. Before I loved Anna you died and I have forgotten your name. My wife, now dead.

Death is nothing. You see?

Yes, I have loved you all my life and it is nothing. Death is nothing

186

and God is an illusion like petals pink and crawling, wailing when they fall.

I know the world is not as I see it. I know my brain is bleeding, painting pictures with my blood. The spider is a hand to hold me, and its web but a crack in the glass. The petals are not babies, I know, and the sky is not green. But my brain did not always bleed, and once I was complete, perceiving things truly. Oh, oh! How strange it is, how funny! Once I was complete, but all my life I have seen things awry — like Lamley on boot polish, seeing crawling life where nothing was — save prison walls. Emily, the dead still living. God, the living dead. Prison walls.

Bleed, brain! Bleed away! The sky is green, but God is *dead*, as I have always wanted him to be.

And now I will confess, now repent. I lusted for my daughter. I coerced her to my lust. I lusted and listed, my cargo had shifted, my ship going down by the head. I wanted my daughter, I beat her and fought her and taught her delight in my bed.

No, you did not. Be calm, Max. You're exaggerating again. You are letting confession go to your head, just because He is dead who never lived except to torment you.

You see, I fell in love with Emily when she was sixteen. I wanted her then, but she left me, and others took her while I sailed the sea. Took her. When she was mine she was never mine, because others had taken her, the woman I loved more than life.

And I thought . . . I thought when she died I had been given a second chance. Anna could not leave me because I was her father.

This was the way of it; that I knew men's souls and thought I knew the souls of women. I thought they would do anything for the thing they needed most. Delaney would not cry for his broken arm. He would not beg. But he cried when they kicked his coffee and let it bleed between the planks. He was cold, you see, and if the goon had given him more coffee he would have kissed his feet.

I knew Anna loved me. She had loved me since the first minute I held her, small and snuffling in my arms. She was Daddy's little girl when she was one hour old. I thought she would do anything for love. I made sure she had no one else to love her — only me — and I kicked her love until it bled between the planks. I kicked her, made her cry. And then I loved her. I taught her the solace of love. I taught her to beg for warmth, gentleness, the sweetness of my kisses, the murmur of my voice. I taught her to unload her pain and her pride, to give it into my

187

arms, and when she was naked I kicked her again. That was the way of it. Coercion. Manipulation. And all so that when she was sixteen I would take Emily, take her for myself, and all my own!

I knew it was wrong. I cared about it more than I would admit. I hated myself, and hating myself, hated Anna; hating blindly as the goons hated the Irish. I gave her nothing. She had nothing, save me. And when she cried, she cried in my arms for there was nowhere else she could go.

But as she grew older she took to herself a woman's soul, a soul I did not know and could not reach. It was a bright light shining from a distance, hurting my eyes in the dark. I could not put it out. Though I tried and tried, though I beat her and fought her, the light was too far from me and the closer I came to it the fiercer it burned in my eyes. Oh, Anna! I loved you too much! You blinded me with your bright, burning soul!

Blind then (and this was the way of it), blind and refusing to see what had happened – that she had ceased to be Emily and become another, more dearly loved – I beat Anna for the last time and took her, weeping in my arms. I kissed her face, her eyes, her sweet, bewildered tears. I laid my hand on her belly and touched her breasts with my fingertips. I unbuttoned her throat, caressed her, gentled her. She was mine.

'Daddy put you to bed?'

(Daddy stroke you, fondle you, pluck your maiden-head with his fingers and milk the juice of your aching heart? Daddy fold you in his arms, hold you in his loins, ride your desire till you scream? Daddy tame you? Daddy put out your light, my darling one?)

She blushed and smiled. She nestled closer, and on my lap, her buttocks moved with desire. She was mine.

She laughed. 'I'm too old,' she said, and jumped up and kissed me; and I was stricken by her light and forced to see – not Emily, but Anna, my daughter.

In my heart I knew I had wasted my life, wasted my lust, but still I would not give in. I re-read the tale of my grievous life and knew that I could not let her go, even now. I could not waste so much.

Eighteen. When she was older and could understand me. Eighteen, when I could tell her at last that I loved her and beg her love in return. Eighteen. I would take her abroad, woo her with sunshine, sweet words, dry champagne. But something happened . . . I do not recall her eighteenth birthday. Something happened, and God was not there. God is dead.

Why do I feel so sad, so full of grief?

I am sorry! I am most grievously sorry! There. But you are dead, thank God, and cannot hear me.

I have been sleeping and feel very strange. I never sleep during the day, but it is pleasant to wake, knowing that the hours are dead and painless behind me, and Anna has come to kiss me, and put an end to loneliness.

'What's leaping on due tea?' she asks, tousling my hair.

What indeed? I wonder what she means. She is more beautiful than ever.

'Half eel in awe light, Daddy?'

'Bu?'

'Are you feeling all right?'

That made sense. I know it did, for a moment. Now I have forgotten what it meant. 'Bu?'

'Are you well? You look a bit funny.'

It does not matter. I know you are happy and it is all the meaning I need, but I wish you would sit on my knee and curl up there like you used to do. As the world becomes stranger and more insubstantial I long to be held and to hold you, to know that you are real.

Chapter Twenty-Eight

After the initial shock, Frank's suggestion that I get a job caught my imagination, and I took to scanning the Situations Vacant column the way some people scan the football results, fantasising about money.

'Oooh, Frank, I can buy some new clothes! And some perfume! And a sports car, of course. You can have one too, if you like.'

He laughed, and I guessed he was wondering what had happened to the stair carpet. 'Thank you,' he said drily. 'What'll you do with your second pay cheque? Get an aeroplane?'

'No. A cleaning lady.'

'That,' he said, with a meaningful glance at my father, 'should be first on the list.'

Of course. I was furious with myself for not thinking of it. How could I leave my father alone all day? I crossed both sports cars off the shopping list and searched the paper for part-time jobs. There weren't any, except for cleaning ladies.

I had kept in touch regularly with Libby since leaving college and after reading her latest letter I handed it over to Frank with a groan of envy.

'Libby's got a teaching job at last, damn it!'

'Damn it?'

'I'm beginning to wish I'd done the post-grad teaching course. I'd be in clover now, wouldn't I?'

'You'd be up the creek by now, I imagine. You'd make a rotten teacher.'

'I would not – I, I've got lots of patience, and – and – '

'And a stammer.' He held up his hand to silence my howl of protest. 'Oh, I know, I know. You only stammer when you're angry, but teachers do sometimes get angry, believe it or not.' He grinned. 'And believe it or not, Anna darling, the average fourteen-year old is six inches taller than you.'

'Oh, shut up. Authority isn't just a matter of size, Frank.'

'And discontentment isn't just a matter of money, Anna. Think about it. People who envy their friends' jobs and possessions aren't necessarily in need of jobs and possessions, are they?'

'The job,' I reminded him aloofly, 'was your idea, if you recall.'

'No.' He stood up and reached for his car keys, his gaze never wavering from mine. 'Think again. Ask yourself just what it is you want, Anna, and then, for the love of God, *do* something about it!'

I asked myself. No reply – at least, none I could do anything about – came to mind. I wanted something, and it wasn't a stair carpet. Neither was it a sports car, although both of them would have been very nice. I was still a child, and I wanted to be a woman. I was still a dependant; still an inferior. In the past, when my father had talked about my mother, I had imagined their relationship; the way he had looked at her, the way she had looked at him. With respect; a respect that had been greater than love, because their love had depended on it. That was what I wanted! And if I couldn't have it from my father, I wanted it from Frank, from anyone, preferably from everyone.

I spent the afternoon writing to Libby. Writing letters was one of the few things I was good at. I lost my inhibitions when there was a pen in my hand; found all my words, and even better, my sense of humour.

The words I found that afternoon were frustrated, angry ones, disguised as jokes to make Libby laugh. I said I wanted to do something, to be someone, to shake off, once and for all, the feeling that I was something small, furry and pathetic the cat had brought in. Libby rang me almost as soon as she'd read it.

'Hiya, mouse. Cat eaten you, yet?'

'What? Oh, that! No, you've missed the point. It's not a matter of life and death, Lib. It's more a matter of having to crawl around in splints, being ministered unto and feeling grateful. I feel useless. Not humiliated, exactly; but not exactly proud of myself, either. You have to be good at things to be proud of them, and there's a limit to the thrill I get out of adding extra parsley to the soup.'

'Sell the recipe!' she joked. 'Write a cook book!'

I laughed, but at that moment Frank came in and, remembering his accusations of envy and discontentment, I changed the subject and asked more about Libby's job.

'Libby says I should write a cook book,' I informed Frank later, knowing he would laugh at the idea too. He didn't laugh. He seemed, in fact, almost annoyed.

'Good,' he said grimly. 'Why don't you?'

'Because I've got a history degree. Anyway, I haven't the least idea about cooking. I just do it. If I began weighing things, I'd make a complete mess of it.'

'Write a history book, then.'

'Crikey, I only got a Second, you know, not a Ph.D.'

'Well, write a history book for idiots, for God's sake! From what Libby tells us about teaching, it would hit the best-seller lists in no time. Good Lord, Anna, if your opinion of yourself gets much lower, you'll be looking for it under the floorboards!'

His exasperation did nothing to hide his contempt for me, and I fled to the kitchen, angrily kicking the wall and wishing it were Frank.

'Anna.'

'Oh, leave me alone! I know I'm bloody useless! Do you think I want to be, damn you? Do you think I want to spend my whole life being g-grateful for sim-simply being tolerated?'

'Anna, that isn't what I meant. I meant –'

'I don't bloody care what you meant! I can't write a book! You know I can't!'

I turned on him, blazing rage from every pore. He stepped backwards, his face a picture of bewilderment which exactly matched the picture of bewilderment on my father's face, just behind him.

I swallowed hard. 'I'm sorry,' I said shakily. 'I'm sorry. It's all right, Daddy. All better now.'

I sniffed. Frank said, 'Bloody hell.' That was that.

But the idea of writing a history book for idiots did not, as I had been determined it should, sink without trace. I was quite certain I wasn't clever enough to do it; but I kept thinking about it, planning it, narrowing my eyes as the ideas came. 'Do you think idiots actually need history books, Frank?'

He laughed. 'No, I shouldn't think so for a moment; but their teachers think they do, and that's all that matters. Why don't you ask Libby? Ring her. Go on.'

I did. We talked for more than an hour, and when we rang off I stared at my ten pages of notes – the rough plan of my book – in happy disbelief. I was going to be a writer!

Frank made love to me that night. I was too excited to notice his kisses, his caresses, the gentle preliminaries which usually drove me mad with irritation. I was thinking about my book.

Afterwards, apparently feeling much happier than usual, Frank pulled me into his arms and kissed me. 'See?' he muttered contentedly. 'Money isn't everything, is it?'

Vaguely sensing that I had missed something important, I stroked his hair and nuzzled my face into his neck. 'Love you,' I murmured, but I was mentally repeating what he had just said. 'Money isn't everything.' But it was! I'd need money to do the research!

'Oh, Lord!'

'What?'

'I love you. Go to sleep, Frank. You're tired.'

Money, when I settled down to think about the book seriously, proved to be a worse problem than I had bargained for. A single day trip to the British Museum would cost almost as much as a week's groceries, and even our grocery bills could turn Frank's face white at times. I felt sick. A history book, even for idiots (whom Libby preferred to call low achievers), required considerably more research than a single day at the British Museum could provide.

'I'll have to forget it.' Hearing myself say it out loud was like hearing a surgeon say, 'Your leg will have to come off.' I couldn't bear it. There had to be another solution.

I asked at the town museum whether any books existed on the subject of local history, and was offered three of them, all very good and beautifully produced. I could have wept.

My father had been unusually excited about my plans to write and had spent the last few days in the workshop, making me a desk. When I came home from the museum I told him not to bother.

'It's no good,' I said drearily. 'I can't do it, Daddy. I can't afford to do

the research for a general book, and local history's been done to death.'
I handed over one of the books I had bought at the museum. 'It's very
good. Only imagination could improve on that, I'm afraid.'

His shoulders had slumped, reflecting the sag of disappointment in
mine, but now he jerked himself upright, glaring at me as if I had sworn
at him.

'Bu! Bu!' It was excitement, not anger in his eyes, and he pointed at
me, smiling, his index finger hooking downwards to indicate that I
must repeat what I had said. I couldn't remember it.

'Local history?'

'Pah!' No! Think again!

'I said – only imagination?'

'Bu!' Yes!

'Sorry, Daddy. I'm not with you.'

My father sighed and bit his lip thoughtfully. He narrowed his eyes,
twirled his finger around on his temple.

'Think? No. Imagination.'

'Bu.' He pointed to the book, beckoned as if to draw it towards him,
then again twirled his finger against his temple.

'Imagine the book? No? Oh! Oh, you mean write a novel? An
historical novel? I couldn't, Daddy! I wouldn't have a clue!'

'Bah!' He looked amazed. How any daughter of his could be so
stupid was still, apparently, a source of great disappointment to him.
'Bu! Mem, mem, memma!'

'Mummy?'

'Bu!' He mimed writing, scribbling his finger across the table top in a
frenzy of excitement.

'Mummy wrote a novel?'

I couldn't believe it! Was there anything she hadn't done? I had a
sensation of vertigo, as if, having embarked on a tightrope walk across
the Niagara rapids, I had heard my father jeer from the far side, 'Your
mother did it first!'

'When? I didn't know!'

'Bu . . .' He shrugged, rocking his hand back and forth in a gesture
which meant, 'Dodgy; very dodgy.'

That did it. If Mummy had failed at anything, damn and bless her, I
would do it too, and succeed if it killed me!

I began almost at once, and after a few false starts found it remarkably
easy. The plot (concerning the fortunes of a nineteenth-century lady

from a nearby village) was – I have to admit – virtually written for me in the museum book, and the rest was done – in its rough draft at least – in a scant three months. They were the shortest three months of my life. The happiest, even though so very little had changed. My father was still an invalid; my sex-life was still a graveyard; and the stairs still clattered when we walked on them. But none of it mattered so much.

My father sometimes sat with me while I worked, gazing for hours from the window, his eyes lighting with interest at the merest sign of life in the lane outside. He had his regulars: a woman who passed by with her dog, the children from the farm, and Bob, the farm labourer, who always waved as he drove by on the tractor. When Bob waved to him, my father smiled as if he had just won a fortune, and I felt sick every time he did it, the thought of his boredom too appalling to entertain.

Sometimes, when I saw him sitting at the window, his head proudly tilted, his good hand resting lightly on the arm of the chair, I imagined that he was unchanged, and that he might turn at any moment and speak to me. And sometimes, watching him, I could almost hear him say, 'Anna, come here': the words I had dreaded and now longed to hear again. I missed him. I missed him. Even while he sat in the same room, even while I touched him, held his hand, I missed him as though he were on the far side of the world.

People who write fiction have given themselves a licence to dream. But I could not confine my dreams to the written page, and once I had begun, I found myself dreaming my entire life into a more satisfactory shape. I hated myself for it, but I couldn't stop. I dreamed that I could begin again, be relieved of my domestic responsibilities, of Frank and my father; be stripped of my inhibitions and find the real me, the racy, fun-loving little intellectual who, I was certain, lurked somewhere beneath the dross, just waiting to be let out. Or I dreamed that Frank was a rich, devil-may-care character who whisked me off for sun-lazy holidays and made love to me in the shadow of the pyramids or on Copacabana Beach. But the dream I wallowed in most often, most shamefully, was that Frank did not exist and that I did not exist, except as a child. My father was well and strong, and different. When he said, 'Anna, come here,' it was to call me into his arms, to hold me and love me, to keep me in his heart, at the centre of his world.

I wanted, more than anything else, to be at the centre of the world, but I remained on the periphery still, and nothing I had ever done had drawn me in. My father was now more distant from me than ever. He had withdrawn into his silence, into regions ever more remote and secret. He did not seem to be unhappy there, but I sensed that it was a no man's land, a sad place, full of memories and circuitous dreams in which I, his changeling child, had no part to play.

I was wishing myself into the heart of the dead.

The thought appalled me, and although I still lusted for knowledge of my father's mystery, I knew that I would never fathom it now. I suspected too, that as a young, healthy woman, I should not want to. What should I want? Frank? Yes, I did want Frank. I wanted to know him, to love him, to find my natural place as his wife and his friend. But sometimes he seemed almost as remote from me as my father was, and I still felt that if I died or went away, he would scarcely notice I had gone. I wasn't enough for him. He was a sensitive, sensuous man, with desires too deep for me to understand, let alone satisfy, and I often felt that I was depriving him of something vast, something wonderful, making him long, as I did, for the centre of the world.

On the rare occasions when I could bring myself to talk about it, I begged him to explain what I was doing wrong; but it was beyond his powers of articulation, or perhaps beyond the limits of his self-control.

'I don't know, Anna.'

I was certain he did know, and that the softness of his voice concealed a depth of feeling too terrible to express. Generous and gentle as he was, I suspected that Frank was not incapable of all-out rage, and that if he ever began to tell me the true measure of my shortcomings it would be the end of our marriage.

'Just help me a little,' I would whisper, hoping to coax it from him safely, a bit at a time. 'Tell me what you need.'

'Oh, Anna, I don't know! It isn't something we can search for. If it's there, we'll find it. Just relax, Anna. Let it happen.'

Let it happen? What on earth did he mean? Sometimes I felt that we were hardly communicating. My father and I had developed, over the years, an almost telepathic form of communication which amazed everyone who saw it in action; including Frank. I occasionally suspected that Frank might be jealous of it, because it left him out entirely. But when we were making love I thanked God for his lack of telepathic insight. If he had read my mind at those moments, he would have shrivelled up and died. I rarely rejected his advances in bed, but the feeling they aroused in me was hatred, and sometimes it was all I could do not to scream.

My tenseness occasionally repelled him so much that he would leave me alone, turning from me with a hiss of frustration and taking most of the covers with him. My initial reaction was always one of relief, before guilt and sorrow took over. After a few minutes, while I balanced my fear of intimacy against my horror of rejection, I would sneak my arm around his waist and whisper, 'I'm sorry. Don't be angry.' Then we would make love. Oddly, I never minded it so much the second time round, perhaps because Frank was still too cross to fiddle about trying to turn me on. But I never had an orgasm. I didn't know what an orgasm was. And when our lovemaking was over Frank and I would both fall asleep disappointed, as though we had swum ten miles and then drowned without reaching the shore.

Even worse than my failure to understand what Frank wanted from me was my failure to understand what I wanted from him. Sex, I reasoned privately, was a natural act. It wasn't dirty, it wasn't humiliating, it wasn't wrong. So why didn't I like it? Why didn't I want it? What did I want instead? To be needed. To be respected. To be loved as my mother was loved and I had never been, matchlessly, without equal or rival. I suspected that I could have none of those things without first wanting sex. And I knew that Frank, if he chose, could replace me at the drop of a hat, with someone far more satisfying, both in bed and at the kitchen sink. Why he didn't was beyond me. Most women, after all, did not come with an invalid father in tow.

Yet I could not believe that Frank resented my father. He loved him, cared for him, brushed his teeth and polished his shoes, pressed his trousers, tied his tie. He never complained, and was always thinking of ways to please and interest him. My father called Frank 'Am', which was sufficiently like 'Amma' (he could never manage the harder consonants) to cause some confusion. But if I answered a call which had been meant for Frank, my father made his displeasure at my intrusion painfully clear. 'No! Am! Am!'

'I'll do it for you, Daddy.'

'No, no, no! Am!'

I was childishly hurt by these little rejections, and once, in a fit of pique, I snapped, 'Frank! The great "I Am" is wanted!'

He was grinning when he appeared on the scene a few moments later, giving me the idea that he had quite enjoyed putting my nose out of joint.

As I neared the end of the first draft of my book – often working late into the night as my excitement grew – Frank and my father drew closer together. They played pontoon and draughts and had little chats about cars, politics and the war. My father mimed his bits, and managed, with the aid of Frank's guesswork, to tell quite fluent stories; stories I had never heard until Frank recounted them to me later.

'Max was telling me about when his ship was torpedoed, Anna. He's had a bumpy old life, hasn't he?'

'Has he? I wouldn't know.'

I never quite managed to keep the note of jealousy from my voice, but it had its positive effect, if only to make Frank laugh, and he told me the stories anyway. It was a strange sensation though, to be told my father's life story by a man who had not even known him.

When the book was finished I felt bereaved, crushingly lonely, and I suddenly realised that the growing rapport between Frank and my father was something I had created. Whilst I was writing I had had no time for them. Now they had no time for me. It was a terrifying thought, and the only comfort I could offer myself was that Frank had not looked further afield for company.

But he wasn't angry with me. When I told him I had finished, he smiled with genuine pleasure and said, 'Good. Pleased with it?'

'No, it's a mess. I think I know how to improve it, but I need a second opinion.'

I had hoped that he would volunteer to help. I had hoped the book would draw us close again. But he said, 'Myra's coming for Easter, isn't she? Why don't you ask her to read it for you. She loves giving advice.'

'So do you!'

He smiled tolerantly. 'No,' he said, 'I prefer preaching. Ask Myra.'

I almost wept. I almost threw the stupid manuscript on the back of the fire. Frank's refusal to get involved seemed to rob it of any value. He thought it a nice little hobby, too trivial for his attention, doomed to fail. He probably wanted it to fail, if only to teach me that fantasy was no substitute for the love and companionship of my husband. I had learned that. But writing had taught me something else: to question motives, to return to my sources. And the source of my book, the motive which had originally fired it, had been my need for self-importance and respect. I still wanted respect. The book was my only hope of getting it.

'Yes,' I said calmly. 'You're right. I'll ask Myra.'

We hadn't seen her since the wedding, and Frank, whom I suspected of having more than a casual affection for 'the old girl' (she was two years his junior) put on his best suit and bought a bottle of gin in her honour. I was excited too, although we both restrained ourselves enough to allow my father the first hello. It was like a scene from a tragic opera. They stood staring at each other, she as paralysed and as mute as he; and then they stepped into each other's arms and wept.

'You old goat,' Myra sniffed. 'You old devil.'

'Bu, bu, bu,' my father crooned, and he stroked her hair until she laughed and blew her nose.

After an appreciative glance at Frank, Myra directed her next insults at me. 'What have you done to deserve it?' she demanded. 'Here's me, lovely as the bloody dawn, and I can't get a man for love or money; and there's you –'

'Ugly as an old boot,' Frank supplied helpfully.

'– with two of the most gorgeous ones I've ever laid eyes on! How do you do it?'

It had been ages since I had thought Frank particularly good looking, but I watched him while he poured our drinks and realised how accurate Myra's description had been. Good food, and the hard work he had done on the cottage, had built Frank up a bit since the wedding, and he filled his suit rather better now than he had then. Worry, and perhaps discontentment, had also played a part, and his face had acquired a few grim, rather attractive lines which somehow made his eyes seem more intensely blue. He was gorgeous. And I loved him. Why on earth weren't we happy?

I thought Myra would never finish my book. She wasted almost the whole of Good Friday on some hare-brained expedition to a show garden. My father loved it. He held her hand and burbled sweet nothings among the daffodils and rhododendrons, while I ground my teeth and prayed that she would turn out to be a fast reader. She did; but she finished only an hour before she was due to leave on Easter Monday.

'It's good,' she said simply. 'It's very good. Have you got an agent yet?'

'No, I didn't think. Why? Is it really all right?'

'Of course it's all right. You know it's all right. I cried my eyes out when Gregory died. Is that based on truth? I'm sure the sexy bits are. They're terrific.' She grinned. 'Randy little devil, aren't you? Is it lovely, being married?'

We were both rather surprised when, instead of making the appropriate reply, I burst into tears. It was partly relief about the book; but it was mostly grief.

'No,' I wailed. 'No, it isn't lovely at all! I don't know what to do, I don't know how to *be* married!'

Myra held my hand and patted it until I stopped crying.

'Oh, Lord, I'm so sorry, Myra. What on earth must you think of me?'

'No change,' she said softly. 'Still jealous. Have you told him how you feel?'

'No. I don't know how I feel. That's the trouble! I love him, Myra, but I can't *do* anything about it. There's something missing!'

'Perhaps you need a baby,' she said, her voice quite unsurprised and matter-of-fact.

To be needed, respected, to be loved without equal or rival . . .

'It sounds very nice,' I said wistfully, 'on the face of it. But it isn't the answer. Not yet, Myra. For one thing, I haven't really got a marriage yet, and I think, perhaps, a marriage comes first. For another . . . well, I'm twenty-two, which is quite old enough to have a child; but I don't feel old enough. When Daddy was well he wouldn't let me grow up, and since then I've not had time to grow up. I lived with Libby for seven months. I've had seven months of freedom, Myra. I don't know anything – except that I'm not ready to have a child.'

'And that you can write.'

I smiled. 'And that I can write.'

When we had waved Myra goodbye, and my father, weeping, had gone indoors to watch *Disney Time*, Frank suggested that we take a walk in the garden to 'see how the nettles are coming on'. Like my father, Frank was not a keen gardener, and I silently reflected that it was typical of him to imagine that we still had any nettles when I had broken my back to get them out and plant daffodils instead.

'It looks very nice,' he said grimly. He seemed tense and sad, and I thought he was probably wishing he could cry too, because Myra had gone.

'She's fun, isn't she?' I offered pathetically.

'Yes. What did she say, Anna?'

'Say?' I blushed, thinking that he had somehow overheard everything.

'You've been crying. Didn't she like it?'

'Oh! Yes. Yes, she did.'

Frank threw back his head and laughed with relief. 'Well! Thank the Lord for that! I didn't dare ask while she was here. So? What's next?'

I was amazed. I stared at him, my heart thudding with a strange, fierce joy which, for a moment, defied all my attempts to identify it. It wasn't pride, though pride was there, and it wasn't love, which had always been there. It was sharing. Having something of my own, and sharing it. So simple!

'You're pleased, Frank? I thought you weren't interested.'

He smiled and shrugged as if to say 'a lot you know', which curiously added to my excitement.

'I'll have to do another draft, of course. And she says I should get an agent.'

'Good. Get an agent.' He kissed my nose and frowned. 'What's an agent?'

His name was Tom Hawdern and I found him in the list in the *Writers' & Artists' Yearbook*. I sent him a synopsis and the first three chapters of my book, which I had called *The Stone Veil*. His chillingly brief reply said that he would be interested to see the completed manuscript. I read his letter ten times over, searching it for a word of encouragement, and at last decided that 'interested' was it.

'He's very interested!' I crowed as I handed Frank the letter.

Frank, too, read it ten times over, but I think he was searching for the 'very' I had conjured out of the air. I felt vaguely angry, and wrote the second draft of the novel with a grim, I'll-show-'em air, sharpening my critical faculties to an edge which at times threatened to cut everything I had previously written – except the sexy bits. I knew I couldn't improve on those: I had cribbed them all from other people's novels.

I waited two months for a response from the agent. During the first week I imagined him reading it with gasps of delight for my brilliance. During the second week I imagined him reading it with groans of despair for my stupidity. During the third week I watched for the postman and when, day after day he ignored me, I sank into a state of gloom which nothing – save a growing desire to kill someone – could relieve. I picked quarrels with Frank which he resolutely unpicked, usually by walking out. My father, less well equipped for rapid departures, turned up the volume on the television and pretended I wasn't there. I had never in my life behaved so badly. I didn't enjoy it much, but no one seemed in the least inclined to stop me.

When, at last, Tom Hawdern's letter arrived, I took it to the study and sat down, staring at the envelope hopelessly, knowing that the book was useless, that I was a failure and that once I had read the letter I would have nothing. I remembered what my father had said about education being a ticket to freedom, reflecting that I was no freer now than I had ever been. I was still hung in chains, my life still depending, as it always had, upon a few precious words which were never spoken. 'Good. Good girl.' I opened the letter. The sense of it touched my consciousness before the words did, and I slid off my chair in a daze.

'A remarkable first novel . . . beautifully written . . . excellent historical detail . . . will be glad to offer it . . . congratulations . . . fine book.'

Good. Good girl.

I felt like a cripple who had been told to get up and walk, but I did not thank God for healing me. The words I uttered were nothing like prayer.

'Mummy,' I whispered, 'can you see me?' And then I stood up and shouted it for all of heaven to hear. 'Mummy! Mummy! Can you *see* me?'

Frank had gone to work, but it didn't matter. I wanted to tell my father first; I wanted him to be the first to congratulate me.

'Daddy! Daddy? Oh, Daddy, guess what! The agent says my novel's remarkable! He says it's a *fine* book!'

I explained it very carefully, but he shrugged and opened his hand palm upwards, as though to say, 'So what? What's all the fuss about?'

'Daddy, the agent knows what he's talking about. If he likes it, it's almost certain to get published! I'll be famous!'

'Bu.' He nodded; but he was not interested. He did not care.

I couldn't believe it. What did he want of me, for Christ's sake? What did he *want*? I had done well; very well! A good degree, a good husband, a good home – and now the promise of success in my own right. I had been a good daughter to him and was well on the way to meeting my mother on equal terms. What more did he *want*? He had spoiled everything. Again. It had been his life's work, I knew it now, to avenge my mother's death on me, continually to goad me into competing with her and continually to deny that I was winning.

And I was winning. I was! She had been handed success on a plate, while I had fought; fought *him* and all he stood for, *her* and her damned precious memory, every inch of the way!

I was still grieving over it when Frank came home that evening. He did his best to cheer me up, and I cheered up for all I was worth. But I wasn't worth much, and after dinner I retired to the kitchen to sulk my way through the washing-up.

Frank followed me. 'I don't think he understands what it means,' he said gently. 'His brain –'

'Of course he understands! God, Frank, it was his bloody idea! He *made* me write that book; I would have given up if it hadn't been for him! "Write a novel," he said, "Write a novel. Your *mother* did!" He just won't *let* me be a success! He was always the same! Always!'

As usual, when there was trouble afoot, my father came to investigate, and stood by the door, saying, 'Bu, bu?' in a soft, pleading voice. He knew I was angry with him and now he was sorry; but it was too late. This time I would not forgive him. He'd have to be pleased with me eventually, when my book was published; and if he praised me for it then, I'd turn away from him, just as he had turned from me. I'd never forgive him.

I sniffed and turned back to the sink, but it was dark outside and my father's face was mirrored clearly in the window, his eyes filling with tears, his mouth trembling as he struggled, as usual without success, to master his emotions. He looked so pitifully bewildered. I forgot I was angry with him and ran into his arms, crying into the hard, fleshless plate of his chest while he patted my shoulder and said, 'Bu, bu, bu,' into my hair.

'Bu, bu.' There, there, my darling. All better now. Don't cry.

I heard it quite clearly, though it was years since he had said such things to me; and I sagged there, clinging to him, knowing that I had never grown up, never would grow up while my father still lived. And I did not want him to die.

Chapter Twenty-Nine

I was certain you were dead, you old goat; but you were just hiding, sniggering in the dark. For a little while I thought I was dead too, but no. Don't you want me? No, of course not. After all, I am an unbeliever, for ever burning in my stubborn unbelief. I thought I was dead, but I am merely deader than before, and still living. A heart, lungs and all that is left of my brain. It isn't much, and sometimes it escapes me entirely. The little I have left has no concept of time. I do not know how long I have been here, and although I still see the hands of my watch creeping slowly from number to number, I can't remember what their movements imply. My vision is sometimes clear, sometimes fragmented, but I have forgotten the shape of reality and everything is meaningless.

The place is pleasant. I know that; and there are many pleasant sensations which relieve my fear from one moment to the next. I am not afraid now, but fear has been with me recently and I see it waiting for me in the corner. It wears a mischievous, lopsided smile, loving me, lusting for me. I've seen that smile somewhere before. I have a sensation of hope, but it is merely the hope that fear will stay in the corner and not touch me again. Fear is a sad companion, but it stays with me, smiling. All others come in and go out, speaking softly or speaking loudly. Sometimes I hear them and do not understand. Sometimes I understand and do not care. It is all one.

'Tie forth or rubbed ear!' A cheerful voice. A trolley. A bowl of stringent fluid. A rhythm to the words I recognise. I am not afraid. She will turn me and rub my heels and buttocks, which are sore because I can no longer move. I forget why. No, I remember tumbling into dark pain and a screaming and a beloved face weeping. My wife? My child? My lover? I do not know, but her face is lovely and drives fear from me, even from the corner where it lurks, smiling.

'Hits a love lead aim, stir nightie. A love lead, eh?'

Love. Yes, it is a word I know, but it means nothing. I have loved. I have loved. And it brought me here. Love is a mighty thing, with fists of steel to break a man of iron.

'There! Clean as a whistle! No bed-sores in Camley Cottage, Mr Knighton! We haven't had a bed-sore in Camley for five years! No need for them, I always say!'

Have I been here five years? It seems a long time. Is eternity so long?

'Good nursing and tie them up to dither properly. Buttons hose at two munching ease daze!'

Yes, indeed. Keep talking. I haven't a clue what you're saying, but it keeps me content until the thing I am waiting for happens. I do not know what I am waiting for. I am waiting, that is all.

'Time for your rub, dear!' Ah, she is going, addressing her kind words to another man, across the room. I am alone again and fear leaps –

No! I will close my eyes and wait in the dark. At least I can still close my eyes. Sometimes I open them, close them, just for the sake of controlling a part of myself, of feeling in control.

I close my eyes, and see – nothing. A red glow. Something else. A tall archway? No, an arched door. A church door opening and a monk – no, a priest. Whatsit? Whatsisname? Can't remember. The parson, anyway. Good sort. Did a lot of fishing and cursing in his spare time and called the lads young blighters. There wasn't much to choose between a parson and a bobby in those days. Schoolmasters were the worst, but they were all good men – of a kind.

Oh, I've forgotten! A red glow. A red glow. I am waiting. A church door opens and out steps old Bones in his dog-collar, smiling. The suspense is killing me. A girl comes out in a pink dress and my heart leaps. No, it is not she. Disappointment. A red glow . . . Waiting . . .

A man in Sunday best, a woman in a straw hat with cherries, two small children.

'Thank you, Mr –' What was his name? We called him Bones, but he – Damn! Damn! Oh, work you bastard brain!

A church door. People crowding around, shaking hands, coming down the steps with straight backs, faces stern or smiling. I am waiting. Trying not to jump up and down but too excited to keep still!

Emily! Oh, Emily, you beauty, you beauty, with your long black hair and your darkling eyes!

'Thank you, Mr Skelton. It was a beautiful service.'

Skelton! That's it! Good old Emily, I knew you'd remember.

'Hello, Emily.'

'My name is Emma, as I believe I have informed you on several previous occasions, Max Knighton. Now, if you'll excuse me?'

'No, I won't. Little girls like you shouldn't be allowed to walk home alone. Anything might happen. A boy might offer to hold your hand, for instance.'

'Huh!'

My, how that girl could blush. She turned my heart to a fluttering fledgeling, fresh from the egg. She tossed her head and marched away, and I did not follow. Even at sixteen I had more sense. But I began going to church again, having given it up at thirteen, as soon as I was safely confirmed, one of God's own children. My mother, who had called me a wicked little heathen ever since, loved me again and never knew that lust had engineered my Christian reawakening.

Eventually I walked home with Emma, and eventually too I held her hand, but she consented to this chiefly out of pity. My boyish bragging never impressed her. Bullying took me nowhere. Wooing was wicked. But for pity Emma would do anything. She was a sentimental little thing. I went away soon afterwards and it was not until I came home on leave a year later that Emma fell in love with me. I had grown three inches, my shoulders were oaken beams, and my skin was the colour of sweet sherry. I had also learned a lot about girls. Emma blushed and lowered her eyes, and realising where they had lighted, closed them.

'Hello, Emily.' And touch her hair.

'My name is Emma,' she whispered.

'Hello, Emily.' And touch her hand.

'Hello, Max.'

Aaaaah.

I am waiting. I am waiting, but I forget why, and for what.

'Dinner time, Mr Knighton!'

Perhaps this, but I doubt it. I am in a chair. How long have I been in this chair? I forget. Eternity is a long time without knowing time. I am in eternity and this stew is a part of it. I remember a *daube* of beef with cloves and oranges, but that was yesterday, or when I was a boy. I remember currant duff and golden syrup. I remember raw turnips. This stew is a limbo between raw turnips and currant duff. I have no idea where my mouth is. At least, I know it is not in my lap, where most of the stew is.

Fear is in the corner, smiling. Laughing because I cannot find my mouth.

Am I dead?

God, am I dead?

I'm buggered if I know.

I am waiting. For Emily? No, she is dead. I'm certain of that. But how did she die? When, and why? Shut your face, you grinning bastard! I am not afraid! I am not, but I wish it would come, the thing I am waiting for. She went away to college. Yes. And when she came home she was twenty-one and we got engaged. Yes, I remember that. I was very sure of myself. I knew a great deal. I had seen South Africa, the Americas, Russia, the Mediterranean. I knew the difference between bloater paste and caviare, Woodbines and Havana cigars, bad women and good girls. I was a Royal Navy snob, an officer, a gentleman of the world; but I loved Emily more than I loved myself. Am I waiting for – ? No, no. She is dead.

Ah! There it is! A spoonful of food has travelled in the right direction at last and I am relieved. Was I waiting for food? Was I – am I – hungry? I think I must be, because I feel excited now and can't eat quickly enough. When I have finished what is left on my plate, I'll eat the bits from my lap. Waste not spoils the broth.

'Stooge Battle and Custer, Mr Knighton?'

Yes, I believe he did. Was I there? No, it was in America. The Red Indians won, but I can't imagine why you mention it now.

Oh, pudding. I am not dead. This sickly yellow pulp confirms it. Except – why does the woman talk about Red Indians, if I am not dead?

205

I am waiting and feel I shall weep if it does not come. I am afraid. What if it does not come? What if I wait and wait and wait and never know what I am waiting for? Fear has me by the hand and is leering into my face.

'What's this? No, no, don't cry. Anna will be here soon, Mr Knighton. She'll cheer you up, won't she? Only another hour and Anna wobble ear. Seesaw gurgle. An chew brow doffer?'

I forget. It is what I am waiting for, isn't it? Say it again, slowly. Slowly. Make me understand.

No. She cleans my face, combs my hair and smiles into my eyes. She cannot hear me screaming and fear still holds my hand. I will close my eyes and not see it. I will close my eyes and see nothing – save redness, redness, a fire beyond the horizon. The British at Bremen. Liberation. Joy and grief. Is Emily married? Have I hoped all these years for nothing?

'Oh, Max! It isn't that I don't love you, but because I love you too much! You consume me. You overpower me. When I am with you I forget my own name!

My name is Emma.

Oh, think nothing of it, my dear. I quite understand. So your barrister friend is a thoughtful, quiet chap, is he? Makes you feel strong, does he? That is because he is a weak little swine who will suck your blood, you stupid – *I cannot live without you.*

'Daddy? Don't cry, Daddy. I'm here.'

Ohhh! She has come! Oh, my darling, darling, hold me in your arms. I'm so lonely, so afraid, and I've been waiting so long. I do not know who you are. Talk to me! Tell me!

'I've brought you some peppermints, Daddy. Frank had a late patient, but he'll be here, soon. It's lovely outside; really warm. Look, there are still some roses outside the window. Daddy, I had a letter from Tom Hawdern today. You know, my agent? Daddy, oh, Daddy, he says my book's going to be published! You remember my book, Daddy?'

I have not understood a word, but she looks so happy. Should I be happy too?

Slowly, slowly. Please. Tell me what is happening to me. Tell me if I will die soon. I want to die. I am no longer afraid of death. Hell cannot be worse than this, and eternity on the far side of the grave cannot hurt more. They told me there was still something to do, but what can I do now? What am I for? Oh, pretty, pretty woman with your slick, slick

206

lipstick, your bright-light God-loved soul, ask Him, beg Him: let me die!

'Daddy? My book? I called it *The Stone Veil*, remember? I'd never have done it if it hadn't been for you, Daddy, and now it's going to be published! Aren't you glad? Aren't you proud of me?'

I remember that you believed in God. You were always asking silly questions about Him, and saying your prayers in the night. 'Oh, please, God, let Daddy love me!'

Yes, I heard you. So did He. Ask Him again. Ask, 'Oh, please, God, let Daddy die!' They said there was still something I must do, but I only want to die, you see. I can't do anything else.

'I do so want you to be proud of me!'

Her face is like a painting of a dream I cannot remember. Like Mary at Golgotha, half pride, half grief, with love in her eyes. There should be more than love. There should be hatred too, for the God who tortured and murdered her beloved. But it is not there. I cannot understand her speech, only her eyes. She takes my hand and kisses it, and tears fall there, scalding, to remind me again of something I cannot remember. How sad I am. And the comfort I crave is not here. I am still waiting.

The woman wipes her eyes and turns to greet a newcomer, who brings a stab of joy to my heart. Is this what I have been waiting for, this good, gentle man? Yes, perhaps. He smiles and touches my shoulder. There is strength in his hand. 'Hello, Max.'

Hello. Take me away? Take me from this woman who loves me? She cannot reach me, and though I long to comfort her, I have to go away. I am nothing now and can give nothing.

My need is all I am.

I need to die.

Chapter Thirty

My father suffered another major stroke when he was fifty-four. He could no longer walk, no longer say the few useful words he had used for so long. 'Bu' disappeared completely. Nothing could be done for him, and after a few weeks at the teaching hospital, fifteen miles away, he was moved to the tiny community hospital at Camley, only a mile from home. It was a lovely place – gone now – with only six 'chronic' beds, a small general ward and a maternity wing. We knew most of the staff, and the only doctors were the patients' own family practitioners. My father seemed to have accepted what had happened, but we could not know. He rarely wept now, rarely smiled, and without 'bu' he became quite isolated, beyond our reach.

When I was seventeen, hearing that sound for the first time, I had thought I would never understand what it strove to convey, but my father had made a passable language of it, with mime, facial expression, changes of tone. It could express anger, interest, sympathy. It could command, demand, beg, thank. It could be amused or sad or puzzled. Sometimes, when we all worked hard at it, it could even be rhetorical. Now he said nothing save an occasional 'Uhh', like the dying notes of a fog horn heard from a distance on a wintry night. There were times when his eyes would spark into life for something we said or did, but it was the same spark for a packet of peppermints as for Frank's announcement that he'd bought a new car – something which, in the old days, would certainly have interested him.

'It's got a heater, Daddy!' I said, desperate to please him. 'And windscreen wipers which both work at the same time!'

'Uhh,' my father said, and the light in his eyes faded and died.

I visited him every day for a few months, but he seemed not to care whether I came or not, and was more interested in what the nurses were doing than in what I had to say. My visits faltered to four times a week, then twice: Wednesdays and Sundays. When I did not see him I longed to see him, but on Wednesdays and Sundays there was a weight on my mind, and, afterwards, relief that it was over. Between times I made mental notes of things to say, knowing that otherwise I should be struck dumb with pity. When I saw him I recited my part, getting the punctuation and breathing all wrong, wanting not to talk to him, as I knew I should, but to hold him in silence, suffering his silence as if it were my own.

My love for him had undergone many changes since he first fell ill, but, in spite of his dependency upon me, he had always been greater than I, always the light upon which my shadow depended for its existence. My father had not diminished, but I wished he had, for then I might have found a way to comfort him. The humiliations he suffered in his helplessness were my humiliations, and when he shifted restlessly in his bed, wincing at some pain whose source he could not describe, I felt the pain too, perhaps more sharply than he felt it, and when I left him I knew that his pain – which I could so easily leave behind – would hold him every moment until I returned.

At home I missed the discipline of his dependency and, missing it, pretended a dependency for Frank which he swiftly scotched, pushing me away as if I were an over-demonstrative aunt and he a tough little boy. 'Gerroff!'

'But you've got egg on your chin!'

'So what? I put it there, and it's my responsibility to wash it off. I'm not an invalid, Anna!'

I desisted, realising how little I knew him, wondering if I would ever know, or if I was doomed to live with men who kept their hearts secret from me.

I went to London to meet Tom Hawdern, my literary agent, and on his advice began another novel, developing two of the minor characters from *The Stone Veil*. Two publishers had by now rejected this, but Tom was still optimistic about it and was encouraging me to develop a saga. His enthusiasm gave me a new sense of purpose and made me think of writing as a career instead of a desultory occupation which might, if I were lucky, pay off. Luck seemed far less important now. Tom was a professional who knew what he was doing, and if he were willing to invest his time, money and effort in my work I owed it to him, as much as to myself, to earn him his ten per cent. That responsibility, the first I had known outside familial duty, was a kind of growing up. It made me feel important.

But I felt younger too, freer. Although I did not admit it, even to myself, my father's departure from home was an extraordinary release. Even my weekly trip to town for the groceries was more enjoyable for not having to rush back, worrying myself into a frenzy in case I missed the bus. I could play my Joe Cocker album at full blast, have a bath without locking the door and go to the cinema with Frank without having to feel guilty about the time. I still did feel guilty. It was a habit. The nice part was when I realised I didn't have to feel guilty.

But liberation stopped short at the bedroom door. I was shocked to discover that guilt could control my body, as well as my mind. It was as if my muscles had not yet learned that they were free; and when Frank made love to me, I still lay like a keeled-over tombstone, and I still gritted my teeth when the bedsprings creaked.

I had almost finished the first draft of my second novel when Tom's letter arrived, telling me that a 'major publishing house' had made an offer for *The Stone Veil*. I had done it!

My first triumphant thought was of my mother's manuscript, a failure which had never seen the light of day. I couldn't wait to tell my father, to see his eyes light up, if only for a moment, with pride in me. I had done it! I had matched her, outmatched her! He could no longer say I was not good enough!

But I was shaking as I approached his bed, and I hesitated for several minutes before I told him. I kissed him, held his hand, told him that it was a fine day, that he looked a little better. The words I wanted to say seemed to have stuck in my throat, and when I eventually said them, I stammered, and had to begin again.

'Daddy, my book's going to be published! I had the letter today.'

My father looked at me blankly, moving his shoulders as though to shrug me off. I told myself he had not heard. I smiled, encouraging him to concentrate.

'Daddy? The book? Remember how you told me to write it? I wouldn't have done it if it hadn't been for you, and now it's going to be published! Aren't you glad, Daddy? Aren't you proud of me?'

He closed his eyes, his mouth hardening against the discomfort of his forced inactivity. But this time I did not flinch in sympathy. He had turned me away and I could not bear it, would not endure it without a word of protest. Before, always before, I had had something else to offer; a safety clause. 'Wait,' I could say, 'wait until I pass my O-levels [until I get to college/get my degree] then I'll prove myself worthy of you.'

Now there was nothing to wait for. I had given him the best – and the last – of myself, and he had rejected it. I begged him: please, please be proud of me! *Please*, just once before you die; but at that moment Frank came in, and my father turned to him, and smiled.

I spent the evening crying. I shut myself in the bathroom and cried, watching myself in the mirror and calling myself ten thousand kinds of fool. But I was beginning to understand. My father could never have loved me as he had loved my mother because he had been *in* love with her. He was sexually bonded to her. And I was his daughter, his child, another person entirely. In my mother, making up the woman he loved, had been elements which could never be a part of me, and a knowledge of my father as a man, a lover, which I could never have learned. But the important thing was my realisation that I was not only my mother's equal but someone quite different, quite independent of her because I was a part of my father too, the product of his blood and his training. His training. What had he trained me to be? A spaniel, a lackey. Without him to strive for, without him to kick me into action, I was nothing. Even the book had been his idea. What would I do now, without him?

Eventually, and chiefly because he wanted a shower, Frank knocked on the bathroom door. 'Come on,' he said. 'You'll have a headache.'

I went out and he put his arms around me. 'What's it all about? What's wrong?'

'I don't know. I've just realised that I've spent my whole life swimming around in circles. The place I was going – it isn't there!'

Frank listened quietly while I told him about my mother, about wanting to be as good as she was and only now realising that I was as good, but different. When I had finished he did not speak, but I had an idea he was holding his breath.

'Frank?'

'I thought you'd never get round to it,' he said. 'Good old Max. He's done more for you today than he's done in a lifetime, Anna.'

'What?' I was confused. 'What's he done? He's destroyed –'

'The only thing he's destroyed is the whip he drove you with. Most people realise the futility of striving for perfection, Anna, but they usually realise it much earlier in life than you've done. They also realise something which seems to have escaped you, even now. Perfection doesn't exist, Anna. You aren't your mother, but little bits of you are probably very close approximations of little bits of her. Has it never once occurred to you that some of those little bits might be your faults? She had *faults*, Anna, and smelly physical functions, just like yours and mine.'

No, it had never once occurred to me. I was shocked. I stared at Frank in utter amazement; not at the idea of my mother's faults and smelly physical functions, nor even at my own stupidity in not realising that she had had them. I was amazed because, for the first time in my life, I could think of my mother with love, regretting sincerely that I had never known her.

Frank laughed and pushed me away for a moment to see how I was taking it. 'Feeling better?'

'Yes, but I don't quite know where to go next, or rather, how to. My motor's broken down.'

'Get a new one. Now that you know you can't please your father by mimicking your mother, why don't you try pleasing yourself for a change? And *be* yourself for a change. Are you sorry you wrote the book? Are you ashamed of it?'

'No!'

'Do you wish it weren't going to be published? Would you rather not have the money?'

'No, of course not.'

'Then Max doesn't matter, does he? It's yours, Anna, and it's for you to be proud of, all by yourself. You don't need anyone else's approval. You've got your own.'

It was a very surprising thing to realise. I was, actually, very proud of myself. Frank was right about the whip, too. I had forgiven, almost forgotten, the numerous occasions when my father had physically beaten me, but the hope I had cherished that one day he would love me had been a relentless punishment which had bent me double; until now. It was strange and sad, almost frightening. I felt like a convict newly released from jail, trembling on the brink of freedom. The world seemed big, dangerous and exciting, and I, with my prison pallor, my brown-paper parcel, was bereft without the familiar walls to confine me and keep me safe.

'I'm on my own, then.'

'No,' Frank said. 'You've still got me.'

I began to feel that Frank had come closer to me after this. We seemed to have come level again in a curious way. I thought at first that it was because his view of me had changed and I only gradually realised that it was because my view of myself had changed. Daddy's little girl had gone away and left a woman in her place. For the first time in my life I was not conscious of being physically small. This might have had something to do with having only one six-footer in the house instead of two; but it seemed more likely that it was because my father had ceased to overshadow my mind, not my body. I still loved him, still visited him and held his hand; but he had lost his power over me. I had grown up, calmed down, accepted myself. I had a new identity now. I was a professional author.

Frank seemed to like it. He seemed, almost, to have fallen in love with me again. On our second wedding anniversary he came home bearing a dozen real red roses and tickets to the charity Christmas Ball, which was the biggest social event our town had to offer. I was thrilled, but the only thing I could find to say was, 'I haven't anything to wear!'

Frank grinned. 'Buy something. I saw some lovely frocks in Woollies!'

I hit him, and blew the remainder of my tiny publisher's advance on a moiré silk dress, new shoes and ear rings. A glimpse of my reflection in a shop window made me gasp with astonishment. I looked terrific, glowing with confidence and high spirits. Frank met me in the car, and on the way home I told him about it.

'I didn't realise it was me! I thought, "Gosh, she's pretty!" I even turned round to get a closer look at her. And it was me!'

Frank didn't seem particularly amused. He looked as if he were trying to find the words to comfort me.

'Oh,' he said, 'didn't you know? I've told you often enough.'

'Yes, but this was different. Before . . . Well, I knew that my eyes and my nose were arranged quite nicely, but it was like looking at a pretty child. I felt . . . unfinished. But when I saw that reflection in the shop window just now, it was as if –'

Frank laughed at last. 'Someone had moved your nose?'

'Yes! From ground level to six feet high!'

Going to the biggest dance of the year was the most exciting thing that had ever happened to me; much more exciting than my wedding, which I had survived in a state of tearful disbelief. Now I couldn't stop giggling.

'But I can't dance, Frank! I've only waltzed twice in my life; both times with Daddy, and he could teach a goat to waltz!'

'You've waltzed three times in your life,' Frank reminded me, 'and for your information, twinkle-toes, *I* can teach a goat to dance the Valeta.'

'What's the Valeta?'

'A refined way of giving yourself a heart attack. How do I look?'

He had finished dressing in the bathroom, and he swept into the bedroom now with a flourish of white pleats, gold cuff links and a perfectly knotted bow tie. I scarcely recognised him. I laughed, almost stammering a reply.

'You look . . . gorgeous. Have you seen my husband anywhere?'

'Forget him!' He swooped his arms around me, a predatory move which ended, with due regard for my make-up, in the most fleeting caress. 'You're wasted on him, my darling. Forget him, and come out with me. I'll sweep you off your size threes.'

It was like a first date, so charged with romance that I was overcome with shyness, and could only stare at Frank as we drove into town, admiring his good looks and gulping with amazement to remember that I was married to him, and had been married to him for two years without ever feeling like this.

I hadn't believed that his dancing would be much more expert than mine; we had 'moved' together once or twice, but the only time we had attempted to dance properly had been a year ago, on New Year's Eve, and that hadn't been too impressive. But he dragged me on to the floor as soon as we had said hello to his partner and their friends, his hand hard around my waist.

'Hey, put me down, you beast.' I was embarrassed and scared, for even if he could dance, I could not, except with the most expert guidance; and one of my size threes was loose. 'Frank, I can't! Wait until there are more people!'

He ignored me, gathering me against him in a hold so firm that I jerked back my head with surprise. This was Frank? I spent the first few minutes of the waltz staring at his buttonhole in confusion. It only gradually dawned on me that we were dancing, and that my feet were not tangling with his, and that my shoes weren't falling off. The floor felt like a cloud. So did I.

It was a wonderful evening. We drank champagne and flirted outrageously, mostly with each other, but after a while with everyone in sight. After a few sedate waltzes and foxtrots, the music grew wilder, the dancing more hectic, and if I felt drunk it was the movement and the freedom which had intoxicated me, not the champagne. After supper we danced the Gay Gordons (which I had learned at school), and then the famous Valeta, the most beautiful dance ever invented. It was a series of entrapments and escapes, being clutched close and whirled off my feet, being released and twirled around like a top. I loved it.

Frank had told the entire town about my book, and I was treated as a celebrity. That was intoxicating too. 'Oh, it's early days, yet,' I smirked, but even my modesty was a flirtation; 'I still have enormous potential for fizzling out.'

'Nonsense!'

Yes, nonsense! I could have gone on for days, just dancing and flirting and talking nonsense. But it ended. Quite suddenly. The band stopped playing, packed up, went home. The Master of Ceremonies said goodnight and wished us a happy Christmas.

I was outraged. How could they send us home, as if we were children? How could the band stop playing when I wanted to dance all night?

But I continued to dance in the car, tapping my feet, humming, laughing, telling Frank how wonderful he was, how happy I was.

'I don't want to go to sleep. I want to dance for ever!'

'You will, if you play your cards right.' He slid his hand up my leg and I laughed, still flirting; but I knew the fun was over.

I pretended it wasn't. I felt trapped, scared, hearing the echo of my father's voice: 'That's enough, Anna. You're over-excited.'

I giggled, halted at the foot of the stairs and reversed squiffily into Frank's chest. 'I'm over-excited, Frank!'

'Good. That's how I like you. Upsadaisy, beddybyes.'

I wanted to cry. I didn't want to go to bed. I didn't want to take off my new dress, my ear rings, my shoes. *I didn't want Frank to touch me.*

He kissed me; his fingers unfastening my dress, sliding next to my skin, his touch soft and tentative. I wanted to kick him. He had spoiled it all. I had known he would want to make love, but why did he have to make such a meal of it, as if he were turning over lettuce leaves in search of onions? I was tired. My head ached. I hated him.

'I'll just brush my teeth.'

'Anna.' I ignored the plea in his voice and kicked off my shoes, trying not to seem too urgent in my dash for the bathroom.

'Anna, come here!'

I stiffened, hearing the ring of dreadfully familiar bells. The rage in his voice snapped again, this time with an obscene curse, and I felt my stomach turn with the old terror of punishment and humiliation. Frank was close behind me when I turned to face him, his shirt open to show the long, silky hairs on a remarkably solid chest. He had never seemed so big before, but I had never been scared of him before.

'Frank? What's wrong? I was only –'

'Asking for it!' He grabbed my arm and dragged me back to the bedroom, pinning me against the wall to kiss me again, stripping off my clothes, hurting me. Could a man rape his own wife? A man like Frank? I couldn't believe it, but it seemed to be happening.

'Frank, please! I was – I wasn't going . . . What's *wrong*?'

Frank took a massive breath. When he released it, I knew, it would be to tell me everything that was wrong – with me. I wished I hadn't asked. But he thought better of it, perhaps knowing that once he began, he wouldn't be able to stop until he had killed me.

I sat on the edge of the bed, knees together, arms crossed defensively over my breasts. I would have made another dash for the bathroom, but Frank had apparently anticipated this and was undressing with his back to the door. His pupils had dilated and his hands were shaking with rage. I decided to be firm with him, as I was with bus conductors who called me darling and affected to admire my legs.

'Frank, this is silly. There's no need to –'

'Shut up.'

I flinched, biting my lip against the shock, not at what he had said, but at the way he had said it. It was his dentist's voice: cold, clinical and detached. Nothing would stop him now, and I could not even look forward, as his patients did, to a smile and a joke when it was over.

'Lie down.'

'No! Frank, you can't! It isn't – I won't – I'm not ready!'

'*Ready?* You're never bloody ready! What so special about tonight?'

He pushed me backwards and knelt over me, pinning my shoulders with his hands.

'No! I don't – I won't –'

'You'll do as you're damn well told. Move over.'

I didn't know him. I vaguely understood that he wasn't raping me, but I hadn't a clue what he was doing instead. He would not let me lie, as I usually did, passively suffering his caresses; and the things he did were, save for the occasional kiss aimed at the most unlikely parts of my anatomy, nothing like his usual caresses. He pushed, pulled, turned and lifted me, his hands seeming to be everywhere at once; hurting here, yet, as I registered the hurt, hurting there, the pain so fleeting that it was no pain at all.

I had lost my bearings. While my body went one way, my stomach went another, lurching violently; a feeling too close to terror to be endurable. I knew it was not terror, but I was certain that if I did not hold on to something solid, I would die. I held on to Frank, dragging him down, tightening my arms to crush him, or at best to keep him still. He laughed in my face, and I blushed, hiding my scarlet in the shadowed curve of his arm.

Frank sank his teeth into my shoulder, nibbling roughly, and the laughter came to my throat like an unexpected fish bone, almost choking me with surprise. I loved it, loved him, oh, I loved him! I didn't know him.

It was dark and Frank was sleeping, his lips still softly parted against my breast. I had the odd idea that instead of consummating a marriage, I had fallen in love with a complete stranger. He had been beautiful and angry, and he had danced with me!

I went rigid and stopped breathing. My skin turned clammily cold. 'Anna, come here!' Frank had said it, but not Frank; and although it had terrified me, it had excited me more. I had not known him. I knew him now. I had made love to my father, and loved it, for I had wanted him all my life.

Frank woke up and gathered me into the crook of his arm. 'What's up? Why are you crying?'

I didn't mean to tell him, but before I could prevent it, my father's name drifted over my lips, like an involuntary curse.

Frank's arm fell away. 'Daddy,' he repeated wearily, 'always Daddy. God, how I hate that man.'

I was shocked and scared, but the words he had said gave me a strange feeling of hope. Frank was not stupid. Perhaps he had known all along, and loved me in spite of it.

'You hate him?' I whispered.

Frank sighed heavily. 'No. No, not really. I don't know him, do I? The man I know – that poor, pathetic, drooling old man – is not your daddy, is he?'

The outrage I felt at hearing him describe my father so brutally did not survive long. It was true. Why had I never seen him like that? Even when he wept, dribbled, spilled his food, he was always the same to me: the same sad, handsome hero, the man I could not reach and did not know. I had never known him.

'I thought you loved him, Frank. You've been so good to him.'

'No. I've been good to you. I've cared for him because I've had to, for your sake. Oh,' he sighed again, 'and for his sake, I suppose. He was helpless, Anna. I would have done as much for a sick cat. I didn't hate him. I just hated the man you thought he was, because you loved him more than you loved me.'

The bitterness in his voice did not hurt me. Why should it? It was a gift I had never imagined possible. I smiled, reached in the dark for his hand.

'No. I just thought I loved him more, Frank, because he didn't love me. He treated me like dirt. I thought he was a hero, but the more I think about it . . . Frank, I'm not even sure he was alive. He was a robot, patterned to love one woman and no one else. I might just as well have tried to get a stone wall to love me, or a motor car. He wasn't real, Frank. You're real.'

'Well!' Frank switched on the light and looked down at me quizzically.

'What's brought all this on? Your dirty night out?'

'Yes. I got a bit muddled, Frank.'

'Muddled?' He frowned. 'What about?' But I could see his mind

217

working, his face freezing as understanding dawned. 'I see,' he said coldly. 'That was a very nasty thing to do, Anna.'

My stomach lurched. I was doing it again!

'No, no,' I said desperately. But it wasn't shame I felt, it was despair. My father had trained me to feel desire only through fear. He had ruined me, perverted me, and left me as he had kept me, on the edge of nowhere, with nothing to do but fall. I had been trained, too, to weep for my sins, to beg forgiveness; but I knew it was futile. If Frank forgave me, if he loved me again, he would love me as before, gently, giving me nothing. And if he did not forgive me, if he left me, he would leave me with nothing. I couldn't bear it. 'Oh, forgive me, Frank, please!'

Frank knelt beside me and pulled me upright, twisting me around to face him. 'No, Anna,' he said gravely. 'No. I won't forgive you. It was a terrible thing to do.'

'No, I won't forgive you.' My father had never said that! My father had always forgiven me.

'It was a terrible thing to do,' Frank repeated thoughtfully, 'and I know how terrible it was because I've done it myself.'

'Done what?'

'Imagined you were someone else. No one in particular, of course. Just someone a bit livelier. A lot livelier.' He kissed my ear. He laughed into it. 'How else could I have had any fun?'

I felt very weak and confused. It was a bit like making love. I had lost my bearings. The problem kept jumping around, and I couldn't hold it long enough to know if it hurt.

'You don't hate me?'

'No. Why should I? We were both in the wrong.'

'But I was more wrong than –'

Frank laughed. 'Oh, no you don't, madam! No more guilt. It's a waste of time, and we've wasted enough time already, thanks.'

He was holding me, rubbing my back to warm and comfort me, not forgiving me, but accepting me, just as I was. 'Anyway,' he went on, 'it doesn't really matter who you think about, just as long as you enjoy it. Forget it, Anna. As I've told you before, it's only sex.'

'But sex is important, Frank.'

'Important, but not serious. It's supposed to be fun, Anna. It's almost bound to go wrong it you take it too seriously. Think about it. It's messy, silly and thoroughly uncivilised. And it hurts. Afterwards, you feel sore all over and you realise you've done things which would be agony if you'd done them stone cold. But it's a lovely feeling, Anna, like a lasting after-image of the pleasure.'

'You mean I'm not a pervert?'

Frank smiled, his eyes crinkling warmly at the corners. I laughed. I felt quite uncivilised.

'Let's do it again,' I said.

The phone rang at five o'clock in the morning and five minutes later we were driving up the lane at eighty miles an hour. I was crying.

Daddy was looking for us, staring patiently at the door. His face was ashen, his lips bloodless, and his fine, hooked nose was like the fleshless beak of a great bird shot from the sky. Frank hung back at the door and I went to my father's side and took his hand.

'I'm here, Daddy.' I could not stop crying, but I did it as quietly as I could. He did not blink, but his eyes seemed to sink and fade, and I was aware of the shadows around them darkening. Frank touched my shoulder and leaned forward.

'Hello, Max.'

My father's eyes brightened and a faint smile moved his lips. His eyes locked on to Frank's face, watching as he went around the bed. Then, using the last of his strength, he reached out his wasted right arm with its soft white hand and Frank took it and pressed it gently.

'It's all right, Max,' he said.

Daddy smiled and closed his eyes. A nurse came and stood beside me. It went very quiet.

'Is he dead?' I whispered.

'Yes,' the nurse said, 'and we must be glad for him.'

I was glad. Yes, I was very glad; but I cried for a long, long time. He had not smiled for me. He had smiled for Frank. It was the final rejection, the last punishment. I deserved it. I accepted it. It was over. But I wished I could have told him that I had found the centre of the world.

Chapter Thirty-One

I will not sleep, nor close my eyes. Oh, that I had died as my darling died, oh, that I had died! She turned in her sleep and cried out in a strange, strange voice, in an agony which left her stricken and cold. For a week I watched her, white and small in her hospital bed. Her mouth dragged down at one corner. Her eye drooped. Smaller and smaller she became as I watched and wept, and she never heard me call her name.

Emily, my Emily! Don't, don't die! I cannot live without you!

I will not sleep, nor close my eyes, but my life unrolls like a worn carpet beneath my feet.

'Touch! You're "It"!'

'You hurt me! I'll tell Mother! I'll tell her you hurt me, you beast!'

I never liked that girl. She was too much like me, bless her heart. What a burden to bear, being so much like me.

And who am I? Who knows? I loved my father, but he had a cruelty I was never aware of, a cruelty which taught Dorothy to hate men. I loved my mother, but she had a malice, a cold, puritan streak which taught me – what? What am I? I forget, and it no longer matters.

I am waiting.

A plate of food and my father's hands.

Sunlight on water.

A song, soft in the dark.

I am waiting. I am tired and I long to sleep, but the waiting is for ever.

'I'm here, Daddy.'

'I will never leave you, Daddy.'

Who said that? It does not matter. It is all so long ago, and I am waiting. Waiting. For what?

'Hello, Max.'

For *this*! Oh, I've waited so long!

Hello . . . You are not as I expected.

No horns? No tail?

Of course! I confused you with the other fellow! Is he coming too? Aren't you tired of him yet?

But I've – sinned.

Everyone does, my dear chap. It's part of being human.

And hell? Am I not –?

You've been there. You said so yourself.

But I thought . . .

Oh, eternity! You've served it. You said so yourself.

I lusted for my child!

No, you loved your wife.

I wanted to die with her. Die with Emily.

You did.

I turned from you, denied you.

Did you?

When you might have comforted, strengthened and supported me . . .

I did, Max. I was always with you. You would not let me go. Come, take my hand with your strong right arm. It's all right now, my little one. It's all right.